THE GENERATION OF POSTMEMORY

Lorie Novak, *Postmemory*. *Courtesy of Lorie Novak, www.lorienovak.com*

INTRODUCTION

> The guardianship of the Holocaust is being passed on to us.
> The second generation is the hinge generation in which received,
> transferred knowledge of events is being transmuted into history,
> or into myth. It is also the generation in which we can think
> about certain questions arising from the Shoah with a sense of
> living connection.
>
> —Eva Hoffman, *After Such Knowledge*

The "hinge generation," the "guardianship of the Holocaust,"
the ways in which "received, transferred knowledge of events
is being transmuted into history, or into myth"[1]—these, indeed, have been my preoccupations for the past two and a half decades.
I have been involved in a series of conversations about how that "sense
of living connection" can be maintained and perpetuated even as the
generation of survivors leaves our midst, and how, at the very same
time, it is being eroded. For me, the conversations that have marked
what Hoffman calls the "era of memory"[2] have had some of the intellectual excitement and the personal urgency, even some of the sense of
community and commonality, of the feminist conversations of the late
1970s and 1980s. And they have been punctured, as well, by similar kinds
of controversies, disagreements, and painful divisions. At stake is precisely the "guardianship" of a traumatic personal and generational
past with which some of us have a "living connection," and that past's
passing into history or myth. At stake is not only a personal/familial/
generational sense of ownership and protectiveness, but an evolving ethical and theoretical discussion about the workings of trauma, memory,

and intergenerational acts of transfer.[3] It is a discussion increasingly taking place in similar terms, regarding other massive historical catastrophes. These are often inflected by the Holocaust as touchstone or, increasingly, by the contestation of its exceptional status.

Urgently and passionately, those of us working on memory and transmission within and beyond the study of the Holocaust have argued about the ethics and the aesthetics of remembrance in the aftermath of catastrophe. How do we regard and recall what Susan Sontag has so powerfully described as the "pain of others?"[4] What do we owe the victims? How can we best carry their stories forward, without appropriating them, without unduly calling attention to ourselves, and without, in turn, having our own stories displaced by them? How are we implicated in the aftermath of crimes we did not ourselves witness?

The multiplication of genocides and collective catastrophes at the end of the twentieth century and during the first decade of the twenty-first, and their cumulative effects, have made these questions ever more urgent. The bodily, psychic, and affective impact of trauma and its aftermath, the ways in which one trauma can recall, or reactivate, the effects of another, exceed the bounds of traditional historical archives and methodologies. Late in his career, for example, Raul Hilberg, after combing through miles of documents and writing his massive, 1,300-page book *The Destruction of the European Jews*—and, indeed, after dismissing oral history and testimony for their factual inaccuracies—deferred to storytelling and to poetry as skills historians need to learn if they are to be able to tell the difficult history of the destruction of the Jews of Europe.[5] Hilberg is recalling a dichotomy between history and memory (for him, embodied by poetry and narrative) that has had a shaping effect on the field. But, nearly seventy years after Adorno's contradictory injunctions about the barbarity of writing poetry after Auschwitz, poetry is now only one of many media of transmission.[6] Numerous testimony projects and oral history archives, the important role of photography and performance, the ever-growing culture of memorials, and the new interactive museology reflect the need for aesthetic and institutional structures that broaden and enlarge the traditional historical archive with a "repertoire" of embodied knowledge that had previously been neglected by many traditional historians.[7] For better or worse, these various genres and institutions have been grouped under the umbrella term "memory." But, as Andreas Huyssen has provocatively asked, "What good is the memory archive? How can it deliver what history alone no longer seems to be able to offer?"[8]

If "memory" as such a capacious analytic term and "memory studies" as a field of inquiry have grown exponentially in academic and popular importance in the last two and a half decades, both have, to a significant degree, been fueled by what has been considered the limit case of the Holocaust and by the work of (and about) what has come to be known as "the second generation," or "the generation after."[9] "Second generation" writers and artists have been producing artworks, films, novels, and memoirs, or hybrid "postmemoirs" (as Leslie Morris has dubbed them), with titles like *After Such Knowledge*, *The War After*, *Second Hand Smoke*, *War Story*, *Lessons of Darkness*, *Losing the Dead*, *Dark Lullabies*, *Breaking the Silence*, *Fifty Years of Silence*, and *Daddy's War*, as well as scholarly essays and collections like *Children of the Holocaust*, *Shaping Losses*, *Memorial Candles*, *In the Shadow of the Holocaust*, and so on.[10] The particular relation to a parental past described, evoked, and analyzed in these works has come to be seen as a "syndrome" of belatedness or "post-ness" and has been variously termed "absent memory" (Ellen Fine), "inherited memory," "belated memory," "prosthetic memory" (Celia Lury, Alison Landsberg), "mémoire trouée" (Henri Raczymow), "mémoire des cendres" (Nadine Fresco), "vicarious witnessing" (Froma Zeitlin), "received history" (James Young), "haunting legacy" (Gabriele Schwab), and "postmemory."[11] These terms reveal a number of controversial assumptions: that descendants of victim survivors as well as of perpetrators and of bystanders who witnessed massive traumatic events connect so deeply to the previous generation's remembrances of the past that they identify that connection as a form of *memory*, and that, in certain extreme circumstances, memory *can* be transferred to those who were not actually there to live an event. At the same time, these members of what Eva Hoffman calls a "postgeneration" also acknowledge that their received memory is distinct from the recall of contemporary witnesses and participants.[12] Hence the insistence on "post" or "after" and the many qualifying adjectives and alternative formulations that try to define both a specifically inter- and transgenerational act of transfer, and the resonant aftereffects of trauma. If this sounds like a contradiction, it is one, and I believe it is inherent to this phenomenon.

"Postmemory" is the term I came to on the basis of my own "autobiographical readings" of works by second-generation writers and visual artists.[13] Like some of the writers named above, I felt the need for a term that would describe the *quality* of my own relationship to my parents' daily stories of danger and survival during the Second World War in Romanian Cernăuți and the ways in which their accounts dominated my postwar childhood in Bucharest. As I was reading and viewing the work of second-generation writers and artists, and as I was talking to fellow children of survivors, I came to see that all of us share certain qualities and symptoms that make us a *postgeneration*.

Why could I recall particular moments from my parents' wartime lives in great detail and have only very few specific memories of my own childhood, I began to wonder? Why could I describe the streets, residences, and schools of pre-World War I Czernowitz and interwar Cernăuți, where they grew up, the corner where they evaded deportation, the knock on the door in the middle of the night, the house in the ghetto where they waited for deportation waivers—all moments and sites that preceded my birth—when I had lost the textures, smells, and tastes of the urban and domestic spaces in Bucharest where I spent my own early life? It took a long time for me to recognize and to name these symptoms—the magnitude of my parents' recollections and the ways in which I felt crowded out by them. These moments from their past were the stuff of dreams and nighttime fears for, as a child, it was at night, particularly, that I imagined myself into the lives they were passing down to me, no doubt without realizing it. My postmemories of the war were not visual; it was only much later, after leaving Romania and the censored history to which my age-mates and I were exposed there, that I saw images of what I had until then only conjured in my imagination. But neither were my postmemories unmediated. My parents' stories and behaviors, and the way that they reached me, followed a set of conventions that were no doubt shaped by stories we had read and heard, conversations we had had, by fears and fantasies associated with persecution and danger.

kinu 20
cultural trauma

"Postmemory" describes the relationship that the "generation after" bears to the personal, collective, and cultural trauma of those who came before—to experiences they "remember" only by means of the stories, images, and behaviors among which they grew up. But these experiences were transmitted to them so deeply and affectively as to *seem* to constitute memories in their own right. Postmemory's connection to the past is thus actually mediated not by recall but by imaginative investment, projection, and creation. To grow up with overwhelming inherited memories, to be dominated by narratives that preceded one's birth or one's consciousness, is to risk having one's own life stories displaced, even evacuated, by our ancestors. It is to be shaped, however indirectly, by traumatic fragments of events that still defy narrative reconstruction and exceed comprehension. These events happened in the past, but their effects continue into the present. This is, I believe, the structure of post-memory and the process of its generation.

The "post" in "postmemory" signals more than a temporal delay and more than a location in an aftermath. It is not a concession simply to linear temporality or sequential logic. Think of the many different "posts" that continue to dominate our intellectual landscape. "Postmodernism" and "poststructuralism," for example, inscribe both a critical distance and a profound interrelation with modernism and structuralism; "postcolonial" does not mean the end of the colonial but its troubling continuity, though, in contrast, "postfeminist" *has* been used to mark a sequel to feminism. We certainly are, still, in the era of "posts," which— for better or worse—continue to proliferate: "posttraumatic," of course, but also "postsecular," "posthuman," "postcolony," "postracial." Rosalind Morris has recently suggested that the "post" functions like a Post-it that adheres to the surface of texts and concepts, adding to them and thereby also transforming them in the form of a Derridean supplement.[14] Post-its, of course, often hold afterthoughts that can easily become unglued and disconnected from their source. If a Post-it falls off, the post-concept must persist on its own, and in that precarious position it can also acquire its own independent qualities.

"Postmemory" shares the layering and belatedness of these other "posts," aligning itself with the practices of citation and supplementarity that characterize them. Like the other "posts," "postmemory" reflects

a Structure

an uneasy oscillation between continuity and rupture. And yet postmemory is not a movement, method, or idea; I see it, rather, as a *structure* of inter- and transgenerational return of traumatic knowledge and embodied experience. It is a *consequence* of traumatic recall but (unlike posttraumatic stress disorder) at a generational remove.

I realize that my description of this structure of inter- and transgenerational transfer of trauma raises as many questions as it answers. Why insist on the term "memory" to describe these transactions? If postmemory is not limited to the intimate embodied space of the family, how, by what mechanisms, does it extend to more distant, adoptive witnesses or affiliative contemporaries? Why is postmemory particular to traumatic recall: cannot happy or otherwise transformative historical moments be transmitted across generations with the ambivalent intensity characterizing postmemory? What aesthetic and institutional structures, what tropes and technologies, best mediate the psychology of postmemory, the continuities and discontinuities between generations, the gaps in knowledge, the fears and terrors that ensue in the aftermath of trauma? And why have visual media, and photography in particular, come to play such an important role here?

This book addresses these and a number of related questions. It was written during the remarkable emergence and rapid evolution of Holocaust studies, and its chapters respond to urgent and immediate questions within this scholarly field, as well as related developments in visual culture and photography studies. But, as I came to Holocaust studies from feminist criticism and comparative literature, the book also gestures broadly and comparatively in the direction of the layered and intertwined transnational memorial landscape that marks the particular epoch of its genealogy from the mid-1980s through the first decade of the twenty-first century. In attempting to look back to the past in order to move forward toward the future, it asks how memory studies, and the work of postmemory, might constitute a platform of activist and interventionist cultural and political engagement, a form of repair and redress, inspired by feminism and other movements for social change.

BEGINNINGS

We've learned to be suspicious of origin stories, but somehow I know with unusual clarity that, for me, it began in 1986. Not personally, of course, but intellectually and professionally. The School of Criticism and Theory (SCT) had just come to Dartmouth College, where I was teaching, and its presence made for an intense academic summer, replete with lectures, seminars, and public events. It was a contentious time, as well, because the SCT, like the world of high theory in the U.S. academy, was still a male stronghold, and women, especially feminist theorists, were both clamoring for recognition and busy toppling and reimagining basic assumptions. In 1986 Elaine Showalter was one of the first women invited to teach at the SCT, and feminists on the Dartmouth faculty and in the School closed ranks around her to help ensure her success and the doors it would open for others.

Showalter's presence and that of Geoffrey Hartman, the SCT's director, helped initiate a transition in my work from feminist literary and psychoanalytic criticism to feminist Holocaust and memory studies. The occasion I remember with such lucidity was a public showing, in Dartmouth's Loews' Theater, of Claude Lanzmann's monumental film *Shoah*, released in France the previous year. I had read about the film and was quite hesitant to go see it, not because of the stamina required by its two-part showing on two consecutive days (five hours on the first day and four and a half on the second), but because I had spent decades assiduously avoiding films about the Holocaust. Although I did not yet think of myself as a child of survivors (that term was not available to me), I could not bear to see any graphic representations of the events that had dominated my childhood nightmares. I had found myself totally unprepared at a showing of Alain Resnais's *Night and Fog* as a college student, and, fifteen years later, I had not yet recovered from the shock of the evening in which I had literally become ill in the bathroom of the auditorium at Phillips Academy, where I was teaching summer school.[15] Even by the late 1970s, I could not bear to look at more than half an episode of the television series *Holocaust*. And yet I knew that everyone would be talking about *Shoah* in Hanover and at Dartmouth, and I thus bravely decided to try watching it, though *Night and Fog* was still burned into my eyelids. I sat right next to the door so as to be able to bolt if the images became too hard to look at. My husband, Leo, himself a child of Viennese Jewish refugees from the Nazis and born in Bolivia during the war, held my hand.

Something quite amazing and life-changing happened on that July afternoon, however: I did not leave the theater but became so fascinated with the very horrific details of persecution and extermination that I had systematically banished from my visual consciousness for many years as to watch the film in these two sittings, see it again many times, teach it and write about it, and spend the next decades thinking and writing about the subjects it opened up. Was it because Lanzmann eschews archival images and relies on oral testimonies that evoke the horror without showing it that I was able to sit through the film without leaving? Or was it his own curiosity, his mediating persona that engaged me so deeply as a viewer? When the film was over, I knew that something had shifted in my relationship to this horrific past. And not just for me: others in the audience were also profoundly affected; sensing this, Geoffrey Hartman organized a discussion about the film for SCT participants and members of the Dartmouth faculty. We gathered on a Friday afternoon in the elegant Wren Room in the English Department to talk about the film. I don't remember very much about the conversation, except that, at one point, looking at each other across the room, Elaine Showalter and I simultaneously exclaimed: "Where are the women in the film?" The question was quickly dismissed: attempting to detail the very process of extermination, the film focused on the Sonderkommando who were closest to it—those prisoners forced to clean the gas chambers, gather the victims' belongings, carry out the burning of the bodies—and only men were chosen for these horrific assignments. How could we even ask such a question, colleagues exclaimed; why would gender be relevant in a case where all Jews were targeted for extermination? But other men were interviewed besides the Sonderkommando, I whispered to Leo, who was sitting next to me, why were there so few women? Of the nine and a half hours of film, it seemed that only a tiny fraction had women's faces on screen. Why were women relegated to the role of translators and mediators? Why were they allowed to sing in the film and not to talk about their experiences as the men were invited to do?

And how did the absence of women shape the story told in this remarkable document? These questions remained both with Leo and with me.

Nine months later, in April 1987, *Shoah* was shown on public television over several nights; on one night, PBS aired an interview with the director. Leo and I watched the entire film again, fascinated by its choices. We were still trying to understand the absence of women: how could the film be so brilliant and also so blind? That question soon receded, when, shortly afterward, at a family event, we found ourselves in an entirely new set of conversations. Suddenly Leo's aunt Frieda, her friends Lore and Kuba, and other friends of theirs—all Holocaust survivors—surrounded us in a corner of Frieda's living room and began talking about the camps. Although we had tried to engage Frieda and some of her friends on previous occasions, they had never wanted to say more than a few words about their wartime past. It turned out that they had all watched *Shoah* on television, but it was not the film that they wished to discuss with us; it was their own acts of survival, the deaths of their parents, siblings, and first spouses, the pain, anger and melancholy they had suppressed for too many years. *Shoah* authorized their acts of witness, we quickly understood; it made them feel that they had a story to tell and listeners who might be willing to acknowledge and receive it from them. On that afternoon, we became those listeners, though we did not yet understand the responsibilities that came with this role.

I could not yet imagine teaching *Shoah* (the length alone seemed utterly forbidding), but that same year I had begun to teach another work about Holocaust memory, Art Spiegelman's *Maus*, which had been published the previous year. I was not teaching it in a course on the Holocaust—that would come later—but I thought it the perfect work to use in an introductory comparative literature course and in my first-year seminars. In fact, I soon found myself teaching *Maus* every year, no matter what I was teaching. Spiegelman's foregrounding of the structures of mediation and representation was enormously useful pedagogically. But there was something else that drew me in as well: Artie's persona, the son who did not live through the war but whose life, whose very self, was shaped by it. I identified with him profoundly, without fully realizing what that meant. In class, I was focusing on aesthetic and narratological questions of representation, and I was also interested in discussing the gender issues in *Maus*, the way it was structured as a transaction between men who were mourning the wife and mother who had committed suicide, whose diaries had been burned and whose voice would never be heard.

By 1987 my fascination with *Shoah* and *Maus* came together in plans for an interdisciplinary team-taught summer course, "After Such Knowledge: Culture and Ideology in Twentieth-Century Europe," with a long section on the Second World War and the Holocaust. As we were preparing the class, along with co-instructors Michael Ermarth and Brenda Silver, I attended my first Holocaust conference, "Writing and the Holocaust," held at SUNY Albany in April 1987, organized by Berel Lang and published as a book with the same title the following year. The conference provided a rich introduction to the debates in the field and to its most distinguished scholars and writers. Bringing historians, writers, and cultural critics together encouraged productive if sometimes acrimonious disagreements about fact and representation, as exemplified by Raul Hilberg's unexpected deference to literature and storytelling mentioned earlier. Five years before the historic conference on "Probing the Limits of Representation" that Saul Friedlander organized at U.C. Irvine and that featured now legendary debates between Hayden White and Carlo Ginsburg about White's notion of the "emplotment" of history and the "problem of truth," "Writing and the Holocaust" introduced the ideas of "the memory of history" and of "fiction as truth"—ideas that remain controversial to this day.[16]

Although a number of the speakers at the Albany conference were women, gender did not figure as a category of analysis, and no one raised it as a question—surprising for me, as I had been attending feminist conferences for more than a decade. Even more surprising was the curt dismissal I received when I enthusiastically attempted to compliment Cynthia Ozick after she read, "The Shawl," her crushing and brilliant story about a mother whose baby is brutally murdered by an SS guard before her eyes, to a rapt audience.[17] I was in the process of finishing a book on mothers and daughters in which I argued that, in feminism and in psychoanalysis, the mother's voice is rarely heard, but that the daughter tends to speak for her.

"Your story means so much to me," I started to say when I met Ozick in the bathroom. "Especially since I am writing a book on mothers and daughters in literature."

"Oh, that's not what the story is about at all," she replied and turned away. I had read about Ozick's reluctance to be thought of as a "woman writer," and yet in Ozick's Rosa I found something I had been searching for in my work on *The Mother/Daughter Plot*—a way to represent the subjectivity of the mother, not mediated by the daughter's narrative as in the novels of Colette or Virginia Woolf, for example, but the subjectivity of the mother herself, the unspeakable mother who cannot protect her child, who cannot keep her alive, but who, devastatingly, survives her brutal murder. What did Ozick's disavowal mean? Why was it so troubling to think *women* and *the Holocaust* in the same frame?

Ozick's reading brought me back to another transformative event that had occurred in 1986, compounding these discoveries and drawing me, irrevocably, to the subject of memory and transmission: Toni Morrison's visit to Dartmouth and her public reading of the first chapter of *Beloved* a full year before the novel's publication. When I heard Morrison read Sethe's powerful voice and articulate the story of the traumatized mother and her bodily remembrance, I knew I could not finish my book until I had read the novel in its entirety. I began and ended *The Mother/Daughter Plot* with Sethe, but Ozick's story somehow became part of another narrative and a different, future, project for me. Indeed, I had not yet been able to find the interface between the feminist questions I was asking about female and maternal subjectivity and the work on memory and the Holocaust toward which I would begin to turn, more deeply, in the 1990s. Morrison's novel was the hinge: it made women both the carriers and the narrators of historical persecution. It dramatized the haunting, transgenerational reach of trauma, and it showed me that latency need not mean forgetting or oblivion. Generations after slavery, Morrison was able to convey its impacts and effects more powerfully than contemporary accounts. How is trauma transmitted across generations, I began to wonder? How is it remembered by those who did not live it or know it in their own bodies? This is the story of Denver in the novel, as it is the story of Spiegelman's Artie. In some ways, I began to acknowledge, it is my story as well.

I had just begun to conceive some of these questions when Dartmouth College announced a new initiative funded by the Mellon Foundation: the opportunity to gather an interdisciplinary group of scholars from Dartmouth and beyond to pursue work around a common topic in the context of a term-long humanities institute. With several colleagues, I participated in a series of meetings that resulted in an institute in the spring of 1990 on "Gender and War: Roles and Representations." We invited Klaus Theweleit to be our resident senior fellow because he had done some of the most interesting work on masculinity and war that we had read: aware of how easily the notion of gender can be conflated with women, we wanted to ensure that the topic of the institute would indeed be "gender and war" rather than "women and war." Theweleit's presence, and that of the other fellows and guest lecturers, created an intense and supportive atmosphere in which to look at the gendered structures not only of war, but of what we then understood as "representation." It gave Leo and me the time and the context to work on Lanzmann's *Shoah*, one of the most challenging works we had ever encountered. Watching the film again, discussing it with colleagues in the institute, and going to hear Claude Lanzmann speak at Yale propelled the first collaborative publication project we undertook, our essay "Gendered Translations: Claude Lanzmann's *Shoah*."[18] In *Shoah*, we argued, women are not simply absent: they tend to function as translators and as mediators carrying the story and its affective fabric, but not generating it themselves. A few Polish witnesses and one German informant do provide some important testimony, but Jewish women in the film merely cry or sing; they are haunting voices in the rubble of the Warsaw ghetto, rather than key witnesses to the workings of extermination or to suffering and survival. Indeed, it is their silence and visual absence that enables the act of witness from "inside" the spaces of death that characterizes the film and allows a horrific past to erupt and invade the present. This analysis of *Shoah* was, for each of us, our first foray into the study of the Holocaust and its memory and our first essay on a visual work. It inspired a set of preoccupations that would engage both of us, in and across our respective disciplines—history and literary and cultural studies—for the next decades.

And yet I still did not think of myself as a Holocaust scholar, but, following on *The Mother/Daughter Plot*, I had begun to work on family photographs and family narratives as media of memory and loss. I was working with the theories of Roland Barthes, Walter Benjamin, and Victor Burgin, on writers like Marguerite Duras and Jamaica Kincaid, and on artists like Edward Steichen, Cindy Sherman, Lorie Novak, and Sally Mann when, in 1991, Art Spiegelman's *Maus II* appeared. In the midst of the drawings of mice and cats there were two photographs of people, one of his lost brother, Richieu, on the dedication page, the other of his father, Vladek, at the end. With the photograph of his mother, Anja, and himself as a young boy in the first volume, Spiegelman had allowed photography to reconstitute his nuclear family, a family destroyed by the Holocaust and its traumatic aftereffects. An analysis of the use of photographs in the graphic pages of *Maus* became the first chapter of my book on family photographs, *Family Frames*, and the inspiration for the idea of postmemory.

Even as I was continuing work on the familial look and gaze, and on the autoportrait and the maternal look, I found that I could not evoke the power that family photos hold in our imagination without writing personally, about my own pictures and the power they hold for me. And, for me, I realized, that power is intimately bound up with my family's displacement and exile, and with the familial and collective losses that were provoked by the Second World War in Europe. *Family Frames* could easily have morphed into two books, and at times I felt that the compelling issues raised by the memory of the Holocaust (not just in *Maus*, but also in the memorial writing and visual installations of Eva Hoffman, Christian Boltanski, Shimon Attie, and the newly opened United States Holocaust Memorial Museum) threatened to overshadow and overtake the critical and theoretical concerns related to family photography with which I had begun the project. I was writing out of a very particular location and a subject position I had never before seen as my own, that of the daughter of survivors—not camp survivors, to be sure, but survivors of persecution, ghettoization, and displacement. I was writing as someone who had inherited the legacy of a distant and incomprehensible past that I was only just beginning to be ready to study and to try to understand from a larger historical and generational perspective. Family photos became my own media of postmemory and helped me define the notion, though not yet refine or focus on it closely. That focus would follow in two subsequent projects, *Ghosts of Home* and *The Generation of Postmemory*, both in response to images and stories that captured me and drew me in for years to come.

Indeed, the book that Leo Spitzer and I coauthored on the afterlife of my family's city of origin in Jewish memory was, in essence, a work both of and about postmemory. *Ghosts of Home* emerged from the "return" trip Leo and I were able to take to present-day Ukrainian Chernivtsi with my parents, a trip that finally allowed me to anchor my postmemories in a specific time and place. It emerged from the urgency we felt to tell a little-known story of my family's largely assimilated cosmopolitan Eastern European Jewish culture that was destroyed and displaced but that persisted in the memory and the identity of its survivors and their children. While working on *Ghosts of Home* together—traveling to Chernivtsi on several occasions, as well as to Romania, Western Europe, and Israel and throughout the United States to collect oral histories from survivors, including family and friends—we had a great many opportunities to reflect more theoretically and critically on the workings of memory and intergenerational transmission. Not all of those reflections had a place in a book written on a closely focused theme and for a more general audience. Our analyses of the methodologies mobilized by this postmemorial work, and our thinking about the archives and objects we were using to write this history, found their way into conference papers and invited lectures and into the two collaboratively written essays included here. My own essays on memory, visuality, and gender were certainly inspired by this personal postmemory work, but they also emerged from the theoretical discussions in the evolving field of cultural memory; from my teaching, and co-teaching with Leo, of courses on Holocaust, memory, and testimony; and, strangely, from my obsessive reading and viewing of images and testimonies of the camp experiences that my parents were fortunate to evade. After decades of avoiding them, I now found I had to look and to try to understand.

Admittedly, the discussions that inspired and inflected this work—in my collaboration with Leo, in the classroom, at conferences, and on the pages of journals, edited volumes, and special issues—were not just scholarly or professional: many of them were intensely personal. It turned out that throughout the late 1980s, the 1990s, and the early 2000s, many of my feminist colleagues and friends had also turned to the study of memory and trauma; they had come to the field out of both their individual histories and their political commitments. At breakfasts and lunches, and over coffee or drinks at various conferences and on the campuses where I was presenting this work, I came to learn of the family histories, some quite traumatic, of colleagues I had known for years, but in different contexts. We began to talk about what it means to be children of Holocaust survivors, members of the "second generation," and, later also, as Leo had experienced, the "1.5 generation" of child survivors. Did we share similar experiences? Was it a syndrome? Was it different for children of camp survivors, or for children of those who had survived in hiding, by fleeing east to the Soviet Union or west to the Americas, with false papers or with special waivers, as my parents did? Was it different for those whose parents talked readily about their experiences and those whose parents were silent? What was our stake in their story, what were our motivations, what was the source of our urgency? Why now? Were we appropriating their stories, overidentifying, perhaps—and this always in a whisper—envious of the drama of their lives that our lives could never match? Were we making a career out of their suffering? And what about other traumatic histories—slavery, dictatorships, war, political terror, apartheid? Among my fellow travelers on these journeys, I found a number of feminist scholars known for their work on women writers and artists and for their theoretical work on sex and gender, on power and social difference. Like me, they had begun to explore personal histories either indirectly, or more explicitly in their critical and theoretical work on trauma and transmission. But, although for all of us working on different sites of trauma and different historical contexts, this work on memory was intensely personal and urgent, it was not necessarily autobiographical or familial.

Thinking back, I now see that along with other feminist colleagues, I turned to the study of memory out of the conviction that, like feminist art, writing, and scholarship, it offered a means to uncover and to restore experiences and life stories that might otherwise remain absent from the historical archive. As a form of counter-history, "memory" offered a means to account for the power structures animating forgetting, oblivion, and erasure and thus to engage in acts of repair and redress. It promised to propose forms of justice outside of the hegemonic structures of the strictly juridical, and to engage in advocacy and activism on behalf of individuals and groups whose lives and whose stories have not yet been thought. At the same time, feminism and other movements for social change also offer important directions for the study and work on memory. They make activism integral to scholarship. They open a space for the consideration of affect, embodiment, privacy, and intimacy as concerns of history, and they shift our attention to the minute events of daily life. They are sensitive to the particular vulnerabilities of lives caught up in historical catastrophe, and the differential effects trauma can have on different historical subjects. It is important, also, to note that they bring critical attention to the agents and the technologies of cultural memory, particularly to its genealogies and the traditional oedipal familial structures where these often take shape. They scrutinize and refuse the sentimentality attached to the figure of the lost child that often mediates traumatic stories, enjoining us to queer that figure and to engage in alternative patterns of affiliation beyond the familial, forming alternate attachments across lines of difference.

Recently, at a panel on memory studies in New York, a historian skeptical of the field's rapid growth and widening reach outlined what he saw as its genealogy and named its "founding fathers"—Maurice Halbwachs, Pierre Nora, and Michel Foucault.[19] Although these theorists are certainly foundational, this was neither my genealogy nor that of other feminists in the audience. Had one of us been asked to tell an origin story, we exclaimed during the coffee break, we would have named Sigmund Freud and Melanie Klein; Virginia Woolf, Marcel Proust, and Toni Morrison; Hannah Arendt, Shoshana Felman, and Cathy Caruth. We would have gone back to the early days of feminist scholarship, especially to women's history and its search for a "usable past," and we would have discussed the political valences that, for us, inflected the field.

And yet, although feminist/queer scholarship and memory studies have shared a number of central preoccupations and political commitments, the two fields have developed along parallel and mostly nonintersecting tracts over the last two and a half decades. In our 2002 coedited issue of *Signs*, titled "Gender and Cultural Memory," Valerie Smith and I argued that "to date there have been very few sustained efforts to theorize in such general and comparative terms about memory from the perspective of feminism," and we viewed our issue as an opportunity for an overdue "interdisciplinary and international dialogue between feminist theories and theories of cultural memory."[20] That dialogue happened in the issue and has been evolving elsewhere, but I would maintain that it has not yet resulted in a developed theoretical elaboration on memory and gender or on a sustained effort to theorize memory from feminist and queer perspectives. As some of the following chapters will show, and as my evocation of that 1986 discussion about *Shoah* at the SCT suggests, this effort is particularly fraught when it comes to catastrophic historical events like the Holocaust. Most of the chapters comprising this book were written in the attempt to offer some suggestions about the terms such a broader theorization might take.

If gender and sexuality have entered Holocaust studies in the last twenty years, they have primarily been used to create a lens through which we can understand the particularities found in women's testimonies and memoirs, and to shape a platform that has enabled those stories to emerge and be heard in a context in which masculine and heteronormative stories had for the most part dominated. My own interest in this book joins a different set of feminist approaches that explore the rhetoric and the politics of memory and transmission, in some of the ways suggested by the analysis of *Shoah*.[21] As Claire Kahane has put it: "If hysteria put gender at the very center of subjectivity, trauma, in its attention to the assault on the ego and the disintegration of the subject, seems to cast gender aside as irrelevant. . . . Does feminist theory of the past several decades make a difference in my reading of Holocaust narratives? . . . Could—and should—the Holocaust even be considered within the context of gender?"[22] In response, my broader aim in this volume is to suggest a reframing of the discussion of gender in Holocaust studies. On the one hand, I want to avoid what I see as an unfortunate and all too common opposition between erasing difference and exaggerating it to the point of celebrating the skills and qualities of women over those of men. On the other hand, I would like to think beyond "relevance" or "appropriateness" as analytic categories. Indeed, the analyses in the book's chapters find that gender, as sexual difference, can fulfill a number of functions in the work of memory. It can serve as a figure that can mediate the ways in which certain images and certain narratives have been able to circulate in the culture of the postgeneration. In traumatic histories, gender can be invisible or hypervisible; it can make trauma unbearable or it can serve as a fetish that helps to shield us from its effects. It can offer a position through which memory can be transmitted within the family and beyond it, distinguishing mother-daughter transmission from that of fathers and daughters or fathers and sons, for example. It can offer a lens through which to read the domestic and the public scenes of memorial acts. And even when gender seems to be erased or invisible, feminist and queer readings can nevertheless illuminate not just what stories are told or forgotten, or what images are seen or suppressed, but how those stories are told and how those images are constructed. In its awareness of power as a central factor in the construction of the archive, moreover, feminist analysis can shift the frames of intelligibility so as to allow new experiences to emerge, experiences that have heretofore remained unspoken, or even unthought.

THE TASKS OF MEMORY

Most of this book's chapters were written during a period when anxieties about the death of the generation of survivors and the responsibilities they were transferring to their descendants were at a peak. This is also the period when Holocaust studies developed as a field. Although I use the Holocaust as example and historical frame of reference in these chapters, I am also sensitive to the fact that at the beginning of the second decade of the twenty-first century—after the brutal dictatorships in Latin America; after Bosnia, Rwanda, and Darfur; during the aftermath, globally, of the events of September 11, 2001; and in the midst of the Israeli/Palestinian conflict—the Holocaust can no longer serve simply as a conceptual limit case in the discussion of historical trauma, memory, and forgetting. Certainly, my analysis is in dialogue with numerous other contexts of traumatic transfer that can be understood as postmemory. In fact, the process of intergenerational transmission has become an important explanatory vehicle and object of study in sites such as American slavery; the Vietnam War; the Dirty War in Argentina and other dictatorships in Latin America; South African apartheid; Soviet, East European, and Chinese communist terror; the Armenian, the Cambodian, and the Rwandan genocides: the Japanese internment camps in the United States; the stolen generations in aboriginal Australia; the Indian partition; and others. It is precisely this kind of resonance I was hoping for in developing the idea of postmemory throughout my writing on this subject, and, in the book's last section, I explicitly engage in such connective and intersecting analyses that I have come to see as absolutely necessary if we are to move forward in the field.

Although I am drawn to the challenge of comparative approaches to memory studies, I have also experienced the risks of such frameworks and the ways in which comparison can slip into problematic equation and distressing competition over suffering. At a conference on testimony focusing on the Holocaust and the South African Truth and Reconciliation Commission held in the late 1990s, for example, it soon became obvious that different emphases and goals were driving the memory work of the different survivor communities. On the one hand, historians and psychoanalysts engaged in Holocaust survivor testimony stressed the unspeakability and incommensurability of trauma and the long reach of its symptoms. Ethically and politically, also, it seemed important to them to "keep the wounds open" so as to warn against forgetting and oblivion, to underscore the injunction "Never again." On the other hand, justices, commissioners, and scholars of the TRC articulated a very different discourse of truth-telling, reconciliation, forgiveness, and reparation, a pragmatic process to serve a "democratic future" within a space in which former victims and former perpetrators needed to coexist. These different approaches, based on divergent histories, are difficult to articulate in neutral terms, and the conference did, at certain moments, acquire an unfortunate and unproductive competitive tone. I saw how easy it is for comparative frameworks to be become unfairly weighted toward certain cultural strategies of working through a traumatic past at the expense of others.[23]

Some of the same debates that have inflected comparative approaches to memory, however, have thrown a dark shadow within Holocaust studies as well. Here also different subject positions compete over authority and authenticity. Virulent critiques of the work on the second generation, including my own, have been based on an assumption that children of survivors want to equate their suffering with that of their parents, appropriating it for their own identity purposes. According to Gary Weissman, second-generation writers and scholars suffer from "fantasies of witnessing," and he contests the very notion of a "post-Holocaust generation."[24] Ruth Franklin, in *The New Republic* and in her recent book *A Thousand Darknesses*, attributes to us baser motives still: "driven by ambition or envy or narcissism, a number of the children of survivors—commonly referred to as 'the second generation'—have constructed elaborate literary fictions that serve to elevate their own childhood traumas above and even beyond the sufferings of their parents."[25] Some volumes on the second generation do, in fact, open themselves to such critique. Even the title of Melvin Bukiet's anthology *Nothing Makes You Free* hints at the appropriation of suffering, underscored by the exclusively biological definition of second generation that Bukiet applies in his selection of writers to include. Names and appellations are important: we are not, I would maintain, "second-generation survivors" or "second-generation witnesses," as Alan L. Berger has written in his *Children of Job*.[26] Many scholars working on the postgeneration have tried to find the delicate balance between identification and distance, and they do so, most successfully, by discovering and analyzing the complex and multiply mediated aesthetic strategies of second-generation artists and writers from different historical contexts, such as the ones who have inspired the chapters of this book.[27]

Other critiques focus on the ways in which Holocaust memory, along with the paradigm of trauma that has developed around it, has functioned as a readily available and appropriable victim identity position and screen memory in the United States, occluding other, more proximate histories of violence.[28] The challenge may be how to account for contiguous or intersecting histories without allowing them to occlude or erase each other, how to turn competitive or appropriative memory into more capacious transnational memory work. Such an expansion does not in any sense aim to diminish or relativize the experiences and suffering of European Holocaust survivors. On the contrary, its goal would be to incorporate these memories into an enlarged global arena, making room for additional, local, regional, national, and transnational memories. The notion of "connective histories" that I use in this book aims to think divergent histories alongside and in connection with each other. A number of recent "connective" transnational projects have, to my mind, responded to this challenge and have begun to chart a future direction in both Holocaust and memory studies. Among these, I would single out Daniel Levy and Nathan Sznaider's *The Holocaust and Memory in a Global Age*, Michael Rothberg's *Multidirectional Memory: Remembering the Holocaust in the Age of Decolonization*, Andreas Huyssen's careful and critical formulation of palimpsestic and interwoven histories that result in related memorial aesthetics across vast cultural divides, and Gabriele Schwab's personal and theoretical reflections on "haunting legacies" emerging from the intertwined histories of victims and perpetrators, the Holocaust and colonialism. Levy and Sznaider propose that the European memory of the Holocaust can itself have a broader effect by "facilitat[ing] the formation of transnational memory cultures, which in turn, have the potential to become the cultural foundation for global human rights politics."[29] In a different approach, Rothberg's notion of "multidirectional memory" calls attention to a series of imbrications between memory of the Holocaust and postwar movements of decolonization and civil rights. And Gabriele Schwab adds, "It is not so much that our memories go in or come from many directions but rather that they are always already composites of dynamically interrelated and conflicted histories."[30]

I believe it is indeed now time for such a "multidirectional" or "connective" approach with different starting and reference points and different models, suggesting paradigms and strategies for working through and, yes, also, without forgetting, for moving beyond a traumatic past. I hope that the notion of postmemory can provide a useful framework for such connective approaches. As the next chapters will show, I am interested in exploring affiliative structures of memory beyond the familial, and I see this connective memory work as another form of affiliation across lines of difference.

In addition, media theorist Andrew Hoskins has recently used the notion of connective memory in relation to the "connective turn" memory has taken in the digital age. Along with José van Dijck, he argues that in the digital, memory is neither *collective* nor *re-colllective*, but, instead *connective*—structured *by* digital networks, and constituted "through the flux of contacts between people and digital technologies and media."[31] Memory, they argue, is constituted not only through individuals and through social institutions, but also through technological media. Tracing a history of the second half of the twentieth century through the first decade of the twenty-first that moves from analog to digital media of memory, this book features memory's connectivity in both these senses.

The first part of the book, "Familial Postmemories and Beyond," focuses on the workings of familial memory, on its problematics and its limits. The first chapter examines some of the fundamental assumptions behind the idea of postmemory. It defines the workings of intergenerational transmission and scrutinizes them from a feminist perspective. In responding to three key questions—why memory? why family? why photography? it clarifies an important distinction I develop and carry through the volume between "familial" and "affiliative" postmemory. Two enormously influential texts, Art Spiegelman's *Maus* and W. G. Sebald's *Austerlitz*, reveal how the work of postmemory falls back on familiar, and unexamined, cultural images that facilitate its generation by tapping into what Aby Warburg saw as a broad cultural "storehouse of pre-established expressive forms"—in this case the images of the lost mother and the lost child. Read together, these two texts map the chronology of the works discussed in the book, from the mid-1980s to the early 2000s.

The second chapter, co-authored with Leo Spitzer, "What's Wrong with This Picture?," begins with a mysterious picture from my parents' family album and looks at it in relation to other archival images from a painful past that are reframed in second-generation fiction and artwork. We argue that, rather than giving information about that past, archival images function as "points of memory" that tell us more about our own needs and desires, our own fantasies and fears, than about the past to which they supposedly bear witness. The notion of small "points of memory," inspired by Roland Barthes's *punctum*, connects productively to feminist preoccupations with the subjective, the daily, the intimate and embodied, the affective. The third chapter, "Marked by Memory," asks how the sense memory of trauma—represented by the mark on the skin—can be transferred across generations. It studies this question particularly through the identification and bodily connection between mother and daughter, but it also examines cross-identifications and interconnections—between the memories of the Holocaust and slavery and between African American and Jewish memory cultures, and between a male artist and his female subjects. It defines "postmemory" in contrast to Toni Morrison's "rememory," moving from the familial and embodied workings of rememory to the mediated structures of postmemory.

In the book's second part, "Affiliation, Gender, and Generation," I move more explicitly from familial to affiliative structures of transmission. Chapter 4, "Surviving Images," asks why images become iconic and which ones, and it argues that repetition actually produces rather than screens trauma in the viewer. By invoking the most dehumanizing and impersonal of iconic images—the gate of Auschwitz and the bulldozer burying corpses, for example—it shows, like the following two chapters, that gender can modulate intolerable images and acts of dehumanization, and that acts of witness are fundamentally gendered. Chapter 5, "Nazi Photographs in Post-Holocaust Art," asks how artists of the postgeneration can use perpetrator images structured by a genocidal Nazi gaze to memorialize victims. This chapter examines tropes of feminization and infantilization that neutralize these images and enable them to be reframed in the art of the postgeneration. Chapter 6, "Projected Memory," wonders why images of children—and which images of children—have so easily become iconic and looks at the ways in which the identification with the endangered child can promote affiliative postmemory. In the co-authored chapter 7, "Testimonial Objects," Leo Spitzer and I read two books produced in concentration camps as "testimonial objects." We ask, particularly, what it means to read for gender in a context of hunger, threat, destruction, and dehumanization in which gender easily disappears from view. In imagining the camp community that produced these books, the analysis moves beyond familial structures to other forms of attachments and alternative structures of transmission.

While several of the essays in the first two parts touch on sites beyond the immediate context of the Holocaust, the essays in the third part, "Connective Histories," engage in more explicitly comparative memory work. Chapter 8, "Objects of Return," explores the role that objects (photographs, here read for their material qualities, domestic interiors, household objects, items of clothing) play in stories of return to a lost home. I develop further the idea of the "testimonial object" that shows how we inherit not only stories and images from the past, but also our bodily and affective relationship to the object world we inhabit. Here again, the familial and gendered image of the lost child returns as a powerful figure of extreme dispossession in the context of the familial ruptures caused by war, genocide, and expulsion. In focusing on Jewish and Palestinian stories of return, this chapter performs a connective approach to memory work. The book ends with a ninth chapter, "Postmemory's Archival Turn," that examines the archives of postmemory, here specifically the album and its digital afterlife on the World Wide Web. It asks what happens to the materiality of images when they circulate on the Web by looking at two postmemorial albums, drawn from the different historical and political circumstances of Polish Jews and Kurds. Collected in the aftermath of historical catastrophe and destruction, they attempt to reconstruct the traces of lost communities on the basis of images and artifacts. Looking specifically at women collectors, the chapter reaches beyond family and historical specificity to explore transnational aesthetic structures after the Holocaust and in the digital age.

I like to think of these capacious, nonessentialist approaches to memory as practices of "reparative reading" in the terms that Eve Kosofsky Sedgwick has so usefully inspired.[32] Unlike "paranoid reading," which is "anticipatory," "monopolistic," demystifying, and confident of exposing a "true knowledge," "reparative reading" offers alternative ways of knowing. In the terms of postmemory, it might offer possibilities of knowing that are, in Sedgwick's terms, "contingent," "additive," and "accretive," "mutable." Such a reparative approach to memory would be open to connective approaches and affiliations—thinking different historical experiences in relation to one another to see what vantage points they might share or offer each other for confronting the past without allowing its tragic dimensions to overwhelm our imagination in the present and the future.

The techniques of projection and superimposition Lorie Novak uses in her evocative *Postmemory*—the cover image of this book—bring some of these layered contradictions to the surface. Incongruously, two hands hold a photo album in a luminous forest setting, announcing the many hands, and the many different protective acts of holding memory, that we will see in the images populating this book. The album is open and features two photos: on the left, a young family, parents and a little boy, arms embracing, all looking intently toward the right of the camera lens. The summer dress and short sleeve shirts, the bright light, indicate a summer day in freedom. On the facing page a woman in a light suit stands alone in front of a large open wooden door. Both these images are taken outdoors, though the second leaves an opening to a dark domestic interior, invisible to our eyes. Photo corners are used to affix the images to the album's elegant paper. It's an ordinary family photo album, created in seemingly ordinary circumstances, but here it is placed into the decidedly extraordinary setting of these woods. And, uncannily, several children's and young women's faces escape from the album: there are no photo corners to hold them in. One smiling girl hangs over the right page, a boy over the left; others float eerily among the trees. These images hover over the album, exceed its boundaries, co-existing with one another but, unintegrated, they do not cohere.

The landscape of *Postmemory* is peopled by faces from the past, by images in and out of the family album, by photos of victims and of survivors. Images originating in Vienna, La Paz, New York, and Izieu, France, from private and public albums and archives are superimposed on trees in upstate New York, near the artist's home. Memory is mediated, cultural, but it has also escaped through the open doorway in the photograph to haunt the natural landscapes of the present. The ghosts have become part of our landscape, reconfiguring the domestic as well as the public spaces of the postgeneration. Despite these invasions, however, the woods themselves continue to replenish in the bright sunshine, the trees persist in reaching upward, indifferent witnesses to the layered connective histories projected onto them.

I.

FAMILIAL POSTMEMORIES AND BEYOND

1.1 Art Spiegelman, from *The First Maus* (1972). First published in *Funny Aminals*. *Courtesy of Art Spiegelman*

1

THE GENERATION OF POSTMEMORY

When Art Spiegelman first began to draw his father's story
of survival in Auschwitz, and his own childhood reception
of that story, he relied on familiar visual archives and narrative traditions that he then transformed in radical and surprising ways.
The three-page *First Maus*, published in 1972, begins as a bedtime story
"about life in the old country during the war."[1] Visually, a small drawing
of the house in Rego Park opens out to a larger frame of the child's bedroom, where the partially pulled shade, the toy figure holding up the
lamp, the polka-dot pajamas, the checkered blanket, and the cozy hug
create a seemingly safe scene in which the father can evoke for his son the
most brutal stories of wartime violence and persecution, fear and terror.

The mice and cats in the flashback images have not yet achieved the
visual economy they will eventually find in the subsequent *Maus* volumes, but the condensed account of the liquidation of the unnamed
ghetto, the attempts at hiding, and the murders, betrayals, and deportation to Auschwitz already connect personal and public memory, present
and past, in paradigmatic ways. The window shade is only partially
pulled down, after all, and the postwar childhood is not protected from

the history it has inherited. Indeed, that history is absorbed in the most vulnerable moments of childhood: the intimate exchange of the bedtime story. As Spiegelman will say later, in the subtitle of *Maus I*, "My father bleeds history."[2]

And indeed, blood flows on this page, off the title letters spelling MAUS that bleed into the large, half-page title image that will remain foundational for Spiegelman, serving as the cover image of the second volume and appearing in a number of other frames. It is a drawing of a widely circulated 1945 photograph by Margaret Bourke-White of liberated male prisoners in Buchenwald, standing behind a barbed wire fence and all facing the photographer, huddled in blankets and torn uniforms, some holding on to the fence. Spiegelman's early drawn version of the photograph is distinct from its later incarnations not only in its drawing style, but also in the photo corners on the edges that show how this public image has been adopted into the private family album. Indeed, the arrow pointing to a mouse figure in the back row and identifying him as "Poppa" clarifies that the son can only imagine his father's experience in Auschwitz by way of a well-known image from the public archive. Even the most intimate familial transmission of the past is, it seems, mediated by public images and narratives.

But if the scene of narration in the first *Maus* takes place between father and son in the striking absence of the mother, it is the powerful image of her loss that will mediate the adult father/son relationship and the narrative of the second generation developed in the later volumes. Maternal abandonment and the fantasy of maternal recognition, announced by implication in the first *Maus*, are paradigmatic tropes for the psychology and aesthetic of the postgeneration, and for the workings of postmemory. "Mickey's" mother appears in the early drawings, led along by her husband from one hiding place to another. But it is the father who is the narrator of her story, as well as his own. When *Die Katzen* capture the couple and send them off to "Mauschwitz," the father hugs his wife, who covers her eyes with her hands. Like the silent women in *Shoah*, she has no voice, but she provides a mute emotional backdrop to the horrific tale in which she is inscribed. Her absence from the bedroom, her inability to modulate her child's reception of the father's history lesson, leave him exposed and undefended.

The aesthetic and representational choices characterizing Spiegelman's early *Maus* and the later volumes make it a generative text with which to begin to scrutinize the workings of the transgenerational structure of postmemory, and the conjunction of several of its prevalent elements that will become key terms in the chapters that follow—memory, family, and photography.

WHY MEMORY?

Do children of survivors, like Artie in *Maus*, have "memories" of their parents' suffering? The bedtime scene of childhood transmission that Spiegelman draws suggests how the father's violent experiences can acquire the status of fairy tale, nightmare, and myth. It suggests some of the transactive, transferential processes—cognitive and affective—through which the past is internalized without fully being understood. These "acts of transfer," to use Paul Connerton's term, not only transform history into memory, but enable memories to be shared across individuals and generations.[3]

Certainly, we do not have literal "memories" of others' experiences, and certainly, one person's lived memories cannot be transformed into another's. Postmemory is not identical to memory: it is "post"; but, at the same time, I argue, it approximates memory in its affective force and its psychic effects. Eva Hoffman describes what was passed down to her as a fairy tale: "The memories—not memories but emanations—of wartime experiences kept erupting in flashes of imagery; in abrupt but broken refrains."[4] These "not memories," communicated in "flashes of imagery," and these "broken refrains," transmitted through "the language of the body," are precisely the stuff of the *postmemory* of trauma, and of its return.

Jan and Aleida Assmann's work on the transmission of memory clarifies precisely what Hoffman refers to as the "living connection"[5] between proximate generations and accounts for the complex lines of transmission encompassed in the inter- and transgenerational umbrella term "memory." The Assmanns have devoted themselves to elucidating, systematically, Maurice Halbwachs's enormously influential notion of *collective* memory.[6] I turn to their work here to scrutinize the lines of transmission between individual and collective remembrance and to specify how the break in transmission resulting from traumatic historical events necessitates forms of remembrance that reconnect and re-embody an intergenerational memorial fabric that is severed by catastrophe.

In his book *Das kulturelle Gedächtnis*, Jan Assmann distinguishes between two kinds of collective remembrance, "communicative" memory and what he calls "cultural" memory.[7] Communicative memory is "biographical" and "factual," and is located within a generation of contemporaries who witness an event as adults and who can pass on their bodily and affective connection to that event to their descendants. In the normal succession of generations (and the family is a crucial unit of transmission for Jan Assmann), this embodied form of memory is transmitted across three to four generations—across 80 to 100 years. At the same time, as its direct bearers enter old age, they increasingly wish to institutionalize memory, whether in traditional archives or books, or through ritual, commemoration, or performance. Jan Assmann terms this institutionalized archival memory "kulturelles Gedächtnis."

In her elaboration of this typology, Aleida Assmann extends this bimodal distinction into four memory "formats": the first two, "individual" memory and "social" memory, correspond to Jan Assmann's "communicative" remembrance, while "political" memory and "cultural" memory form part of his "cultural" memory.[8] A fundamental assumption driving this schema is, indeed, that "memories are linked between individuals." "Once verbalized," Aleida Assmann insists, "the individual's memories are fused with the inter-subjective symbolic system of language and are, strictly speaking, no longer a purely exclusive and unalienable property. . . . they can be exchanged, shared, corroborated, confirmed, corrected, disputed—and, last not least, written down."[9] And even individual memory "include[s] much more than we, as individuals, have ourselves experienced."[10] Individuals are part of social groups with shared belief systems that frame memories and shape them into narratives and scenarios. For Aleida Assmann, the family is a privileged site of memorial transmission. The "social memory" in her schema is based on the familial transfer of embodied experience to the next generation:

it is intergenerational. "Political" and "cultural" memory, in contrast, is not inter- but transgenerational; it is no longer mediated through embodied practice but solely through symbolic systems.

Jan and Aleida Assmann's typological distinctions do not specifically account for the ruptures introduced by collective historical trauma, by war, Holocaust, exile, and refugeehood: these ruptures would certainly inflect these schemas of transmission. Both embodied communicative memory and institutionalized cultural memory would be severely impaired by traumatic experience. They would be compromised as well by the erasures of records, such as those perpetrated by totalitarian regimes. Under the Nazis, cultural archives were destroyed, records burned, possessions lost, histories suppressed and eradicated.

The structure of postmemory clarifies how the multiple ruptures and radical breaks introduced by trauma and catastrophe inflect intra-, inter-, and transgenerational inheritance. It breaks through and complicates the line the Assmanns draw connecting individual to family, to social group, to institutionalized historical archive. That archive, in the case of traumatic interruption, exile, and diaspora, has lost its direct link to the past, has forfeited the embodied connections that forge community and society. And yet the Assmanns' typology explains why and how the postgeneration could and does work to counteract or to repair this loss. Postmemorial work, I want to suggest—and this is the central point of my argument in this book—strives to *reactivate* and *re-embody* more distant political and cultural memorial structures by reinvesting them with resonant individual and familial forms of mediation and aesthetic expression. In these ways, less directly affected participants can become engaged in the generation of postmemory that can persist even after all participants and even their familial descendants are gone.

It is this presence of embodied and affective experience in the process of transmission that is best described by the notion of memory as opposed to history. Memory signals an affective link to the past—a sense, precisely, of a material "living connection"—and it is powerfully mediated by technologies like literature, photography, and testimony.

The growth of our memory culture may indeed be a symptom of a need for individual and group inclusion in a collective membrane forged by a shared inheritance of multiple traumatic histories and the individual and social responsibility we feel toward a persistent and traumatic past. As Aleida Assmann writes, "the memory boom reflects a general desire to reclaim the past as an indispensible part of the present," and she suggests that the idea of "collective memory" has become an umbrella term that has replaced the notion of "ideology," prevalent in the discourses of the 1960s, 1970s, and 1980s.[11]

WHY THE FAMILY?

Maus locates the scene of transmission in the bedtime connection between parent and child. The language of family, the language of the body: nonverbal and precognitive acts of transfer occur most clearly within a familial space, often taking the form of symptoms. It is perhaps the descriptions of this symptomatology that have made it appear as though the postgeneration wanted to assert its own victimhood, alongside that of the parents, and to exploit it.

To be sure, children of those directly affected by collective trauma inherit a horrific, unknown, and unknowable past that their parents were not meant to survive. Second-generation fiction, art, memoir, and testimony are shaped by the attempt to represent the long-term effects of living in close proximity to the pain, depression, and dissociation of persons who have witnessed and survived massive historical trauma. They are shaped by the child's confusion and responsibility, by a desire to repair, and by the consciousness that her own existence may well be a form of compensation for unspeakable loss. Loss of family, home, of a sense of belonging and safety in the world "bleed" from one generation to the next.

For those of us in the *literal* second generation, as Eva Hoffman writes, "our own internal imagery is powerful" and linked both to the particular experiences communicated by our parents, and to the way these experiences come down to us as "emanations" in a "chaos of emotions." Even so, other images and stories, especially those public images related to the concentration and extermination camps, also "become part of [our] inner storehouse."[12] I would argue that, as public and private images and stories blend, distinctions and specificities between them are more difficult to maintain, and the more difficult they are to maintain, the more some of us might wish to reassert them so as to insist on the distinctiveness of a specifically *familial* generational identity.[13]

The photo corners at the edges of Art Spiegelman's early drawing, and the arrow pointing at "Poppa," show how the *language* of family can literally reactivate and re-embody an archival image whose subjects are, to most viewers, anonymous. This "adoption" of public, anonymous images into the family photo album finds its counterpart in the pervasive use of private, familial images and objects in institutions of public display—museums and memorials like the Tower of Faces in the United States Holocaust Memorial Museum or certain exhibits in the Museum of Jewish Heritage in New York—which thus construct every visitor as a familial subject. This fluidity (some might call it obfuscation) is made possible by the power of the *idea* of family, by the pervasiveness of the familial gaze, and by the forms of mutual *recognition* that define family images and narratives.[14]

Throughout this book, however, I argue that postmemory is *not* an *identity* position but a *generational* structure of transmission embedded in multiple forms of mediation. Family life, even in its most intimate moments, is entrenched in a collective imaginary shaped by public, generational structures of fantasy and projection and by a shared archive of stories and images that inflect the broader transfer and availability of individual and familial remembrance. Geoffrey Hartman's notion of "witnesses by adoption" and Ross Chambers's term "foster writing" acknowledge breaks and fractures in biological transmission even as they preserve a familial frame.[15] If, however, we thus *adopt* the traumatic experiences of others as experiences we *might ourselves have lived through*, if we inscribe them into our own life story, can we do so without imitating or unduly appropriating them?[16]

This question applies equally to the process of identification, imagination, and projection of those who grew up in survivor families, and of those less proximate members of their generation or relational network who share a legacy of trauma and thus the curiosity, the urgency, the frustrated *need* to know about a traumatic past. Still, their relationship to the past is certainly not the same. Eva Hoffman draws a line, however tenuous and permeable, between "the postgeneration as a whole and the *literal* second generation in particular."[17] To delineate the border between these respective structures of transmission—between what I would like to refer to as *familial* and "*affiliative*" postmemory—we would have to account for the difference between an intergenerational vertical identification of child and parent occurring within the family, and the intragenerational horizontal identification that makes that child's position more broadly available to other contemporaries.[18] But survivor families are often already fractured and disrupted: traumatized parents return from the camps to be taken care of, or to be rejected, by children who survived in hiding; families flee or emigrate to distant lands, and languages in host countries are more easily navigated by children than by parents. Affiliative postmemory is thus no more than an extension of the loosened familial structured occasioned by war and persecution. It is the result of contemporaneity and generational connection with the literal second generation, combined with a set of structures of mediation that would be broadly available, appropriable, and, indeed, compelling enough to encompass a larger collective in an organic web of transmission.

WHY PHOTOGRAPHS?

When Spiegelman adopts the Bourke-White image into his family album and points to an anonymous figure as "Poppa," he performs an affiliative postmemorial act. The key role that photographic images—and family photographs in particular—play as media of postmemory clarifies the connection between familial and affiliative postmemory, and the mechanisms by which public archives and institutions have been able both to re-embody and to re-individualize the more distant structures of cultural memory.

More than oral or written narratives, photographic images that survive massive devastation and outlive their subjects and owners function as ghostly revenants from an irretrievably lost past world. They enable us, in the present, not only to see and to touch that past, but also to try to reanimate it by undoing the finality of the photographic "take."[19]

The retrospective irony of every photograph consists precisely in the simultaneity of this effort and the consciousness of its impossibility. But is not all irony removed from such an act of viewing if violent death on a massive scale separates the two presents of the image?

Photographs, especially analog ones, of course, exist and survive, like memory, in "generations" of reproduction and reproducibility. As aura and authenticity fade in the processes of mechanical reproduction and now digitization, and as the relationship of the image to the original context of its production erodes, the changes images undergo mirror the movement from memory to postmemory.

In C. S. Peirce's tripartite definition of the sign, analog photographic images are more than purely indexical, or contiguous to the object in front of the lens: they are also iconic, exhibiting a mimetic similarity with that object.[20] Combining these two semiotic principles enables them also—quickly, and perhaps too easily—to assume symbolic status and thus, in spite of the vast archive of Holocaust images, the second generation seems to have inherited but a small number of specific images, or kinds of images, that have shaped our conception of the event and its transmission.[21] The power of the intercalated photos in the two *Maus* volumes can serve as illustration: the images of Anja and Richieu function as specters reanimating their dead subjects with indexical and iconic force. The photographs of Vladek in his concentration camp uniform, of Anja with her son, of Richieu as a young boy together reassemble a family destroyed by the Holocaust and consequently fractured in the artist's stylized drawings of mice and cats. They not only refer to their subjects and bring them back in their full appearance; they also symbolize the sense of family, safety, and continuity that has been hopelessly severed. Through the indexical link that joins the photograph to its subject—what Roland Barthes calls the "umbilical cord" made of light—photography, especially analog photography, can appear to solidify the tenuous bonds that are shaped by need, desire, and narrative projection.[22]

Whether they are family pictures of a destroyed world, or records of the process of its destruction, photographic images are fragmentary remnants that shape the cultural work of postmemory. The work that they have been mobilized to do for the postgeneration, in particular, ranges from the indexical to the symbolic. In his controversial book *Images in Spite of All*, the French art historian Georges Didi-Huberman describes the double regime of the photographic image: in it, he argues, we simultaneously find truth and obscurity, exactitude and simulacrum. Historical photographs from a traumatic past authenticate the past's existence, what Roland Barthes calls its *ça a été* or "having-been-there," and, in their flat two-dimensionality, they also signal its insurmountable distance and "de-realization."[23] Unlike public images or images of atrocity, however, family photos, and the familial aspects of postmemory would tend to diminish distance, bridge separation, and facilitate identification and affiliation. When we look at photographic images from a lost past world, especially one that has been annihilated by force, we look not only for information or confirmation, but for an intimate material and affective connection that would transmit the affective quality of the events. We look to be shocked (Benjamin), touched, wounded, and pricked (Barthes's punctum), torn apart (Didi-Huberman). Photographs thus become screens—spaces of projection and approximation, and of protection.[24] Small, two-dimensional, delimited by their frame, photographs minimize the disaster they depict, and screen their viewers from it. But in seeming to open a window to the past, and materializing the viewer's relationship to it, they also give a glimpse of its enormity and its power. They can tell us as much about our own needs and desires (as readers and spectators) as they can about the past world they presumably depict. While authentication and projection can work against each other, the powerful tropes of familiality can also, and sometimes problematically, obscure their distinction. The fragmentariness and the two-dimensional flatness of the photographic image, moreover, make it especially open to narrative elaboration and embroidery, and to symbolization.[25]

What is more, in Paul Connerton's useful terms, photography is an "inscriptive" (archival) memorial practice that, one could argue, retains an "incorporative" (embodied) dimension; as archival documents that inscribe aspects of the past, photographs give rise to certain bodily acts of looking and certain conventions of seeing and understanding that we have come to take for granted but that shape, seemingly re-embody, and render material, the past we are seeking to understand and receive.[26]

Sight, Jill Bennett has argued, is deeply connected to "affective memory": "Images have the capacity to address the spectator's own bodily memory; to *touch* the viewer who *feels* rather than simply sees the event, drawn into the image through a process of affective contagion. . . . Bodily response thus precedes the inscription of narrative, or moral emotion of empathy."[27]

Familial structures of mediation and representation facilitate the *affiliative* acts of the postgeneration. The idiom of family can become an accessible lingua franca easing identification and projection, recognition and misrecognition, across distance and difference. This explains the pervasiveness of family pictures and family narratives as artistic media in the aftermath of trauma. Still, the very accessibility of familial idioms and images needs also to engender suspicion on our part: does not locating trauma in the space of family personalize and individualize it too much? Does it not risk occluding a public historical context and responsibility, blurring significant differences—national difference, for example, or differences between the descendants of victims, perpetrators, and bystanders? And does it not undergird a fundamentally oedipal and heteronormative, reproductive form of social organization? Constructing the processes of transmission, and the postgeneration itself, in familial terms is as engaging as it is troubling.

If particular tropes and particular images become pervasive, they can offer a lens into some of the workings of postmemory and the mediations on which it relies. Close scrutiny of such repeated images enables us to see how postmemory risks falling back on familiar and often unexamined cultural images that facilitate its generation by tapping into what Aby Warburg saw as a broad cultural storehouse of "pre-established expressive forms."[28] Taking shape in the "iconology of the interval," the "space between thought and the deepest emotional impulses,"[29] these forms transmit affect across subjects and generations. For the post-Holocaust generation, these "pre-established" forms often take the shape of photographs—images of murder and atrocity, images of bare survival, and also images of a "before" that signal the deep loss of safety in the world. As "pre-established" and well-rehearsed forms prevalent in postmemorial writing, art, and display, some of these photographic images illustrate particularly well how gender can become a potent and troubling vehicle of remembrance for the postgeneration, and suggest one way in which we might theorize the relationship between memory and gender.

In order to make some of these points more immediately concrete, I want to turn to two images, drawn from Art Spiegelman's *Maus* and W. G. Sebald's *Austerlitz*. Illustrating the pervasive trope of maternal abandonment and the fantasy of maternal recognition, these pictures of lost mothers illuminate the performative regime of the photograph and the gazes of familial and affiliative postmemory that I develop further in the chapters that follow.[30]

WHY SEBALD?

In the late 1980s and early 1990s, Art Spiegelman's *Maus* played an important role in enabling the work of postmemory of an entire generation. That role fell to W. G. Sebald and particularly his 2001 novel *Austerlitz* in the first decade of the new millennium. Both works have spawned a veritable industry of critical and theoretical work on memory, photography, and transmission, and thus the differences between *Maus* and *Austerlitz* are a measure of the evolving conversations of and about the postgeneration. My comparative discussion here aims to bring out some of the elements implicit in these conversations—the continuing power that the familial and the indexical hold for Spiegelman and the less literal, much more fluid, conception of both that characterizes the turn-of-the-century remembrance illustrated by Sebald. In this sense, these two works form bookends to the period covered by the works discussed in the rest of this book.

Maus and *Austerlitz* share a great deal: a self-conscious, innovative, and critical aesthetic that palpably conveys absence and loss; the determination to know about the past and the acknowledgment of its elusiveness; the testimonial structure of listener and witness separated by relative proximity and distance to the events of the war (two men in both works); the reliance on looking and reading, on visual media in addition to verbal ones; and the consciousness that the memory of the past is an act firmly located in the present. Still, the two authors could not be more different: one the son of two Auschwitz survivors, a cartoonist who grew up in the United States; the other a son of Germans, a literary scholar and novelist writing in England.

The narrators of *Maus* are father and son, first and second generation, and their conversations illustrate how familial postmemory works through the transformations and mediations from the father's memory to the son's postmemory. The generational structure of *Austerlitz* and its particular kind of postmemory is more complicated: Sebald himself, born in 1944, belongs to the second generation, but through his character Austerlitz, born in 1934 and a member of the "1.5 generation," he blurs generational boundaries and highlights the current preoccupation with the persona of the child survivor. Austerlitz himself has no memory of his childhood in Prague, which was erased and superseded by the new identity he was given when he arrived in Wales and was raised by Welsh adoptive parents. The conversations in the novel are intragenerational conversations between the narrator and the protagonist who (we assume) were both young children during the war, one a non-Jewish German living in England, the other a Czech Jew. For them, the past is located in objects, images, and documents, in fragments and traces barely noticeable in the layered train stations, streets, and official and private buildings of the European cities in which they meet and talk. Standing outside the family, the narrator receives the story from Austerlitz and *affiliates* with it, thus illustrating the relationship between familial and affiliative postmemory. And, as a German, he also shows how the lines of affiliation can cross the divide between victim and perpetrator memory and postmemory.

Maus, while trenchantly critical of representational regimes and eager to foreground their artifice, remains, at the same time, anxious about the truth and accuracy of the son's graphic account of the father's prewar and wartime experiences in Poland. Indeed, in spite of its myriad distancing devices, the work achieves what Andreas Huyssen has called a "powerful effect of authentication."[31] That authentication, and even any concern about it, has disappeared in *Austerlitz*. The confusion experienced by Sebald's character, the profound losses he has suffered, his helpless meanderings and pointless searches, and the beautiful prose that conveys absence and an objectless and thus endless melancholia, all this combined with blurry, hard-to-make-out photographic images, speak somehow to a generation marked by a history to which they have lost even the distant and now barely "living connection" to which *Maus* uncompromisingly clings.

While *Maus* begins as a familial story, *Austerlitz* becomes so only halfway through: familiality, and thus also gender, anchor, individualize, and re-embody the free-floating, disconnected and disorganized feelings of loss and nostalgia that come to attach themselves to more concrete and seemingly authentic images and objects. Still, the world around Sebald's character does not actually become more readable, nor does his connection to the past become more firm, when he finds his way back to a personal and familial history, to Prague, where he was born and where he spent a very few years before being sent to England on the Kindertransport, and to the nurse who raised him and knew his parents.

The images Austerlitz finds, I want to argue, are what Warburg calls "pre-established expressive forms," that amount to no more than impersonal building blocks of affiliative postmemory. "Our concern with history" Austerlitz says, quoting his boarding school history master André Hilary, "is a concern with preformed images already imprinted on our brains, images at which we keep staring while the truth lies elsewhere, away from it all, somewhere as yet undiscovered."[32] This passage perfectly encapsulates the perils of postmemory. The images already imprinted on our brains, the tropes and structures we bring from the present to the past, hoping to find them there and to have our questions answered, may be screen memories—screens on which we project present, or timeless, needs and desires and which thus mask other images and other, as yet unthought or unthinkable concerns. The familial aspects of postmemory that make it so powerful and problematically open to affiliation contain many of these preformed screen images. What image is more potent than the image of the lost mother, and the fantasy of her recovery?

In *Maus*, the photograph of mother and son, a postwar image embedded in the inserted "Prisoner on the Hell Planet: A Case History," anchors and authenticates the work (figure 1.2). As the only photograph

1.2 Art Spiegelman, *Trojan Lake, N.Y., 1968. From* Maus I: A Survivor's Tale/My Father Bleeds History, *by Art Spiegelman, copyright 1986 by Art Spiegelman. Used by permission of Pantheon Books, a division of Random House, Inc.*

in the first volume, it solidifies the mother's material presence even as it records her loss and suicide. Maternal recognition and the maternal look are anything but reassuring: in fact, when the artist draws himself wearing a concentration camp uniform, he signals his complete transposition into his parents' history and his own incorporation of their trauma in Auschwitz activated by the trauma of his mother's suicide.[33] Still, there is no doubt in the work that this photo is a photo of Anja and Art Spiegelman. Taken in 1958, it shows not the war but its aftermath. Through the angle at which it is drawn, it breaks out of the page, acting as a link between the comics medium and the viewer, drawing the viewer into the page and counterbalancing its many distancing devices (the multiple hands holding the page and the photograph, the expressionist drawing style that yanks the reader out of the comics style of the rest of the book, and the human forms that challenge the animal fable to which we have become habituated in our reading, to name but a few). The maternal image and the "Prisoner" insert solidify the familiality of *Maus*'s postmemorial transmission and individualize the story. At the same time, Anja's suicide in the late 1960s can also be seen as a product of a broader post-Holocaust historical moment—a moment at which other Holocaust survivors like Paul Celan and, a few years later, Jean Améry, also committed suicide.

The two "maternal" images in *Austerlitz* function quite differently: rather than authenticating, they blur and relativize truth and reference. After following his mother's deportation to Terezín, Austerlitz is desperate to find more concrete traces of her presence there. He visits the town, walks its streets, searches the museum for traces, and finally settles on the Nazi propaganda film *The Führer Gives a City to the Jews* as the last possible source in which he might find a visual image of his mother. His fantasies revolve around the extraordinary events of the Red Cross inspection of Terezín, in which inmates were forced to participate in performances of normalcy and well-being that were then filmed for propaganda purposes: "I imagined seeing her walking down the street in a summer dress and lightweight gabardine coat, said Austerlitz: among a group of ghetto residents out for a stroll, she alone seemed to make straight for me, coming closer with every step, until at last I thought I could sense her stepping out of the frame and passing over into me."[34] The fantasy is so strong that, against all odds, Austerlitz does succeed in finding in the film an image of a woman who, he believes (or hopes), might be his mother.

The film to which he finds access in a Berlin archive is only a 14-minute version of the Nazi documentary, and after watching it repeatedly, he concludes that his mother does not appear in it. But he does not give up:

1.3 Film still from *The Führer Gives a City to the Jews*, a Nazi propaganda film. *Reprinted in W. G. Sebald,* Austerlitz, *translated by Anthea Bell (New York: Modern Library, 2001)*

he has a slow-motion, hour-long copy made of the excerpt and he watches it over and over, discovering new things in it, but marveling also at the distortions of sound and image that now mark it. In the very background of one of the sequences contained in these distorted slow-motion fragments of a propaganda film of fake performances of normalcy, Austerlitz does eventually glimpse a woman who reminds him of his image of his mother (figure 1.3). In the audience at a concert

> set a little way back and close to the upper edge of the frame, the face of a young woman appears, barely emerging from the back shadows around it. . . . She looks, so I tell myself as I watch, just as I imagined the singer Agáta from my faint memories and the few other clues to her appearance that I now have, and I gaze and gaze again at that face which seems to me both strange and familiar, said Austerlitz.[35]

Far from the fantasy of recognition and embrace Austerlitz spun out for the novel's narrator—"she alone seemed to make straight for me, coming closer with every step, until at last I could sense her stepping out of the frame"[36]—the woman's face is partially covered by the time indicator showing the 4/100 of a second during which it appears on the screen. In the foreground of the image, the face of a gray-haired man takes up most of the space, blocking the backgrounded woman from view.

In the novel, this picture can at best become a measure of the character's *desire* for his mother's face. It tells us as little about her and how she might have looked, what she lived through, as the photo of an anonymous actress Austerlitz finds in the theater archives in Prague. His impression that this found image also looks like Agáta is corroborated by Vera, who nods, but the link to truth or authentication remains equally tenuous. Austerlitz hands both images over to the narrator along with his story, as though for protection and dissemination, at once.

What, with this precious image, is the narrator actually receiving? Even for the familial second (or 1.5) generation, pictures are no more than spaces of projection, approximation, and affiliation; they have retained no more than an *aura* of indexicality. For more distant affiliative descendants, their referential link to a sought-after past is ever more questionable. The images Austerlitz finds, moreover, are in themselves products of performances—his mother was an actress before the war, and, what is more, in the propaganda film in Terezín, all inmates were violently forced to play a part that would further the workings of the Nazi death machine. Unlike the picture of mother and son in *Maus*, which was probably taken by the father, the presumed image of Agáta in the film inscribes the gaze of the perpetrator and thus also the genocidal intentions of the Nazi death machine and the lies on which it was based.[37] The numbers in the corner, of course, recall the Auschwitz numbers and thus anticipate the fate of the Terezín prisoners. They overpower the figures who shrink beneath the fate that awaits them. But who are these figures? Has Austerlitz, has the narrator, found what they were seeking?

Austerlitz's description of the film still throws ever more doubt on the act of postmemorial looking. Austerlitz focuses on one telling detail: "Around her neck, said Austerlitz, she is wearing a three-stringed and delicately draped necklace which scarcely stands out from her dark, high necked dress, and there is, I think, a white flower in her hair."[38] The necklace, I believe, connects this image—whether deliberately or not—to another important maternal photograph, that of Roland Barthes's mother in *Camera Lucida*, perhaps *the* image exemplifying the trope of maternal loss and longing and the son's affiliative look that attempt to suture an unbridgeable distance.

The necklace appears in Barthes's discussion of a picture by James van der Zee not so much as a prime example of Barthes's notion of the punctum as detail, and of the affective link between the viewer and the image, but of how the punctum can travel and be displaced from image to image. Barthes first finds the picture's punctum in the strapped pumps worn by one of the women; a few pages later, when the photograph is no longer in front of him, or of us, he realizes that "the real punctum was the necklace she was wearing; for (no doubt) it was this same necklace (a slender ribbon of braided gold) which I had seen worn by someone in my own family."[39] In a brilliant reading of Barthes's notion of the punctum, Margaret Olin takes us back to the initial image to expose Barthes's glaring mistake: the women in van der Zee's image wear strings of pearls and not "slender ribbons of braided gold."[40] The slender ribbon of braided gold, she argues, was transposed from one of his own family pictures that Barthes had reproduced in his *Roland Barthes by Roland Barthes* and entitled "the two grandmothers."[41]

Olin uses this example to call into question the very existence of the famous winter garden photo of Barthes's mother in *Camera Lucida*, showing how some of the details in his description might have been drawn from another text, Walter Benjamin's description of a photograph of the six-year-old Kafka in a "winter garden landscape."[42] The mother's picture may instead be one that is indeed reproduced in *Camera Lucida*, titled *La Souche* (*The Stock*).[43] These displacements and intertextualities, which Olin delineates in fascinating detail, lead her usefully and yet dangerously to redefine the photograph's indexicality: "The fact that something was in front of the camera matters; what that something was does not. . . . What matters is displaced," she provocatively states.[44] In her conclusion she proposes that the relationship between the photograph and its beholder be described as a "performative index" or an "index of identification," shaped by the reality of the *viewer's needs and desires* rather than by the subject's actual "having-been-there."[45]

I believe that the maternal image in *Austerlitz* can be inserted into the inter-textual chain Olin identifies, especially since, amazingly, Austerlitz also makes a mistake about the necklace, which, in the photo, only has two strings and not three, as he claims. To call reference into question in the context not just of death, as with Barthes's mother, but of extermination, as with *Austerlitz*, may be more provocative still, but this is indeed how photographs function in this novel. As *Austerlitz* shows, the index of postmemory (as opposed to memory) is the performative index, shaped more and more by affect, need, and desire as time and distance attenuate the links to authenticity and "truth." Familial and, indeed, feminine tropes rebuild and re-embody a connection that is disappearing, and thus gender becomes a powerful idiom of remembrance in the face of detachment and forgetting.

The generation of affiliative postmemory needs precisely such familiar and familial tropes to rely on. For feminist critics, however, it is particularly important to perceive and expose the functions of gender as a "preformed image" in the act of transmission. The photograph of the mother's face is a "preformed image" at which we stare while, as Austerlitz says, "the truth lies elsewhere, somewhere as yet undiscovered."[46] At our generational remove, that elsewhere may never be discovered. Thus the maternal image in *Austerlitz* provokes us to scrutinize the unraveling link between present and past that defines indexicality as no more than performative. The gendered familial figures we retrieve from our storehouses of expressive forms can be as elusive, and as in need of authentication, as memory itself.

And yet, for better or worse, one could say that for the postgeneration the screens of gender and of familiality, and the images that mediate them, function analogously to the protective shield of trauma itself: they function as screens that absorb the shock, filter and diffuse the impact of trauma, diminish harm. In forging a protective shield particular to the postgeneration, one could say that, paradoxically, they actually reinforce the *living* connection between past and present, between the generation of witnesses and survivors and the generation after.

FAMILY ROMANCES

In *Austerlitz*, the performative index structures every one of the photographs included, and even the very identity of the protagonist. Named after its main character, the novel's cover displays a photograph that is later revealed to be of that character as a child (figure 1.4). As we read, we have to ask ourselves, who *is* the curly-haired blond boy on the cover

1.4 *The Queen's Page. From W. G. Sebald,* Austerlitz, *translated by Anthea Bell (New York: Modern Library, 2001)*

of the book? If, as Barthes says, the photograph is evidence for someone's presence in front of the lens, who *was* in front of the lens and what is his relationship to the fictional Austerlitz? This photo is only one in several fictional devices to throw doubt on every element of the plot and to leave readers disoriented. Jacques Austerlitz, after all, is named after a train station that figures in the text, and that station refers to the site of a famous Napoleonic battle. And, of course, "Austerlitz" also recalls the name of the most famous Nazi death camp, Auschwitz. Placing us in the midst of a play of signifiers, the novel nevertheless uses photographs to gesture toward historical authenticity.

Austerlitz receives the photograph of himself from his nurse, Vera, who says to him "this is you, Jacquot, in 1939, about six months before you left Prague."[47] The precise date, 1939, underscored by the precise connection to his departure from Prague, and also the fact that the date is 1939, the year of the start of the war, all serve as forms of authentication. But when he gets the image, Austerlitz does not recognize himself. What makes the scene in the photograph come back to him is not the visual image but the *words* Vera says his grandfather said to him in Czech, *paže růžové královny*. But when that scene comes back to him, he does not find himself but loses himself altogether: "Once again I saw the live tableau with the Rose Queen and the little boy carrying her train at her side. Yet hard as I tried . . . I could not recollect myself in that part. I have studied the photograph many times since . . . I examined every detail under a magnifying glass without once finding the slightest clue."[48] Austerlitz goes to the picture for information about the past, but all he finds is the affects and emotions associated with it. He reports being "speechless," "uncomprehending," filled with "blind panic." The emotions are so strong that they leave him incapable of imagining "who or what I was," but they do enable him to fantasize in great detail his parents' return to the apartment, still alive.[49] The photograph confirms his feeling that "time does not exist at all, only various spaces . . . between which the living and the dead can move back and forth as they like."[50] As Barthes suggests, the photographic referent is the revenant, the ghost that returns to haunt those who look at the image, but Sebald goes further than Barthes in making the viewer himself or herself the ghost who haunts the photograph.

The picture of the little pageboy on the book's cover and inside it itself materializes like a revenant from the dead. Vera finds this image and another one of the two parents on stage acting in "*Wilhelm Tell*, or *La Somnambula*, or Ibsen's last play" by chance.[51] Tellingly, she finds it in a copy of *Le Colonel Chabert*, Balzac's novel about the survival and haunting return of a colonel in the Napoleonic wars who had been left for dead, but who climbs over the other corpses on the battlefield around him and returns home, only to have his identity contested by his wife and other heirs and to end up alone, destitute, and embittered. The photographs of Jacquot and his parents also function as revenants, and their identity is no less contested or ambiguous than the colonel's.

Unlike the photographs of Vladek and Anja in *Maus*, the parents in *Austerlitz* are minuscule figures on an enormous stage, actors in an undetermined play. Their costumes and size in the image make them unrecognizable. And Jacquot is not the little boy who was sent off to England and who returns as an adult to find himself, but the Rose Queen's page, dressed up in a costume in an empty field, in a scene he can neither remember nor locate.

These acts of myth making, these elaborate costumes and elegant stage sets, are the scenarios of a Freudian family romance and its ambitions. Freud writes that "the child's imagination becomes engaged in the task of getting free from the parents of whom he now has a low opinion and of replacing them by others who, as a rule, are of higher social standing" or, as he writes later, of "better birth."[52] The child becomes the Rose Queen's page or her son. But, in the aftermath of Terezín and Auschwitz, another family romance may be at work altogether, reconnecting a ruptured family rather than enacting the break. This is certainly the case for the three photographs in *Maus*. Could it be that these "family pictures," however staged, merely stand in for other photos from the time, historical photos that might be too difficult to look at? Perhaps the family pictures themselves are mere screen memories recalling a pre-historic time and masking an unbearable visual landscape, a shadow archive, with "preformed" figures of destruction.

This, in fact, might be the post-Holocaust family romance and survivor fantasy: that before the destruction, there was another world, a happier one, one uncontaminated by the violence that followed.[53] When he looks at the photo of himself, Austerlitz says, he feels "the piercing inquiring gaze of the page boy who had come to demand his dues, who was waiting in the gray light of dawn on the empty field for me to accept the challenge and avert the misfortune lying ahead of him."[54] Establishing the existence of such a safe prewar world might enable the fantasy of averting the disaster that was to come.

This need for a "before" is not a matter of reality or indexicality, but of fantasy and affect. As Austerlitz shows, photographs can provide the stage for just such an affective encounter that can bring back the most primal childhood fears and desires for care and recognition. When Austerlitz and Vera look at the two photos she found in the Balzac volume, she begins to speak of the mysterious quality of such photographs when they surface from oblivion: "One has the impression, she said, of something stirring in them, as if one caught small sighs of despair, *gémissements de désespoir* was her expression, said Austerlitz, as if the pictures had a memory of their own and remembered us, remembered the roles that we, the survivors, and those no longer among us had played in our former lives."[55]

It seems to me that this may be the clearest articulation of what we fantasize and expect of surviving images from the past: that they have a memory of their own that they bring to us from the past; that that memory tells us something about ourselves, about what/how we and those who preceded us once were; that they carry not only information about the past but enable us to reach its emotional register. That they require a particular kind of visual literacy, one that can decode the foreign language that they speak, for in Sebald's formulations, they don't just utter "small sighs of despair," but they do so in French, "*gémissements de désespoir.*" The work of postmemory would thus consist of "learning French" (as it were) to be able to translate the "*gémissements*" from the past into the present and the future, where they will be heard by generations not yet born.

2.1 Carl and Lotte Hirsch, Strada Iancu Flondor, Cernăuți, 1942. *Courtesy of the Hirsch family archive*

2

WHAT'S WRONG WITH THIS PICTURE?

(WITH LEO SPITZER)

> Au mois de juin 1942, un officier allemand s'avance vers un jeune homme et lui dit: "Pardon monsieur, où se trouve la place de l'Etoile?" Le jeune homme désigne le côté gauche de sa poitrine.
>
> [In June 1942, a German officer approaches a young man and asks him: "Excuse me, sir, but where is the Place de l'Etoile?" The young man points to his left lapel.]
>
> —Patrick Modiano, *La Place de l'Etoile*

It is the only photograph of Lotte and Carl Hirsch, my parents, taken during the war years, and it is tiny, 2.5 × 3.5 centimeters, about the size of a 35-millimeter negative, with unevenly cut edges. I have always loved this image of a stylish young couple— newlyweds walking confidently down an active urban street. The more difficult it was to make out the details of the faded and slightly spotted black-and-white image, the more mysterious and enticing it became to me over the years. In it, my mother is wearing a flared, light-colored calf-length coat and attractive leather or suede shoes with heels, and she is carrying a dark purse under her arm. My father wears well-cut pants and dark leather shoes, and a tweed jacket that looks slightly too small. Details of their facial expressions are difficult to read, but their strides appear animated, matching, their arms interlaced, my mother's hands in her pockets. The picture must have been taken by one of the street photographers on the Herrengasse in Czernowitz (later, Iancu Flondor in Romanian Cernăuţi; today, Kobylanska in Chernivtsi, Ukraine), who took the photos that populated my parents' albums and those of their friends, photos dating from the 1920s and 1930s. Equally small, they were all no doubt developed and sold to clients on the spot.[1] This picture's radical difference is marked on the back, however, where my father's handwriting reads "Cz.1942."

In 1942, Czernowitz/Cernăuți was again a Romanian city, ruled by a fascist Romanian government that collaborated with Nazi authorities. Two-thirds of the city's Jewish population—some 40,000 persons— had been deported to Transnistria in the fall of 1941, about half of those perishing from hunger and typhus during that winter, or murdered, either by Romanian gendarmes or Nazi troops. Those, like my parents, who were still in the city had been issued special waivers to remain by the city's mayor or the region's governor as Jews who were deemed necessary to the city's functioning. After the Jewish ghetto into which they had been forced was largely emptied and dissolved, they were permitted to return to their own homes, but they were subject to severe restrictions and a strict curfew, and were obliged to wear the yellow star. Men were routinely taken off the street to do forced labor. Later (or earlier, depending on exactly when the picture was taken) in the summer of 1942, Jewish inhabitants would have been vulnerable to a second wave of deportations to Transnistria or farther east, across the river Bug into German-administered territories and almost certain death.[2]

Nothing in the picture betrays the hardship of the time. Carl and Lotte are not visibly suffering; they don't look starved, unhealthy, or afraid. The photo is not comparable to pictures of Jews in Warsaw or Łódz streets taken in 1942—images of acute misery and deprivation in ghettos or other restricted quarters.

"Here we are during the war," my parents once said to me, with what I took to be some amount of defiance. This photograph had been a measure for me of the difference between my parents' way of telling the story about their experiences during the war years and the much more dire and frightening narratives we read and collected from other survivors and witnesses. The photo seemed to confirm Lotte and Carl's version of events: what they thought of as their "relatively lucky circumstances," and the "youth" and "young love" that helped them to endure and keep up their spirits. Still, I became increasingly puzzled by the little picture's incongruities: by its refusal to testify to what I knew to be true of the context in which it was taken—a time of persecution, oppression, and totalitarian constraints in which photography itself took an ominous turn from a medium of personal and familial remembrance to a threatening instrument of surveillance. Flipping the little photo from front to back, I was unable to get its two sides to match up.

THE LITTLE PICTURE

When the two of us began to write about the wartime in Cernăuți, this photo was one of very few images we had on hand from there that might supplement the many written documents, memoirs, and oral testimonies on which we were basing our understanding of the place and time. However small and blurred, however seemingly incongruous, it was a valuable piece of evidence that, we hoped, would give us some greater insight into the texture of wartime Jewish life in this city. Eager for it to reveal itself even more to us, we digitally scanned and enlarged it, blowing it up several times, searching to find what might not be visible to the naked eye (figure 2.2).

Amazingly, as it came up now at about 10 × 14 centimeters on the screen, the image and the story it told changed dramatically—at least at first glance. All of a sudden, it looked like there *was* something on Carl Hirsch's left lapel that had not been noticeable before. A bright light spot, not too large, emerged just in the place where Jews would have worn the yellow star in the spring or fall of 1942. Perhaps the picture was not as incongruous as we had thought: perhaps it would indeed confirm the darker version of the story we had learned and absorbed from so many other accounts. We printed the enlargement, took out magnifying glasses, went up to the window, and used the best lamps in our study to scrutinize the blowup. We played with the enlargement's resolution on the computer in Photoshop, sleuthing like detectives to determine the exact nature of the spot.

The spot's edges remained blurry. But didn't their shape suggest points? This *must* be the yellow star, we concluded; what else could he be wearing on his lapel? We blew the picture up even more, then again, even a little more—yes, of course, it had the *shape* of the Jewish star.

2.2 "A spot?" *Courtesy of the Hirsch family archive*

We began to reread the photograph's content, its message, against Lotte's and Carl's facial expressions and body language that were now also much more clearly visible. We remembered some of their stories about the star, about how they sometimes went out without it, daring fate to buy groceries more easily or simply to re-experience their former freedom and mobility. The stars in Cernăuți were not sewn on but affixed with safety pins: young people like Carl and Lotte sometimes wore them on the *inside* of their coats, illegally, but able to show them should they be stopped by the authorities. But if that, indeed, explained the seemingly missing star in Lotte's case, wouldn't the couple have been afraid to have their picture taken by a street photographer? The smiles with which they greeted the camera and, indeed, the fact that they had stopped to *buy* the photo after it was developed, gave us no such impression.

We sent the enlarged photo to Lotte and Carl. "There is a small spot on my lapel," Carl wrote in an e-mail, "but it could not be *the* star. The stars were large, 6 centimeters in diameter. Maybe I should have written 1943 on the photo. They did away with the stars in July of 1943." "And if that is a star," Lotte wrote, "then why am I not wearing one?" In a later e-mail she said: "Yes, it was definitely taken on the Herrengasse during the war, and to me it looks like a star, but the date is causing us problems." In fact, we later found two other photos of Czernowitz Jews wearing the yellow star (figure 2.3).

Those photographs are dated "around 1943" and "May 1943." Their stars are larger and more distinctive than the spot on Carl Hirsch's lapel, but they also are walking through the city—seemingly on the former Herrengasse—having their picture taken by a street photographer and evidently purchasing the photo after its development. Like Lotte and Carl's, their stroll also seems "normal," as though the temporal and political moment in which they were snapped and the "otherness" that they were made to display were hardly relevant.

It may not be possible to determine exactly what, if anything, Carl has on his lapel. Perhaps it is *dust*—no more than a small dot of dirt blocking light on the print. *Our* reception of the photo, the questions we pose in examining it, the needs and desires that shape our postmemorial viewing, inevitably exceed the image's small size and its limited ability to serve as evidence. Even after its enlargements, the results of our persistent efforts to penetrate beyond its mysterious surface are intriguing, but also inconclusive. No doubt, our determination to magnify and enhance the picture—to zoom in, blow up, sharpen—reveals more about our own projections and appropriations than about life in

2.3 (top) Ilana Schmueli and her mother, Cernăuți, ca. 1943; (bottom) City Dermer, Berthold Geisinger, and Heini Stupp, Cernăuți, 1943. *Courtesy of Ilana Shmueli and Silvio Geisinger*

wartime Greater Romania. As the previous chapter argued, this picture's indexicality is more performative—based on the viewer's needs and desires—than factual.

What, then, can we learn about a traumatic past from photographs? Ulrich Baer notes that such photographs in the context of trauma constitute a kind of "spectral evidence," revealing "the striking gap between what we can see and what we can know."[3] Addressing the Second World War and the Holocaust, in particular, he argues that they mark a crisis of witnessing and "call into question the habitual reliance on vision as the principal ground for cognition."[4]

Nonetheless, as this book suggests, photography has functioned as one of the principal forms mediating the memory of this period. The powerful memorial aesthetic that has developed around archival photographs and objects from this era over the last three decades invites us to look more broadly at what knowledge and insight they can, in fact, offer us about that past and our relation to it. If photographs are limited and flawed historical documents, in an evidentiary sense, they can function as powerful "points of memory" supplementing the accounts of historians and the words of witnesses, and signaling a visceral, material, and affective connection to the past. They thus become both instruments and emblems of the process of its transmission.

POINTS OF MEMORY

Roland Barthes's much discussed notion of the punctum has inspired us to look at images, objects, and memorabilia inherited from the past, like this little picture, as "points of memory"—points of intersection between past and present, memory and postmemory, personal remembrance and cultural recall.[5] The term "point" is both spatial—such as a point on a map—and temporal—a moment in time—and it thus highlights the intersection of spatiality and temporality in the workings of personal and cultural memory. The sharpness of a point pierces or punctures: like Barthes's punctum, points of memory puncture through layers of oblivion, interpellating those who seek to know about the past. A point is also small, a detail, and thus it can convey the fragmentariness of the vestiges of the past that come down to us in the present—small rectangular pieces of paper we invest with enormous power. In addition, such remnants are useful for *purposes of remembrance*—in order to help generate recall—another meaning of the term "point." And points of memory are also *arguments* about memory, objects or images that have remained from the past, containing "points" about the work of memory and transmission. Points of memory produce *touching, piercing insights* that traverse temporal, spatial, and experiential divides. As points multiply, they can convey the overlay of different temporalities and interpretive frames, resisting straightforward readings or any lure of authenticity.

Following Barthes, then, we might say that while some remnants merely give information about the past (what Barthes terms the *studium*) others prick and wound and grab and puncture, like the punctum, unsettling assumptions, exposing the unexpected, suggesting what Barthes describes as "a subtle beyond" or the "blind field" outside the photograph's frame.[6] For Barthes, the punctum is first a detail: the necklace, for example, or the pair of lace-up shoes in the family portrait taken by James van der Zee in 1926.[7] It is a detail only he notices, often because of some personal connection he has with it: as we have seen, he is interested in the necklace because someone in his own family had worn a similar one. This acknowledged subjectivity and positionality, this vulnerability, and this focus on the detail and the ordinary and everyday—all these also belong to reading practices that can be associated with feminist methodologies.[8] And they belong to the work of postmemory.

Even though it is in some ways subjective and individual, the memorial punctum is also mobilized by collective and cultural factors. A point of memory emerges in an encounter between subjects—the parents who lived through a traumatic history and survived, and the daughter who transmits their story to others, along with her irresolvable questions, hopes, and regrets. As encounters between subjects, as acts of reading that are personal as well as cultural, familial as well as affiliative, points of memory are contingent upon the social factors that shape those subjects, and upon the way those subjects experience these. But as acts of reading, they also expose historical and cultural codes of meaning, codes marked by gender and other forms of social difference.

In the second part of *Camera Lucida*, Barthes elaborates his discussion of the punctum, stating: "I now know that there exists another punctum (another 'stigmatum') than the 'detail.' This new punctum, which is no longer of form but of intensity, is Time, the lacerating emphasis of the *noeme* ('that-has-been'), its pure representation."[9] The punctum of time is precisely that incongruity or incommensurability between the meaning of a given experience, object, or image *then*, and the one it holds *now*. It is the knowledge of the inevitability of loss, change, and death. And that inevitability constitutes the lens through which we, as humans, look at the past. The photograph, Barthes says, "tells me death in the future."[10] But, as Michael André Bernstein warns, reading the past backward through our retrospective knowledge is a dangerous form of "backshadowing"—"a kind of retroactive foreshadowing in which the shared knowledge of the outcome of a series of events by narrator and listener is used to judge the participants in those events *as though they too should have known what was to come*."[11] The work of postmemorial reading entails juxtaposing two incommensurable temporalities, and exposing and keeping open the devastating disjunction between them.

THE DARK ROOM

The Dark Room, Rachel Seiffert's 2002 novel about German memory of the Second World War, is structured around three distinct stories that are linked not by their plot, but by their use of photographs as points of memory. Seiffert shows how problems of photographic evidence evolve between the 1940s and the 1990s, between the experience of witnesses and that of their children and grandchildren.[12] The family, in her novel, is not an intimate private space, but is enmeshed in a complex and shifting social and political landscape that determines every private relation and transaction.

Helmut, the protagonist of the first story (which takes place in Germany during the war) is a bystander to its developments. Exempted from

Wehrmacht service due to a severe physical disability, he works as a photographer's assistant, and is able to witness and to record, on film, some of the events in his native city in the early 1940s. In the section's climactic moments, Helmut watches through a camera's viewfinder and photographs a scene the narrative describes through his eyes, but does not interpret: "There are trucks and uniformed men shouting and pushing. . . . Through the lens he sees possessions scattered: clothes, pots, boxes, sacks kicked and hurled across the muddy ground. An officer stands by screaming orders."[13] Helmut is agitated, frightened, but perhaps also exhilarated by what he is seeing, and he photographs furiously. "In the viewfinder his eyes meet the eyes of a shouting, pointing gypsy. Others turn to look, frightened angry faces in headscarves, hats and in uniform too."[14] But when Helmut returns to the studio and develops his film, he is severely disappointed. The blurred, grainy photos just refuse to show what he had observed earlier in the day: the medium is simply inadequate, wrong. "The bright skirts of the gypsy women are just drab rags in his photos. . . . The dark SS uniforms blend into the soot-black walls of the buildings making them almost invisible. . . . He blows up the image, but the grain evens out the angry lines on the face of the officer who was screaming orders by the jeep, and he barely looks like he is shouting" (30). The list of the photographs' failures goes on. Ultimately, deeply disappointed, Helmut throws both the negatives and the prints into the trash can. All that remains is the enormous disjunction between the affect of the scene of witness and Helmut's encounter with his photographs: the frenzy of the moment gives way to frustration, rage, even self-hatred.

Helmut's failed photos illustrate the belatedness of photographic looking and the temporal gap between the moment an image is taken and the moment it is developed and viewed—a gap that, paradoxically, is no less enormous within the very brief time frame of the scene in the narrative (no more than several hours) than it is for second-generation viewers like us. Helmut's photos are destroyed; the most important ones in his act of witnessing were never even taken. Photographs, Helmut's responses indicate, are shaped by intense emotion—in this case, by fear, nervousness, inadequacy. In this first story of *The Dark Room*, Rachel Seiffert establishes the interested nature of photographic evidence, the partial view of the photographer, and the contingency of the images that survive.

And yet, in the book's second story, taking place at the very end of the war amid arrests, flight, relocation, and ensuing chaos, photographs are accorded enough evidentiary power to be burned, torn up, and buried. Here a mother and daughter trying to protect the Nazi father from accusation, and themselves from association with him, destroy photos and family albums that can implicate all of them. But the evidentiary authority of photography is also utterly undermined when, at the end of the section, a mysterious character named Tomas is found to be using an identity card and picture that clearly belongs not to him but to a Jew who, Tomas reveals, had been killed in a camp. Why Tomas is impersonating this Jewish victim, what he is trying to hide under this false identity, what the ID card has to do with the blue number tattooed on his arm, remains as ambiguous as the other photos that are being used as pedagogic displays after the liberation of concentration camps in Germany.

When the daughter, Lore, and her young siblings walk through various small towns on their way to Oma's house in Hamburg, they occasionally confront large blurry photographs tacked up in central locations. Silent crowds of onlookers surround these images.[15] Like Helmut, Lore can take in the scenes depicted on these photos only viscerally; she is incapable of identifying their context or of interpretation: "In front of Lore is a picture of a trash dump, or it might be a heap of ashes. She leans in closer, thinks it could be shoes. . . . She steps forward out of the group, smoothens out the damp creases with her palms. A whisper sets off behind her and makes its way around the group. The pictures are of skeletons, Lore can see that now" (76). These pictures had been glued onto a tree, but the adhesive was still wet and they rippled upon drying. Daring to touch them, to flatten them, to step up close and then back again, Lore reveals their details to the crowd. But neither her stroking touch nor the more distant vantage point of the onlookers helps the girl understand what the pictures reveal. Lore is touched by them in return, and her body responds with sweat, heat, faintness; but her mind is a rush of questions. The images stay with her; they remain visible behind her eyelids. She is relieved when she hears adults suggest that the Americans may have staged the frightening photos. Indistinct, unidentifiable, difficult to connect to her experience, the pictures carry a very different kind of evidence for Lore than the factual one that those posting them had most likely intended. Through their sheer emotional force, they spell out for her that crimes were committed, that those around her, even her parents, may be implicated. Yet they also remain impenetrable and inexplicable: blurry visuals of horrific scenes encountered by onlookers responding with whispers, throat-clearing, silence, or audible protests of denial and rationalization.

In these first two stories, Seiffert's point of view remains close to that of her young, uninformed, yet deeply (if indirectly) implicated German witnesses, and she records their responses in great detail. These illustrate the act of traumatic seeing, in which the image—at first felt affectively and not cognitively—acquires meaning only belatedly, in retrospect. Even later, more meaningful insights and deeper comprehension are blocked by conscious and unconscious needs, by desires and resistances, both individual and collective. Knowledge remains partial, fragmentary, with its enlightening components both partially revealed and blocked from exposure.

The Dark Room's third story then jumps ahead several decades and one generation, focusing on Micha, the grandson of a Waffen-SS officer, Askan Boell, who had served in Belarus and had not returned to Germany from a Soviet prison camp until 1954. The story traces the grandson's painful research into his Opa's past and his difficult realization that his grandfather was present when masses of Jewish civilians were killed in the summer and fall of 1943. Photographs are Micha's main research tools: he takes a 1938 picture of his grandfather to Belarus and shows it to witnesses who recognize Boell as one of the SS Germans who were there in 1943. But, primarily, photographs serve to bring home the disjunction between the kind grandfather Micha remembers and the Nazi killer he suspects him to have been. Micha's sister insists: "They don't show anything, the pictures. They're family shots, you know? Celebrations, always happy. You can't see anything." But Micha "does not want to believe her," does not give up the attempt to find "truth" in the photos: "*He always looked away from the camera, though. Did you notice that? After the war*" (266). Together, grandson and granddaughter, brother and sister, try to read the grandfather's postwar feelings in conventional, opaque family snapshots. Why did Opa look away from the camera in family photos? Did it mean he "had eyes only" for his grandchildren, standing beside him? Or did it mean he was feeling guilty about his crimes?

Micha wants and needs something from the photographs that they cannot possibly convey. However much he studies them, carries them back to Belarus and around Germany, they remain unreadable, always saying either too much or too little. At most they can serve to identify Askan Boell to the Belorussian collaborator Kolesnik and to gain the latter's confirmation of the grandfather's presence in Belarus in 1943. But even here we find out more about Micha's affective response than about participation and guilt. "Micha has put the photo on the table, so that the old man won't see that his hands are shaking" (256). Kolesnik's testimony is general, vague, describing Nazi killings and the Soviet arrests of the culprits, leading Micha to ask again and again: *"Did you see my Opa do anything?"* (258). Repeatedly prodded, Kolesnik eventually admits that, yes, he knows that Askan Boell participated because all the Germans who were there did, with the exception of one who shot himself. Askan must have done it, like the others. The evidence is there, but it is not incontrovertible; the old collaborator had been present, but he was not an explicit eyewitness to Boell's participation in killings. *"There are no pictures of him holding a gun to someone's head, but I am sure he did that and pulled the trigger, too. The camera was pointing elsewhere, shutter opening and closing on the murder of another Jew, done by another man. But my Opa was no more than a few steps away"* (264). Thus, the crucial, confirming photo was not taken, or did not survive, and so the third-generation retrospective witness is left only with the ambiguous evidence carried by the photos that he inherited, and onto which he projects his own anxieties, needs, and desires—feelings disproportionate to what the pictures can, in fact, support. The truth about the past always seems to lie somewhere else, in Barthes's blind field just beyond the frame. As powerful conduits between what was then and what is now, as performative vehicles of affect carried across generations, the photographs can at most gesture toward that elsewhere.

PROJECTIONS

Photographic documents, like the pictures of Micha's Opa, bring the contradictions of the archives we have inherited into the open. Invariably, archival photographic images appear in postmemorial texts in altered form: they are cropped, enlarged, projected onto other images; they are reframed and de- or re-contextualized; they are embedded in new narratives, new texts; they are surrounded by new frames.

Muriel Hasbun's composite memorial images can sharpen our analysis of this postmemorial photographic aesthetic and the psychic structures that motivate it. Hasbun crops and reframes archival photos, superimposes them on one another, reconstitutes them to alter their color, surrounds them with written text, with twigs that look like barbed wire, or with old wooden frames, prints them on linens she inherited from her grandmother, and installs them amid aural recordings of music and conversations about them.

The images that result are often blurry, out of focus, partial, hard to read. In spite of their obscurity, an obscurity the artist actually augments in her installations, Hasbun describes them as a "refuge against silence and forgetting" and as means to "transcend generational amnesia."[16]

Hasbun's work results from her own hybrid background as the daughter of a Polish Jewish mother who survived the war with some of her family in hiding in France and a Palestinian Christian father who emigrated to El Salvador where Hasbun grew up. The images and objects Hasbun includes in her composite photographs and installations stem from multiple sites and archives, coming together through her own combination, synthesis, and recreation. Even the multilingual titles of the projects that recall her mother's survival in France, with their parentheses and question marks, ¿Sólo una Sombra? (Only a Shadow?) (figures 2.4 and 2.5) and Protegida/Watched Over (figures 2.6 and 2.7) inscribe the tentative, ambiguous, and diasporic quality of Hasbun's postmemory work.

In one part of the triptych Protegida: Auvergne- Hélène entitled Mes enfants—Photographe Sanitas, 1943, Hasbun overlays a photo of two young children and a letter dated Paris, 3.1.1942, addressed to "Mes enfants," my children (figure 2.6). "I would love to have some photos of

2.4 Muriel Hasbun, *¿Sólo una sombra? (Familia Lódz)/Only a Shadow? (Lódz Family).*
Selenium gelatin silver print, 16.5" × 12" (32 × 30 cm). *From the series* Santos y sombras/Saints
and Shadows, *1994. Courtesy of Muriel Hasbun, www.murielhasbun.com*

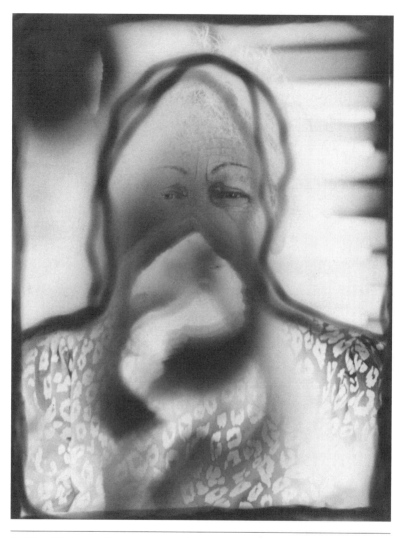

2.5 Muriel Hasbun, *¿Sólo una sombra?/Only a Shadow? (Ester I)*. Gelatin silver print, 18" × 14" (46 × 36 cm). *From the* series Santos y sombras/Saints and Shadows, *1994. Courtesy of Muriel Hasbun, www.murielhasbun.com*

my two dolls," the letter says, "preferably dressed in their winter clothing and taken around the house." Did the writer, the artist's grandfather who was hiding in Paris, receive this studio picture of these two "dolls," his grandchildren hiding with his wife and daughter in Le Mont Dore, or is it Hasbun who now brings together the letter and the photo in an act of retrospective repair? The composite image is as blurred as it is haunting, signaling loss, longing, and desire, but giving no specific insight into the circumstances of the letter or the photo. Exhibiting the material imprint of the writer's hand, the indexical trace of the children who posed for the photo, and of Hasbun's own postmemorial act of reframing, the image becomes a site in which the familial and cultural present and past intersect with one another. But what do we actually learn about Jewish survival in France by looking at Hasbun's images? The composite installations inscribe and highlight the inscrutability of the images and the questions they raise, as well as the artist's [and our] present needs and desires to find out more about her mother's or grandmother's past lives.

Hasbun's images, like those of her contemporaries, resist our desire to see more clearly, to penetrate more deeply. They are often cropped in unexpected and frustrating ways: in *Hélène's Eye* (figure 2.7) we see only half of Hélène's (her great-aunt's) face, and the face is blown up, almost distorted. On the other side of the tryptich, *Hélène B/Hendla F.* (she changed her name from Finkielstjain to Barthel to survive), she holds the photo that was attached to her two identity cards with two different names. We see only her mouth and her hand: we cannot look into her eyes. And yet the voices playing in the background of the pictures of Ester, the sister of Hasbun's grandfather, whom he did not find until 1974, reveal another dimension of knowledge and transmission:

In my darkroom, I was looking at the portrait of Ester, its image projected on the paper. Only a shadow? Impossible. The brittle leaves from an earlier autumn had already been transformed by the light. Upon finishing the portraits, I wrote to Ester: "When I make these pictures—*cuando hago estas fotografías*—it's as if I were finding what has been underneath the shadows—*es como que si encontraría lo que estaba debajo de las sombras*—or what lives inside our

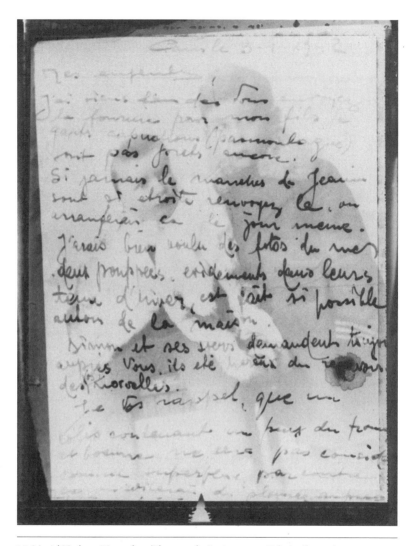

2.6 Muriel Hasbun, *Mes enfants/Photographe Sanitas*, 1943. Gelatin silver print, 13.25" × 10.25" or 20" × 15". *From the series* Protegida/Watched Over, *2003. Courtesy of Muriel Hasbun, www.murielhasbun.com*

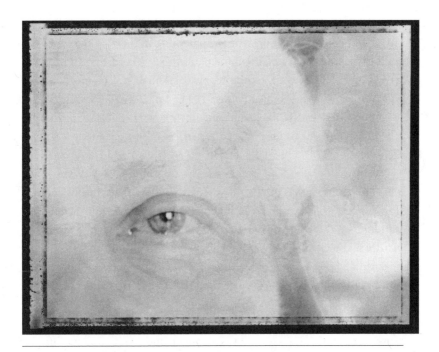

2.7 Muriel Hasbun, *Hélène's Eye*. Selenium gelatin silver print, 10.25" × 13.5" or 15" × 20. *From the series* Protegida/Watched Over, *2003. Courtesy of Muriel Hasbun, www.murielhasbun.com*

hearts—*o lo que vive dentro de nuestros corazones*—." [Ester:] "I remember, in the camp I worked . . . Every Sunday when we don't work, we sit all the girls and look at the pictures. It was not important it was the pictures of us, but pictures from the home . . . The first thing, when I came here, the first thing that I asked, 'Have you pictures,' the first thing."[17]

REPARATIVE LOOKING

In memoir and testimony, and in historical accounts and scholarly discussions, as within new artistic texts, archival images function as supplements, both confirming and unsettling the stories that are explored and transmitted. On the one hand, they are imperfect documents, as Seiffert shows, already deeply problematic when they are taken; on the other hand, as points of memory, they embody an alternate discourse, create an opening in the present to something in the past that goes beyond their indexicality or the information they record. As Andrea Liss writes, they have the "potential to provoke historical memory and to confront the viewer's subjectivities."[18] The fantasies they call forth are deep and often inarticulable and uncontrollable, capable of provoking ethical attempts at mourning and repair but also unwanted and illicit identifications.[19]

When we blew up Carl and Lotte Hirsch's photograph to the point where all contrast was gone, but where it revealed that curious spot on Carl's lapel, we were searching for the confirmation of our own understanding of the past, one that fundamentally contradicted what the picture made visible. We very much wanted to challenge its seeming air of normality—the way it fit like any other everyday snapshot into a page of a photo album without proclaiming the irregularity of the place and time in which it was taken.

Like the artists who reemploy documentary images in their contemporary works, we felt we had to amend, and tweak, and modify the picture—to open up the range of affects and meanings it contained, as well as those we were projecting onto it. Looking at the picture now, we realize that in it Carl and Lotte are *already* survivors, alive within a fortunate minority that had been spared a terrible fate. They are on the former Herrengasse, but they are not supposed to be there; they have outstayed their welcome in this city of their birth. They are looking, shyly, smilingly, toward a future they could not, cannot foresee. This is the knowledge a retrospective witness brings to a photograph that, as Barthes says, "tells me death in the future."[20]

In wanting to restore to Carl and Lotte's photo the hardships it seemed to be eliding, we adopted, we now see, the backshadowing glance that Eve Kosofsky Sedgwick has termed "paranoid reading"— anticipatory, eager to unveil hidden violence and to expose unseen danger.[21] Through this reading, we wanted to find and reveal the negative lurking within and outside the frame of the image and, through our vigilance, somehow, to protect Carl and Lotte, walking down the Herrengasse, from the terrible fate that in hindsight we know could have been —and, in the summer of 1942, could still be—theirs.

But archival photographs also challenge their viewers not to impose retrospection to the point where a photo's own temporality and surface, however delicate and contingent, is erased. While this photo qualifies the grand historical narrative we have of the time, it also requires a more generous "reparative reading" than the paranoid scrutiny we initially employed.[22] Such a reading would leave ambiguities unresolved, providing an expanded context for more affective knowing. Was Lotte and Carl's photo taken in 1942 or 1943? Were they wearing a yellow star, or not? If it was 1942, and they walked on the Herrengasse without it, trying to pass, why didn't they fear a photographic record of their transgression? Why did they stop to buy the photo? Did their purchase accentuate an act of resistance? Or, in a technology that produces a print and no negative, were they buying up the evidence? What was the encounter and the negotiation with the photographer like—was he an interested bystander, or a distant one, above the fray? If they were both, in fact, wearing a star (Lotte, perhaps under a turned-up coat collar), were they humiliated by the photo, yet nonetheless defiant enough to buy it as a record of an outrage Jews were forced to endure? Or, perhaps, was the inscription on the photo's back indeed an error? Was it taken in 1943, after the stars were discontinued in Greater Romania? The Herrengasse stroll, in that case, would attest to a moment of greater freedom, increased hope, following Carl and Lotte's fortunate evasion of mass deportations. But if so, then what is the spot on the lapel? Will we ever be able to know?

Muriel Hasbun's *Mes enfants* raises similar puzzling questions and incongruities. First the date: as Hasbun writes, the letter was written "in the first days of January 1943. The date on the letter is 1942, but the postmark (on the dorso) is 1943, which probably meant my grandfather made a mistake since it was the new year. They had already been hiding in Le Mont Dore since August of 1942."[23] How were her grandparents able to correspond if both were in hiding in different places? How was it possible for Jews who were passing or hiding to have their children's pictures taken in a formal photography studio such as Photographe Sanitas? Would they not have been afraid of detection and exposure through these two revealing media? As though to underscore the dangers that the rather benign if blurry and haunting image seems almost to be eliding, Hasbun includes another image on the back of the pedestal on which this picture is mounted. " 'Mes enfants' has 'El lobo feroz' on its dorso, which I've rephotographed from a book that came out after the war, telling the story of WWII to children, called 'La Guerre chez les animaux,' and the big bad wolf is Hitler (the wolf has a swastika on the armband)."[24]

By considering, rather than dismissing, these multiple and contradictory readings of Jewish existence during 1942 and 1943, by leaving ambiguities unresolved, postmemorial viewers, artists and scholars, like Hasbun, and like us, broaden the boundaries of our understanding and tap into a deeper register of intergenerational transmission. We gain access to what the images and stories about this past do not readily reveal—the emotional fabric of daily life in extreme circumstances, its aftereffects in the process of survival. If our own search into Carl and Lotte's wartime photo was indeed successful in revealing the traumatic wound that seemed so strangely absent from the tiny image in the album, our scrutiny of the picture also reveals the indeterminacy of that wound and the unlocatability of its source. Yet it also reveals that as much as survival might be a struggle against the return of trauma, structured by forgetting or denial, the mark is there, present, even if it remains submerged, disguised, invisible to the naked eye. Extracting whatever information we can from fragmentary documents, unreadable sources, and blurry, indeterminate, spots in a tiny pale image, we also realize that allowing the image to fade back to its initial size, we might be able to make space for the possibility of "life" rather than "death in the future."

3.1 Irma Morgensztern and her daughter, from Jeffrey Wolin's 1997 exhibition *Written in Memory: Portraits of the Holocaust. Courtesy of Catherine Edelman Gallery, Chicago, Illinois*

3

MARKED BY MEMORY

> Even between mother and daughter a certain
> historical withholding intervenes.
>
> —Gayatri C. Spivak, "Acting Bits/Identity Talk."

Toni Morrison's Sethe meets her own mother only once. As she tells her two daughters, one day, when she was still a little girl, raised primarily by Nan, who spoke to her in a language she has since forgotten, her mother took her behind the smokehouse, opened her dress, and showed her the mark under her breast: "Right on her rib was a circle and cross burnt right in the skin. She said, 'This is your ma'am. This,' and she pointed. 'I am the only one got this mark now. The rest dead. If something happens to me and you can't tell me by my face, you can know me by this mark." Sethe's answer expresses her sense of her own vulnerability, and her desire for mutuality and maternal recognition: "'Yes Ma'am,' I said. 'But how will you know me? How will you know me? Mark me too,' I said. 'Mark the mark on me too.' Sethe chuckled. 'Did she?' asked Denver. 'She slapped my face.' 'What for?' 'I didn't understand it then. Not till I had a mark of my own.'"[1]

In telling this story to her daughters, Sethe claims the mark of her slavery as a thing that can be spoken about to those in the next generation who, like Denver, were not there to be marked themselves. For survivors of trauma, the gap between generations is the breach between a memory located in the body and the mediated knowledge of those who were born after. *Trauma*, in its literal meaning is a wound inflicted on the flesh. Roberta Culbertson stresses that "no experience is more one's own than harm to one's own skin, but none is more locked within that skin, played out within it in actions other than words, in patterns of consciousness below the everyday and the constructions of language."[2] The wound inflicted on the skin can be read as a sign of trauma's incommunicability, a figure for the traumatic real that defines a seemingly unbridgeable gap between survivors and their descendants. Paradoxically, the writing on the body that most objectifies its victims by identifying them as slaves or concentration camp prisoners is enclosed within the boundaries of skin, ultimately and utterly private and incommunicable—in Sethe's terms, "a mark of *my own*."

While theorists like Shoshana Felman and Geoffrey Hartman, in writing about the Holocaust, have consistently seen literary language as a privileged medium for the transmission of trauma, a prevalent visual figuration of trauma often takes the shape of a bodily mark, wound, or tattoo. Building on Charlotte Delbo's definition of a "deep" or "sense" memory located in the body (as opposed to the "ordinary memory" out of which stories are made), Jill Bennett comments specifically on its visual figuration:

> It is no coincidence that the image of ruptured skin recurs throughout the work of artists dealing with sense memory. . . . If the skin of memory is permeable, then it cannot serve to encase the past self as other. It is precisely through the breached boundaries of skin in such imagery that memory continues to be felt as a wound rather than seen as contained other . . . it is here in sense memory that the past seeps back into the present, becoming sensation rather than representation.[3]

In this chapter, I want to consider this visual figuration of trauma and transmission, particularly, the dynamics of identification by which the mark, and thus the sense memory that it represents, can, however partially and imperfectly, be transferred across subjects and generatio*ns*. When Gayatri C. Spivak reads the above scene in *Beloved* in relation to the novel's repeated assertion that "this is not a story to pass on,"[4] she reflects on the mother's slap: "even between mother and daughter a certain historical withholding intervenes."[5] "And yet," she continues, "it *is* passed on with the mark of untranslatability on it, in the bound book *Beloved* that we hold in our hands."[6] The mark of untranslatability becomes the untranslatability of the mark. The implication, on the one hand, that interest and empathy are heightened within the matrilineal family in particular, and the articulation, on the other, of the "historical withholding" that intervenes *even* between mothers and daughters, make of Morrison's novel a theoretical text for the contradictions that define the intergenerational legacy of trauma and familial postmemory in particular. I begin this discussion of body memory with *Beloved* to find in Morrison's mother/daughter story a paradigm of relation, through which we might read the connections between the ways in which trauma is transmitted and received in vastly different historical circumstances.[7]

When Sethe's mother points out that "this your ma'am," she identifies the mother with the burned circle and cross on her skin. The mark *is* the mother—"this your ma'am"—and it is also the vehicle for mother/daughter recognition—"you will know me by this mark." When physical identity is altered by the mark of slavery and the daughter is separated from the mother by a radically different history, she both fears having to repeat her mother's story and longs for the recognition that ensures her identity as her mother's daughter. "How will you know me?"[8] The ambivalent desire to be marked, and thus to repeat the mother's trauma, is understandable between mothers and daughters whose bodily relation and resemblance is so violated by the mark as no longer to work as a vehicle of mutual recognition at the heart of the mother/daughter bond.

What concerns me here is how writers and visual artists of the postgeneration have been able to represent this intergenerational dynamic—the desire and the hesitation, the necessity and the impossibility of receiving the parents' bodily experience of trauma manifested in the visual mark or tattoo. In the previous chapter, we discussed and, indeed, performed the postgeneration's ambivalent wish to locate parental trauma in a precise spot—like the spot on the lapel. Here that desire, and that ambivalence, are more intense and more intimate still: it is to identify so strongly as to receive from the parent the wound on the skin, and, at the same time, it is the disavowal of this bodily mirroring.

Witnessed by those who were not there to live it but who received its effects, belatedly, through the narratives, actions, and symptoms of the previous generation, trauma both solidifies and blurs generational difference.[9] What forms of identification and attachment can enable the transfer of body memory, and what artistic idioms can represent them? And what is the role of "historical withholding" in the transmission of trauma? Because of the distinctive cultural expectations bestowed on daughters and the gendered dynamics of subject-formation by which they are shaped, I am particularly interested, in this chapter, in exploring the specificity of the role of daughters in the work of familial postmemory.

REMEMORY AND POSTMEMORY

In the literature on trauma inspired by readings of Freud's work on mourning and melancholia, there is a familiar distinction between two modes of remembering. Variously labeled "mémoire profonde" and "mémoire ordinaire" ("deep" and "ordinary" memory) (Charlotte Delbo), "acting out" and "working through" (Dominick LaCapra), "perception" and "memory" (Juliet Mitchell), "traumatic memory" and "narrative memory" (Bessel van der Kolk and Ono van der Hart), "introjection" and "incorporation" (Nicolas Abraham and Maria Torok), these modes are neither opposed nor mutually exclusive.[10] Rather, relying on a performative notion of language and other forms of expression, they account for varying degrees of working through, coming to terms with, or gaining distance from the past. But postmemorial witnesses are also subject to different, if always overlapping, modes of "remembering." In the stories of transmission on which I focus in this book, I see a range between what Morrison has called "rememory" and what I am defining as "postmemory"—between, on the one hand, a memory that, communicated through bodily symptoms, becomes a form of repetition and reenactment, and, on the other hand, one that works through indirection and multiple mediation.[11] Within the intimate familial space of mother/daughter transmission, however, postmemory always risks sliding into rememory, traumatic reenactment, and repetition.

In her extensive psychoanalytic discussions of children of Holocaust survivors, Judith Kestenberg has found the notion of "identification" insufficient in describing their relationships with their parents: "The mechanism goes beyond identification. I have called it 'transposition' into the world of the past, similar—but not identical—to the spiritualist's journey into the world of the dead."[12] Morrison's rememory is such a form of "transposition," a descent through what Kestenberg calls a "time tunnel of history"[13] into the world of the dead. Rememory is a noun and verb, a thing and an action. Communicable, shared, and permanent, because it is spatial and material, tactile, it underscores the deadly dangers of intergenerational transmission:

> "Some things you forget. Other things you never do. . . . Places, places are still there. If a house burns down, it's gone, but the place—the picture of it—stays, and not just in my rememory but out there, in the world." . . . "Can other people see it?" asked Denver. "Oh yes. Oh, yes, yes, yes. Some day you be walking down the road and you hear something or see something going on. So clear. And you think it's you thinking it up. A thought picture. But no. It's when you bump into a rememory that belongs to somebody else."[14]

In this passage Sethe underscores the materiality and the intersubjectivity of memory and the dire consequences of one person's empathic over-identification and adoption of another's memories.

In *Beloved*, the ultimate ghost story, haunting takes on material shapes. Rememory is the same for the one who was there and the one who was never there, for the I and the you in Sethe's conversation: " 'Where I was before I came here, that place is real. It's never going away. Even if the whole farm—every tree and grass blade of it dies. The picture is still there and what's more, if you go there—you who never was there—if you go there and stand in the place where it was, it will happen again; it will be there for you, waiting for you.' "[15] The "re" in "rememory" signals not just the threat, but the certainty of repetition: "It will happen again."

Children of Holocaust survivors often describe their relationships to their parents' memories in these very terms. In her memoir, *The War After*, for example, British journalist Anne Karpf, the daughter of an Auschwitz survivor, enumerates the bodily symptoms through which she experiences her mother's sense memories of the camps. Her discussion revolves around the mark on the skin. For a long period in her young adulthood she develops terrible eczema and scratches herself irresistibly first on her hands and arms and later her entire body:

> I wanted to divest myself of my skin, slip out of it like a starched dress left standing while my self crept away to hide. . . . My skin no longer seemed able to keep what was inside in. . . . After years of my scratching, a close friend asked whether the place on my inside forearm that I was repeatedly injuring wasn't the same place, indeed the very same arm, where my mother's concentration camp number was inked. I was astonished—it had never occurred to me. But I couldn't believe that the unconscious could go in for such crude symbolism, the kind you find in made-for-TV movies—it seemed like a base attempt to endow my own flimsy desolation with historical gravitas and dignify it with reference to my mother's. (I remain unconvinced).[16]

Her own welcome skepticism notwithstanding, Karpf's symptoms, like Sethe's intense desire to be marked with her mother's mark, illustrates what can happen in the absence, or even in spite of, "a certain historical withholding" between mother and daughter. Anne Karpf's relationship to her mother becomes incorporative and appropriative— more a form of "transposition" than identification. Memory is transmitted to be repeated and reenacted, not to be worked through: "I'd always envied my parents their suffering. This was so obviously shocking that I couldn't have admitted it, had I even been conscious of it. . . . their terrible experiences seemed to diminish—even to taunt—anything bad which ever happened to us."[17] In the absence of a bodily identity with her mother, Karpf, like Sethe, risks losing her sense of herself. She has to feel the same sense of cold and warmth, the same marking of her skin, the same danger and misery: "It was as if I'd finally managed to prise off some particle of my mother's suffering and make it my own. I'd grafted on to myself a bit of her pain."[18]

The child of survivors who "transposes" herself into the past of the Holocaust lives the "burden of a double reality" that makes "functioning" extraordinarily "complex."[19] Karpf receives her mother's memories in her own body as symptoms that plague even as they fail to lead to understanding. In the sense that they repeat the trauma of the past in what she calls an "awful, involuntary mimetic obsession,"[20] her mother's memories are rememories engaging both mother and daughter with equal vehemence. But Karpf's memoir allows us also to distinguish "transposition" from a different form of "identification," and thus "rememory" from "postmemory." When the mother's experiences are communicated through stories and images that can be narrativized, integrated—however uneasily—into a historically different present, they open up the possibility of a form of second-generation remembrance that is based on a more consciously and necessarily mediated form of identification. Postmemory, in this sense, corresponds to what Eve Kosofsky Sedgwick terms "allo-identification" or "identification with" as opposed to the "auto-identification" or "identification as" that is closer to rememory.[21] But how can even such a more distant identification resist the envy and competition we see in Morrison and Karpf's texts? How, particularly, can the bodily memory of the mark be received without the violent self-wounding of transposition?

In *The Threshold of the Visible World*, Kaja Silverman, borrowing the term from Max Scheler, has theorized a "heteropathic" as opposed to an "idiopathic" process of identification—a way of aligning the "not-me" with the "me" without interiorizing it or, in her terms, "introduc[ing] the 'not-me' into my memory reserve."[22] Through "discursively 'implanted' memories" the subject can "participate in the desires, struggles, and sufferings of the other"—particularly, in Silverman's examples, the culturally devalued and persecuted other.[23] Thus the subject can engage in what Silverman calls "identification-at-a-distance"— identification that does not appropriate or interiorize the other within the self but that goes out of one's self and out of one's own cultural norms in order to align oneself, through displacement, with another. Postmemory is a form of heteropathic memory in which the self and the other are more closely connected through familial or group relation—through an understanding of what it means to be Jewish or of African descent, for example. While postmemory implies a temporal distance between the self and the other, daughter and mother, Silverman's heteropathic recollection could depend solely on spatial or cultural distance and temporal coincidence. In both cases, an enormous distance must be bridged and, in the specific case of catastrophic memory—such as the memory of slavery or the Holocaust—that distance cannot ultimately be bridged; the break between then and now, between the one who lived it and the one who did not remains monumental and insurmountable, even as the heteropathic imagination struggles to overcome it.

Silverman's instrument of heteropathic memory is the look, the wounding look of Roland Barthes's punctum, which designates something so unfamiliar and unexpected in the image that it acts like a "prick" or a "wound" interrupting any familiar relation between the viewer and the visible world.[24] The productive look of heteropathic identification can see beyond "the given to be seen," it can displace the incorporative, ingestive look of self-sameness and the familiar object it sees in favor of "an appetite for alterity" that enables an act of recognition across difference.[25]

For postmemorial artists, the challenge is to define an aesthetic based on a form of identification and projection that can include the transmission of the bodily memory of trauma without leading to the self-wounding and retraumatization that is rememory. The desire for this type of nonappropriative identification and empathy, and, of course, its often painful and disastrous flaws and failures, have formed the core of feminist theory and practice in the last thirty years. As Sedgwick writes, "For a politics like feminism . . . effective moral authority has seemed to depend on its capacity for conscientious and nonperfunctory enfoldment of women alienated from one another in virtually every other relation of life."[26] In this light, we might examine Spivak's implications that mothers and daughters are privileged intergenerational interlocutors when it comes to traumatic recollection. Can the daughter, in particular, both maintain the distance of allo-identification and receive a bodily memory that enables the trans-generational transmission of trauma and its empathic reception?

If identifications, learned and practiced within the family, can be expanded to cross the boundaries of gender, family, race, and generation, then the identification between mothers and daughters forms a clear example of how a shared intersubjective trans-generational space of remembrance, based in bodily connection, can be imagined. Because of a bodily closeness that is reinforced by cultural expectations, the case of mothers and daughters might indeed acutely exemplify the danger of an over-identification through which the more distant idioms of postmemory slide back into the appropriations of rememory. Through the care-giving role traditionally attributed to daughters, the pressures of inter-subjective relationships marked by trauma emerge in especially sharp focus. In looking at postmemory through the lens of the daughter, I bring feminist negotiations between commonalities and differences, and feminist theorizations of subjectivity and intersubjectivity, and of political solidarity, to bear on the theorization of memory and trauma. Daughters become paradigmatic insofar as they enable us to define the range of identificatory practices that motivate the art of the familial and the affiliative postgeneration. And yet, even as we consider bodily connections and bodily marks, identities need not be literal or essential. Indeed, as we shall see, identifications can cross lines of difference, and the daughter can function as a familial position or identificatory space open to extra-familial, even male, subjects.

FIFTY YEARS OF SILENCE

I have known since I was a child that my parents were concentration camp survivors, since both of them had a number tattooed on their left arm. I used to spend a lot of time studying their tattoos, wondering what it must have been like. My mother never talked about her experiences. My father only talked about it when he was scolding us, especially about eating everything on our plates. Once when I was at his side on an after-dinner walk, he told a friend the stories of the

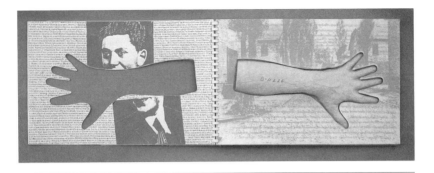

3.2 Tatana Kellner, *Layered Pages. From Tatana Kellner,* B-11226: Fifty Years of Silence *(Rosendale, N.Y.: Women's Studio Workshop, 1992). Courtesy of Tatana Kellner*

medical experiments performed on him and the ten-day transport when people began devouring each other. I think he must have forgotten I was there. I didn't inquire any further for fear of hurting him.[27]

Tatana Kellner's two artists' books *Fifty Years of Silence*, which both begin with the above passage, are the work of a daughter of Holocaust survivors, born and raised in postwar Prague (figure 3.2). After emigrating to the United States and becoming an artist, Kellner invited her parents to help her with a work that would be based on their reminiscences of the war. She wanted to tape their stories, but they preferred to write them for her in Czech, and she undertook to translate their texts into English. "Except for questions I had in terms of accuracy, this is still not something we can talk about," she says.[28]

Fifty Years of Silence is the product of collaboration between the parents and the daughter. The parents' handwritten Czech text, in blue ink on translucent pages, faces its typewritten translation (on opaque white pages) by the daughter. Superimposed on both versions are large silk-screened photographs. Some were taken recently by Tatana Kellner on a trip to Prague and Auschwitz; these are mostly of roads, train stations, and what look like remains and memorial sites in the camp. Others are family photographs from the more than fifty years between the parents' youth in Prague before the war and their old age in an American suburb. On some pages, the superimposed photographs are combined with lists of names and with birth and death dates, taken

3.3 Tatana Kellner, book cover from *B-11226: Fifty Years of Silence. From Tatana Kellner,* B-11226: Fifty Years of Silence *(Rosendale, N.Y.: Women's Studio Workshop, 1992). Courtesy of Tatana Kellner*

from the memorial wall of Prague's Pinkasova synagogue. Strikingly, in the middle of each book, there is a handmade paper cast of her parents' tattooed arms: the daughter took casts to make the handmade paper arms and photographed the tattoos so as to copy them exactly, in her own hand, onto the pink surfaces (figure 3.3). The parents then wrote their stories around the empty hole left by the cast.

By embedding her parents' stories, written in their own language and their own handwriting, into her artwork, Kellner is able, in Paul Celan's terms, to "bear witness for the witness."[29] In editing and trans-lating her parents' texts, in going to Poland to visit the camp where her parents had been interned, and in constructing her books, Kellner has found a mode of receiving and transmitting their testimony even as she attempts to respect their 50 years of silence. Like the stories of Sethe in *Beloved*, Eva and Eugene Kellner's are not stories "to pass on." But in the artwork of their daughter, they are passed on, and with them the process of transmission itself, the work of postmemory. *Fifty Years of Silence* suggests the silence with which Tatana Kellner grew up, as well as her own determined need to know. It represents the daughter's responsive and protective "allo-identification," her effort to elicit the stories, and her continuing childhood fear of "hurting" them further. And Kellner's visual text and the willingness to print the Czech handwriting enables her to respect her parents' "historical withholding," their need for silence and the untranslatability of their story: "this is still not something we can talk about."[30] But, of course, in translating their text and publishing their narratives, she does inevitably violate the silence they had determined to keep. Kellner's work, like all postmemorial texts, situates itself in this paradoxical space.

Rather than listen and talk with her parents, Kellner looks at their tattoos. Like Sethe's paradigmatic look at the mark on her mother's breast—a look both of recognition ("you will know me by this mark") and of nonrecognition ("but how will you know me?")—Tatana's look fundamentally structures her text. She suggests that visual images might expand the current emphasis on oral testimony and active listening as privileged modes of transmission. And the graphic modes she has chosen—casting, tracing, and photography—attempt precisely to convey to her own readers/viewers her parents' bodily wounding. For Kellner, as for other postmemorial artists, visuality is both a vehicle and a figure for the transmission of sense memory. The enlarged photographs dominate the pages of the two books in such a way that the written text itself becomes photographic—more a visual than a textual image—especially since the reception of the books in a museum setting, where I first encountered them, precludes detailed reading of the texts and relegates viewers to an uncomfortable shuttling between the impulse to look and the compulsion to read.

Like the tattoo's, the photograph's indexical relation to its object and the haunting, ghost-like presence of the referent it calls forth makes the photographic image a privileged link between memory and postmemory, a vehicle of the *productive look* that can supplement the active listening of postmemory. Kellner's multimedia work elicits a productive look of "allo-identification" that can see beyond the familiar, displacing an incorporative, ingestive look of self-sameness and familiarization in favor of an openness to the other, a granting of alterity and opaqueness. Its images have the power both of screening the real and of piercing holes that allow the real to show through.

Kellner's text is literally built around a hole, and thus this paradoxical dilemma of transmission structures Kellner's work nowhere more obviously than in the tattooed arm at the center of each book. The arm is almost unbearable to look at in its truncated presence, but it also leaves an empty space in the center of each turned page. Kellner has said that for her, visually, "it began with the arms" and she built the books around them.[31] The arms communicate visually and sensually the wounded skin and thus the bodily presence of trauma by provoking the viewer's own embodied response. At the same time, the empty space on the other side of the page is a reminder of absence, secrecy, silence, untranslatability.

After turning all the pages of *Fifty Years of Silence* one reaches the base on which each book rests: a sheet of pink handmade paper holding the cast of the amputated tattooed arm, a sculpture signed and numbered by the artist. The numbers tattooed on the two arms are thus mirrored in the numbers indicating the edition of the artwork, signed in the artist's hand. Here ultimately is the unbridgeable distance between the experiences of the two generations: while the artist numbers her own work, separate from her body, the parents' arms were themselves numbered—not as works but as bodies deprived of human agency—by their Nazi victimizers. On the daughter's part, creative choice, the sign of artistic power; on the parents' part, a reminder of forcible dehumanization and powerlessness.[32]

One might ask, however, whether Kellner, in numbering her work, has taken care to mark the gap separating her own process of knowledge and *marking* from her parents' experience of *being marked*. Has Kellner, in casting the arm, made too literal a signifier, has she revealed too much, has she slipped into the mimetic repetition that is rememory? She might indeed have, had the arm not been inscribed in the layered, mixed-media work that is *Fifty Years of Silence*. The photographs, the plaster casts and tattoos, combined with the writing, work together to engage us in multiple and complex ways, inviting us to look, to turn pages, to read, to confront the empty space left by the arm. As we shuttle, uneasily, between modes of reception, the text resists understanding and consumption. Indeed, in its very form, *Fifty Years of Silence* comments self-consciously both on the difficulties of remembrance and transmission and on the problematics of the artistic representation of

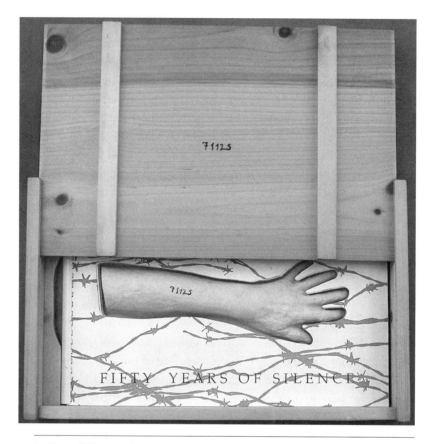

3.4 Tatana Kellner, book covers. *From Tatana Kellner, 71125: Fifty Years of Silence (Rosendale, N.Y.: Women's Studio Workshop, 1992). Courtesy of Tatana Kellner*

the Holocaust from a present vantage point. In its sculptural mode and book form, in its conjunction of narrative and image, Kellner's work creates a sense of depth and the promise of revelation (figure 3.4). At the same time, the excess of text, the flatness and illegibility of the super-imposed images, the materiality of the arm we reach at the end of our reading, and the gaps left in the stories, cannot remove frustration, in-comprehension, and unreality. Kellner's work is no more than an attempt at translation, from Czech to English, from the past to the present, from the camp world to ours. And in that process of failed translation, the second-generation daughter can hold the memory with which she has been entrusted, because she can respect and perpetuate her parents' act of "historical withholding." At the same time, she can acknowledge the inevitability of her own act of violation that emerges from the lack of recognition that marks the relationship of survivors to their children. But in Kellner's text, as in Spiegelman's, it is the father who talks, and the mother who withholds: "I think he must have forgotten I was there."

WRITTEN IN MEMORY

Jeffrey Wolin's 1997 exhibition and book, *Written in Memory: Portraits of the Holocaust*, offers other cross-generational moments of visual and verbal transmission of trauma. In these portraits, Wolin, an American artist born in 1951 as a descendant of Polish and Lithuanian Jews (not Holocaust survivors), photographs survivors and records excerpts from their edited testimony by writing them in his own hand right on the print. While a number of his images illustrate the workings of familial postmemory, one in particular, the image of Irma Morgensztern and her daughter (figure 3.1) figures powerfully the dynamics of mother/daughter transmission. Unlike the mother/daughter stories told by Morrison, Karpf, and Kellner, this one is mediated by Wolin, a male artist who receives the story from his interview subjects, then edits and writes it. Thus, this particular image enables us to envision mother/daughter transmission not as an identity position, but as an affiliative space of remembrance, available to other subjects external to the immediate family. It enables us to see the negotiation between the distance necessary for the allo-identification of postmemory and the closeness that enables the bodily transmission of the mark.

In the image of Irma Morgensztern, born in 1933 in Warsaw, Irma stands hugging a young woman who must be her adult daughter, and they both hold a portrait of a woman who must be Irma's mother. On the facing page is a 1945 photo of the 12-year-old Irma taken in Warsaw at the end of the war (figure 3.5).

The text describes the night Irma escaped from the ghetto. While it tells about her mother and father, no mention is made of the daughter, who is depicted as an earnest listener, witness, and inheritor. The

3.5 Irma Morgensztern, from Jeffrey Wolin's 1997 exhibition *Written in Memory: Portraits of the Holocaust. Courtesy of Catherine Edelman Gallery, Chicago, Illinois*

narrative tells about the complicated name and identity change Irma had to undergo in hiding. "It was terribly tragic the night before I left the Warsaw ghetto when they knew I'm going to be gone the next night. So we were sitting and talking and they were trying to put into my head who I am, that I'm from Warsaw and my name is Barbara Nosarewska, I never should forget. . . . And on the other hand they were trying to put into the other side of my brain that after the war I am Jewish and my name is Irma Morgensztern."[33]

Mother, daughter, and grandmother are intertwined in the image, but there is something terribly anachronistic about the fact that the woman in the portrait, the grandmother, is younger than the adult Irma, perhaps not much older than Irma's daughter, and that she will never age or have aged enough to act as a grandmother to the young woman in the picture. There are several mother/daughter pairs in the image: Irma and her daughter, in the present; Irma and her mother in the past looking at each other across the break of the white page, both smiling; and Irma and her mother in the present: but here the mother is just a portrait, younger than her daughter, frozen in an eternally past present.

Nor is the mother's story told—did she die in the war, did Irma ever find out what happed to her mother and father? The gesture with which Irma and her daughter hold her mother's portrait is protective and tender, as is the gesture with which they hold one another, but their eyes do not meet; each is in her own space, each in her own time zone. Even as the women hug, we sense that this is a fractured family, that the chain of transmission has been broken. With her mother covering most of her chest and the words of her story crowding around her body, Irma is shuttling between that night before she left the ghetto and the present moment, more than fifty years later. Her daughter is in the present, as we viewers are, trying to understand that past moment, to gain access to it. But just as Irma rehearses her separation from her mother and father, and from her past identity—"So while I was sitting with the cows in the pasture I was thinking 'that's me or not me?"[34]—so her daughter looks to her for a form of recognition that might assure her identity. But Irma's gaze is elsewhere: she does not return her daughter's look.

Wolin explains the role of the intercalated archival images when he discusses the founding photo of the exhibit, the image of Mišo Vogel (figure 3.6): "I wanted to show his tattoo, which is in and of itself a powerful visual statement. . . . I also had him hold a photograph of his father who died in Auschwitz. This image acted as a window and Mišo was, for a moment, transported back to a terrible time in his past."[35] So is Irma, transported back to a terrible time in her past, and by holding on to her daughter, she takes her back with her, even as she needs her daughter to take her back out to the present again. The photo is a window to the past, reinforced by the partly open door at the edge of the picture, marking both the invitation to go back and the threshold that is so difficult to cross.

The stylized, obviously posed position of the figures, the framing by the door and the plant and, especially, the writing on the print create a

The handwriting on the photograph reads:

MIŠO VOGEL. Born November 29, 1925. Topolčany, Slovakia. Taken prisoner by Nazis. Entered Novaky, Slovakia 1941-1942. Transferred to Auschwitz 1942 - October 1944. Oranienburg October - December 1944. 1942 - October 1944. Oranienburg 1945. Landsberg January-February-March 1945. Escaped March 1945. All his family murdered in concentration camps. MOTHER: CORNELIA died September 23, 1942, Auschwitz. Age 42. SISTER: MARTA died torture, death at the hands of the Nazis. A badly faded photograph shows Mišo catching a bundle of clothes, frozen by a camera in mid-flight at the rail station of Auschwitz. He was just a teenager. After escaping from concentration camp deep inside Germany, Mišo joined the U.S. Army. On furlough at the end of the war, he returned to his home town in Slovakia to obtain records (birth certificate, medical history, etc.) needed for U.S. citizenship. The same Slovaks who had stolen his father's cattle business and family's home greeted him from the front door of his house. "We thought you were gassed. Thought you were burned like all the rest." Mišo's records, all the records of the Jews were like the Jews themselves gone forever from that part of the world.

September 23, 1942, Auschwitz. Age 10. BROTHER: MAXMILLIAN died September 23, 1942, Auschwitz. Age 8. BROTHER: ARPAD killed Lublin Majdanek, May 1942. Age 16. SISTER: ROZSIE died June 1942, Auschwitz. Age 20. FATHER: HEINRICH VOGEL died November 1942, Auschwitz. Age 44. Owner of a cattle business in Topolčany before the war. Of a family of seven, Mišo the sole survivor. Assigned to a work detail at Auschwitz. "ARBEIT MACHT FREI." He searched the belongings of incoming prisoners stunned after days, weeks on the transports - no food - packed in like cattle - awaiting

3.6 Mišo Vogel, from Jeffrey Wolin's 1997 exhibition *Written in Memory: Portraits of the Holocaust. Courtesy of Catherine Edelman Gallery, Chicago, Illinois*

flat two-dimensionality that removes depth and thus temporality, showing memory to be firmly situated in the present. The past is in the present, spatially in the room, crowding out the figures, encasing them in a story that determines their very movements. Irma's daughter stares at the writing that surrounds her. The writing on the print is "written in memory"—both written in *memory*, out of one's memory, and *written-in* memory, a memory inscribed on the skin of the image itself, as a tattoo might be, as tattoos are in a great number of Wolin's images. Written-in memory, like photography (writing in light), mediates the transmission between memory and postmemory. But the handwriting here, and the photographic gaze itself, expand the familial circle. The artist—a male artist—inserts himself as another co-witness, another viewer and listener who is able to receive the stories and to transmit them, sharing in the familial, mother-daughterly network of looking that he enables. Through his indirection, his extra-familial presence, he can become the agent of the allo-identification or *affiliative postmemory*, the medium of the historical withholding that precisely prevents mother-daughter transmission from becoming incorporative rememory.

In *Written in Memory* Jeffrey Wolin begins to articulate the aesthetic strategies of identification, projection, and mourning that specifically characterize postmemory. In the image of Irma Morgensztern (figure 3.1), he stages and shares in a moment of knowledge for the daughter, who is literally bodily surrounded, marked, by traumatic memories that preceded her birth but that nevertheless define her life. Along with the unnamed daughter, Jeffrey Wolin becomes an affiliative "witness by adoption,"[36] who, in his own hand, reenacts the split identity of Irma Morgensztern (written on the right side of the image) and Barbara Nosarewska (written on the left). The two sides of the photograph mirror the two sides of young Irma's brain. He both creates and severely delimits the space of the encounter between memory and familial as well as affiliative postmemory.

These trans-gendered and trans-generational affiliations mark the subjects of these memories as members of a generation and as witnesses of a particular historical moment. Wolin's text, shaped by identification with the victims, invites viewers to participate in a cultural act of remembrance, or in Shoshana Felman's terms, to "perceiv(e) history— what is happening to others—*in one's own body*, with the power of sight (of insight) usually afforded only by one's own immediate physical involvement."[37] As the daughter's body, like the mother's, is surrounded by the inscription of her mother's story, and as their bodies intertwine, they risk losing their physical boundaries and merging with one another. Yet their eyes do not meet, their hands do not touch, the writing is someone else's.

Photographic writing and the affect it can engender allow bodily sense memory to be passed on beyond the family to those who would witness affiliatively "by adoption." Describing his own affiliative relationship with survivors, James Young has said that their stories are "grafted indelibly into my own life story."[38] Wolin's images reproduce this "indelible grafting." His photographic writing demands reading as well as looking, thus drawing the viewer in even as it pushes us back out. Wolin, this "witness for the witness," re-produces the marking of trauma by enabling the narrative and bodily encounter between mother and daughter and by staging it for others to witness. The challenge for the postmemorial artist is precisely to allow the spectator to enter the image, to imagine the disaster "in one's own body," yet to evade the transposition that erases distance, creating too available, too direct an access to this particular past.

AFFILIATIVE RELATIONS

Our access to the postmemory of the Holocaust has, until recently, been largely shaped by works by and about men, fathers and sons. Male narrators have dominated not only in the first generation (Levi, Wiesel) but also in the second: Art Spiegelman's *Maus*, David Grossman's *See Under Love*, the work of Patrick Modiano, Christian Boltanski, Alain Finkielkraut. Even Anne Michaels, a woman writer, envisions the transmission of the Holocaust along masculine lines in her *Fugitive Pieces*. Vladek Spiegelman boldly erases any gender differentiation when he states about his wife, Anja, who could no longer testify for herself: "She went through the same what me, *terrible!*"[39] Does it then make sense, even in the second generation, to single out the daughter as an agent of transmission? Of course, just as Anja did not go through "the same what me," so the position of the daughter as historical agent is not the same as that of the son.

Yet in thinking about postmemory as a feminist, I have found it fruitful not only to search for female witnesses of the first and second generation, but also to think about a feminist mode of knowing this past. In this effort, it seems to me that the works by Morrison, Karpf, Kellner, and Wolin, and their focus on the position of the daughter, might allow us to theorize not a female or daughterly but a feminist postmemory work defined by a particular mode of knowledge about the other, a particular intersubjective relation or "allo-identification." It is a question of how memory is constructed, of what stories are told or withheld—to whom and by whom. And, of course, it is a question of how family stories are structured and told, and of how they are repressed, suppressed, or silenced, and of how a feminist analysis can expose those structures.

Thus, I would say that some of the characteristics of Kellner and Wolin's postmemorial aesthetic can be fruitfully read through the lens of feminist theories of commonality and difference. Both these artists search for forms of identification that are nonappropriative. The mixture of media and the multiple responses they elicit, the oscillation between reading and looking, in particular, create a resistant textuality for the viewer. The mediated access they open allows for a "historical withholding" that does not absorb the other but grants the pastness and the irretrievability of the past, the irreducibility of the other, the untranslatablity of the story of trauma. The modes of knowledge they engage in are embodied, material, located, and thus also responsive and responsible to the other. But they also thematize the act of *holding*— caring, protective, and nurturing—made palpable in the use of hands as primary figures in their works. The lines of transmission they enact, moreover, are capacious enough to transcend gender and familial role, and thus they expand the circle of postmemory in multiple, inviting, and open-ended ways. In casting daughters as agents of transmission, and through them opening the space of remembrance beyond the line of family, their practice of postmemory, particularly, can become a reparative ethical and political act of solidarity and, perhaps, agency on behalf of the trauma of the other. Significantly, however, both artists enable us also to understand the risks of even such a well-intentioned identificatory practice, and the inevitable appropriations that inflect an empathic aesthetics. The particularities of mother/daughter relations provide the clearest insight into these messy contradictions.

II.

AFFILIATION, GENDER, AND GENERATION

4.1 Image 128, Dora Kraus with her son Jozef and his Polish nursemaid, from the exhibition *And I Still See Their Faces: Images of Polish Jews. From Golda Tencer and Anna Bikont, eds.,* And I Still See Their Faces: Images of Polish Jews *(Warsaw: Shalom Foundation, 1998)*

4

SURVIVING IMAGES

One's first encounter with the photographic inventory of ultimate horror is a kind of revelation, the prototypically modern revelation: a negative epiphany. For me, it was photographs of Bergen-Belsen and Dachau which I came across by chance in a bookstore in Santa Monica in July 1945. Nothing I have seen—in photographs or in real life—ever cut me as sharply, deeply, instantaneously. Indeed, it seems plausible to me to divide my life into two parts, before I saw those photographs (I was twelve) and after, though it was several years before I understood fully what they were about. What good was served by seeing them? They were only photographs—of an event I had scarcely heard of and could do nothing to affect, of suffering I could hardly imagine and could do nothing to relieve. When I looked at those photographs, something broke. Some limit had been reached, and not only that of horror; I felt irrevocably grieved, wounded, but a part of my feelings started to tighten; something went dead, something is still crying.[1]

Susan Sontag was twelve in 1945 when she first encountered those pictures "of ultimate horror" so vividly described in her 1973 book.

Twenty years later, in her 1993 *French Lessons*, Alice Kaplan evokes a similar encounter. Kaplan was in third grade, eight or nine, in 1962 when she found these images of atrocity in the desk of her father, who had been a prosecutor at Nuremberg and who had recently died of heart failure.

> I made a thorough search of my father's desk. I opened every pad and every box in every drawer. . . . In the right bottom drawer I found gray cardboard boxes. There were black and white photographs of dead bodies in them. In several photographs hundreds of bony corpses were piled on top of one another in bony heaps. I had never seen a dead body, not even in a photograph. . . . This is what death looked like.
>
> Not every body in the photographs was dead. People were standing up, but they didn't look human. Their bones stuck out too much. You could see the sockets where one bone connected to the next. Some were naked, some wore striped pajamas that fell off their bones. One man tried to smile. His face was more frightening than the expressionless faces—he was reaching for life, but it was too late. . . . "U.S. Army" and a series of numbers was stamped on the back of each photograph.
>
> My mother told me that the photographs were taken by Mr. Newman. He was a photographer for the Army when they liberated the concentration camps at the end of the war. His photographs were evidence at Nuremberg for what the Nazis did.
>
> I took the photos to class to show the other third-graders what had happened in the camps. My mother had gone through the photos to remove the ones she thought were too upsetting, but I wanted to take all of them, especially the upsetting ones. . . . I believed my friends had no right to live without knowing about these pictures, how could they look so pleased when they were so ignorant. None of them knew what I know, I thought. I hated them for it.[2]

Significantly, both of these encounters with what Sontag calls "the photographic inventory of ultimate horror"[3] occurred in childhood. Although one of these writers is a contemporary of the Holocaust and the other a member of the second generation, both encounters are marked by the same rupture, the same child realization of death, inconceivable violence, incomprehensible evil, the same sense that the world will never again be whole, that "something broke."[4] In both texts, the descriptions of these encounters are carefully dated and situated: they serve to position the authorial subject in a generational space defined by its visual culture, one in which images such as those found in the privacy of the desk drawer or even the public space of the bookstore are the mark of a limit of what can and should be seen. Although these two generations share the same visual landscape and live in it with the same sense of shock, that shock has different effects for witnesses and survivors than it does for their children and grandchildren.

Thus, if Sontag describes this radical interruption through seeing, it is only to show how easily we can become inured to its visual impact: "Photographs shock insofar as they show something novel. . . . Once one has seen such images, one has started down the road of seeing more—and more. Images transfix. Images anesthetize. . . . At the time of the first photographs of the Nazi camps, there was nothing banal about these images. After thirty years, a saturation point may have been reached."[5]

We do not have to look at the images Sontag and Kaplan describe. Now, after nearly seven decades later, they have become all too familiar. The saturation point that "may have been reached" for Sontag almost forty years ago has certainly been surpassed by now, causing many commentators on the representation and memorialization of the Holocaust to express serious concerns and warnings. "Is our capacity for sympathy finite and soon exhausted?" Geoffrey Hartman asked in his 1996 book *The Longest Shadow*.[6] The surfeit of violent imagery that constitutes our present visual landscape, he insisted, has desensitized us to horror, evacuating the capacity for the shocked child vision of Sontag or Kaplan. Hartman feared that we would try to go ever further, surpassing all representational limits to "seek to 'cut' ourselves, like psychotics who ascertain in this way that they exist."[7] In her extensive and classic study of Holocaust atrocity photos taken by the liberating armies, published in 1998, Barbie Zelizer cautioned that through this surfeit of imagery we were, as her title indicates, "remembering to forget," that the photographs have become no more than decontextualized memory cues, energized by an already coded remembrance, no longer the vehicles that can themselves provoke memory.[8]

Hartman and Zelizer voiced an anxiety that would become pervasive among scholars and writers concerned about the transmission of Holocaust memory in the 1990s and early 2000s. In a more recent essay, "Choosing Not to Look: Representation, Repatriation, and Holocaust Atrocity Photography," historian Susan A. Crane echoes these concerns, arguing that the continued circulation of atrocity images impedes historical understanding by banalizing the Holocaust. She makes a strong case for a moratorium on reproducing and looking at Holocaust atrocity images, and for treating them as "inadmissible, . . . ethically compromised" material that should be "repatriated."[9] Crane is inspired by Sontag's more recent questions about the point of continuing to look at atrocity images in *Regarding the Pain of Others*. In this later book, Sontag famously reverses her earlier position: "What is the evidence that photographs have a diminishing impact, that our culture of spectatorship neutralizes the moral force of photographs of atrocities?"[10] Arguing forcefully against the idea of a hypermediated "society of the spectacle" that constructs us all as observers alienated from the real, Sontag mobilizes recent conflicts around the globe to show how "hundreds of millions of television watchers are far from inured to what they see on television. They do not have the luxury of patronizing reality."[11]

In the context of these debates, it is telling that what we find in the contemporary scholarly and popular representation and memorialization of the Holocaust is not the multiplication and escalation of imagery that earlier fears of inurement might lead us to expect, but a striking repetition of the same very few images, used over and over again iconically and emblematically to signal this event. This despite the fact that the Holocaust is one of the visually best-documented events in the history of an era marked by a plenitude and striking range of visual documentation. The Nazis were masterful at recording visually their own rise to power as well as the atrocities they committed, immortalizing both victims and perpetrators.[12] Guards often officially photographed inmates at the time of their imprisonment and recorded their destruction. Individual soldiers frequently traveled with cameras and documented the ghettos and camps in which they served. At the liberation, the Allies photographed and filmed the opening of the camps; postwar interrogations and trials were meticulously filmed as well. It is ironic that although the Nazis intended to exterminate not only all Jews but also their entire culture, down to the very records and documents of their existence, they should themselves have been so anxious to add images to those that would, nevertheless, survive the death of their subjects.

Very few of these images were taken by victims: the astounding clandestine photographs Mendel Grossman succeeded in taking in the Lódz ghetto, hiding the negatives that were found after his death, are a rare exception, as are the images of the Warsaw ghetto taken at his own risk by the German anti-Nazi photographer Joe Heydecker, and the blurred, virtually unrecognizable photos of burnings and executions taken by members of the resistance in Auschwitz that form the core of the notorious debate between Claude Lanzmann and Jean-Luc Godard taken up by Georges Didi-Huberman.[13] The images of perpetrators, resisters, and victims together yield an enormous archive of diverse representations, many of which appeared frequently in the two decades after the war, in Alain Resnais's important 1956 film *Night and Fog*, which is largely composed of this gruesome archival material, and in Gerhard Schoenberger's 1960 volume *The Yellow Star*.[14] With the opening of new archives and museums, more and more imagery has become available, and yet, as the historian Sybil Milton wrote more than a decade before the opening of Soviet archives: "Although more than two million photos exist in the public archives of more than twenty nations, the quality, scope and content of the images reproduced in scholarly and popular literature has been very repetitive."[15] Surprisingly, her assessment is still valid. The repetition of the same few images, moreover, has disturbingly brought with it their radical decontextualization from their original context of production and reception.[16] Why, with so much imagery available from the time, has the postmemorial visual landscape been so radically delimited?

In my study and teaching of Holocaust memory, I have found this repetition puzzling and disturbing. If these obsessively repeated images delimit our available visual archive of this event, can they enable a deeper historical understanding and a responsible and ethical discourse in its aftermath? Do they banalize this painful history, as Crane contends, acting like empty signifiers, clichés that distance and protect us from its impact?[17] Have they become, in Alison Landsberg's terms, mere mass-mediated prostheses?[18] Does their repetition have the power in itself to retraumatize, making distant viewers into surrogate victims who, having seen the images so often, have adopted them into their own narratives and memories, and have thus become all the more vulnerable to their effects? If they cut and wound, do they enable memory, mourning, and working through?[19] Or is their repetition an effect of melancholy replay, appropriative identification?

These questions situate repetition itself as a specifically postmemorial response to an inherited trauma and point to its specific generational function. Cognizant that our memory consists not of events but of representations and reenactments, I argue, we do not experience repetition as desensitizing us to horror, or shielding us from shock, thus demanding an endless escalation of disturbing imagery, as survivors might fear. On the contrary, repetition connects the second generation to the first, in its capacity to produce rather than screen the effect of trauma that was lived so much more directly as compulsive repetition by survivors and contemporary witnesses. We have already seen the work that repetition can perform in Jacques Austerlitz's repetitive search for his mother's image, described in chapter 1, and in my own and Leo's repetitive return to the spot on my father's lapel, discussed in chapter 2.

Thus, while the reduction of the archive of images and their repetition might seem problematic in the abstract, the postmemorial generation, in displacing and recontextualizing these well-known images in their historical, literary, and artistic work, has been able to make repetition not an instrument of fixity or paralysis or simple retraumatization, as it often is for survivors of trauma, but a mostly helpful vehicle of transmitting an inherited traumatic past in such a way that it can be worked through.[20]

Alice Kaplan's relentless search through her father's desk drawers, her exposure of the images he carefully saved, and her insistence that her classmates must join her in the act of looking at what her father saw, illustrate the shift from familial to affiliative postmemory. Her description clarifies the postgeneration's reliance on images, stories, and documents passed down to them. But it clarifies as well how the affective force of these images can overshadow their informative potential. Thus, the repeated images of the Holocaust need to be read not so much for what they reveal but for how they reveal it, or fail to do so. As in themselves figures for memory and forgetting, they are part of an intergenerational effort at reconstitution and repair that Robert Jay Lifton describes on an individual level: "In the case of severe trauma we can say that there has been an important break in the lifeline that can leave one permanently engaged in either repair or the acquisition of new twine. And here we come to the survivor's overall task, that of formulation, evolving new inner forms that include the traumatic event."[21] As much for the generations following the Shoah as for survivors themselves, the work of postmemory is such a work of "formulation" and attempted repair. The repetitive visual landscape we construct and reconstruct is a central aspect of that work and its affiliative availability. To understand it, we must both understand the function of photographs in the act of transfer and read the images themselves.[22]

"TRACES"

Like a number of her short stories and plays, Ida Fink's story "Traces," from her 1987 collection *A Scrap of Time*, stages an intergenerational encounter between a survivor and some unnamed "they" who ask detailed questions about the liquidation of the ghetto in which she was interned.[23] In this particular story, the conversation revolves around a photograph:

Yes, of course she recognizes it. Why shouldn't she? That was their last ghetto.

The photograph, a copy of a clumsy amateur snapshot, is blurred. There's a lot of white in it, that's snow. The picture was taken in February. The snow is high, piled up in deep drifts. In the foreground are traces of footprints, along the edges, two rows of wooden stalls. That is all.[24]

As the woman tries to tell what she remembers, her narrative is arrested, time and again, by the details she can make out in the photo:

"That's the ghetto," she says again, bending over the photograph. Her voice sounds amazed.

. . . she reaches for the photograph, raises it to her nearsighted eyes, looks at it for a long time, and says, "You can still see traces of footprints." And a moment later, "That's very strange." . . .

"I wonder who photographed it? And when? Probably right afterwards: the footprints are clear here, but when they shot them in the afternoon it was snowing again."

The people are gone—their footprints remain. Very strange. (135–36)

This image in Fink's story is a kind of meta-picture illustrating the complicated issues that are raised in the seemingly simple attempt to use a photograph as an instrument of historical evidence, or even, simply, as a memory cue for the witness. What does Fink gain for her story by adding this fictional photograph to the witness's narrative?

The witness in Fink's story underscores what Barthes calls the photograph's *ça-a-été*, the having-been-there, of the past, with her first repeated spoken statement: " 'That's the ghetto,' she says again, bending over the photo. Her voice sounds amazed" (135). She points to the trace (the photo)—which is in itself of a trace (the footprints) and, amazed, she finds there an unequivocal presence ("that's the ghetto").[25] Oral or written testimony, like photography, leaves a trace, but, unlike writing, the photograph of the footprint, a trace of a trace, is the photographic index par excellence. Here is why Fink needed the description of the photograph to underscore the material connection between past and present that is embodied in the photograph and underscored by the witness who recognizes it. The photo—even the fictional photo—has, as Barthes would say, evidential force. It thus illustrates the integral link photographs provide for the second generation, those who in their desire for memory and knowledge are left to track the traces of what was there and no longer is. Pictures, as Zelizer argues, "materialize" memory.

"The photograph . . . is blurred. There's a lot of white in it."[26] In spite of their evidential force and their material connection to an event that was there before the lens, photographs can be extremely frustrating, as fleeting in their certainty as footprints in the snow. What ultimately can we see as we look at an image, or, in Ariella Azoulay's terms, "watch" it?[27] Does it not, like the white picture of footprints in the snow, conceal as much as it reveals? When was the picture taken, the witness wonders, and concludes that it was "probably right afterwards: the footprints are clear here, but when they shot them it was snowing again" (136). The still picture captures, refers to, an instant in time that, when we look at the picture, is over, irrecoverable. If the photograph has evidential force, Barthes argues, it testifies not as much to the object as to time, but because time is stopped in the photograph, one might say it gives us only a partial and thus perhaps a misleading knowledge about the past. Even as it freezes time, however, the image shows that time cannot be frozen: in the case of Holocaust photos such as this one, the impossibility of stopping time or of averting death is already announced by the shrinking of the ghetto, the roundup, the footprints pointing toward the site of execution. In this case, these footprints in the snow are the visible evidence not of the inevitable, non-negotiable march of time, but of its murderous interruption.

Those who question the witness, looking for facts and information, have only traces such as this photograph and the woman's halting narrative to go on. In the scene of transfer, the questioners and the witness perform crassly gendered roles. The story does not tell of the listeners' response, cites only one of their questions. But through the picture it can suggest everything that exceeds their queries and the woman's inadequate answers: it can *produce* affect in the viewer and the reader. The postmemorial viewers do more than listen to the witness; they "watch" the image with her and thus they can relive, in the very sensations of the body, that fateful walk in the snow. As we have seen in the preceding chapter, this connection between photography and bodily or sense memory can perhaps account for the power of photographs to connect first- and second- generation subjects in an unsettling mutuality that crosses the gap of genocidal destruction.

On the one hand, a blurred picture with a lot of white in it, depicting footprints and some wooden stalls in the snow. On the other, a narrative about the massacre of the children and their parents, the last in their ghetto. The two are incommensurable, illustrating the disjunction between the crime and the instruments of representation and even conceptualization available in the aftermath. If the photograph is a trace, then it cannot ultimately refer to the incomprehensible, inconceivable referent that is the extermination of European Jewry, or even just the murder of the last 80 Jews in the town. "The people are gone—their footprints remain. Very strange" (136). Equally strange that the photo, a "copy of a clumsy amateur snapshot" (135), should remain.

More than just evocative and representational power, images also quickly assume symbolic power—the trace in the story becomes not just a footprint in the snow but a trace of the children who were killed. "But suddenly she changes her mind and asks that what she is going to say be written down and preserved forever, because she wants a trace to remain" (136). And thus she tells the story of the eight hidden children who were brought out by the SS to identify their parents but who refused to move or to speak. Children and parents were killed, and the female, maternal, witness holds their memory and decides to pass it on. She asks that it be written down: " 'So I wanted some trace of them to be left behind' " (137).

She alone can connect the two presents of the photograph because she alone survived. The testimony with its ellipses, the suggestion of "tears, instantly restrained" (137) is provoked by the photograph, which, without her elucidation, would remain silent. With her story, the photograph can speak and cry, utter, in Sebald's terms, "small sighs of despair," perhaps.[28] But the particular photograph she uses to tell her story also allows her testimony to figure the very act of witness. Zelizer discusses the symbolic and interpretive power of images, arguing that "the photo's significance . . . evolved from the ability not only to depict a real-life event but to position that depiction within a broader interpretive framework."[29] Photos are "markers of both truth-value and symbolism."[30]

FIGURES

As a figure for the relationship between photography, memory, and postmemory, Fink's fictional photograph enables us to think about some of the emblematic public images used in Holocaust representation and memorialization, images repeated in textbooks and museums, on book covers and in films: (1) the entrance to Auschwitz I with its ironic "Arbeit macht frei" sign, its massive iron gate in whose center is the small sign "Halt! Ausweise vorzeigen" (show documents) (figure 4.2); (2) the main guard house to Auschwitz II–Birkenau depicted from a slight distance with three train lines leading into it and with snow-covered pots, pans, and other belongings in the foreground (figure 4.3); (3) the camp watchtowers connected by electric barbed wire fences, poles, and spotlights (figure 4.4; in some images the signs saying "Halt/ Stop" or "Halt/Lebensgefahr" (Danger/Keep Out) are visible); and (4) the bulldozers moving corpses into enormous mass graves—clearly one of the images that so struck Sontag and Kaplan (figure 4.5).

The specific context of these images has certainly been lost in their incessant reproduction. The gate of Auschwitz I and the tower could be either perpetrator or liberator images; the liberator's signature can clearly be found in the objects in front of the Birkenau gate, and the bulldozer image reveals its production most explicitly at the moment of liberation, although its specific provenance from Bergen-Belsen is immaterial to the uses to which the image has been put.

I would like to suggest, not without some hesitation, that more than simply generalized "icons of destruction," these images have come to function more specifically as tropes for Holocaust memory itself. And they are also tropes for photography, referring to the act of looking itself. It is as such tropes, and not for their informational value about the Holocaust, whether denotative or connotative, that they are incorporated into the visual landscape of postmemory as pervasively as they are. And, at the same time, the repetition also underscores their figurative role.[31]

The two gates are the thresholds that represent the difficult access to the narratives of dehumanization and extermination. As Debórah Dwork and Robert Jan van Pelt say of the gate of Auschwitz I, "For the

4.2 Gate to Auschwitz I, Główna Komisja Badania Zbrodni Przeciwko Narodowi Polskiemu.
United States Holocaust Memorial Museum, courtesy of Instytut Pamieci Narodowej

4.3 The main rail entrance of Auschwitz II–Birkenau just after the liberation of the camp.
United States Holocaust Memorial Museum, courtesy of Yivo Institute for Jewish Research

4.4 Art Spiegelman, Guard towers in Mauschwitz. *From* Maus I: A Survivor's Tale/My Father Bleeds History *by Art Spiegelman, copyright 1986 by Art Spiegelman. Used by permission of Pantheon Books, a division of Random House, Inc.*

post-Auschwitz generation, that gate symbolizes the threshold that separates the oikomene (the human community) from the planet Auschwitz. It is a fixed point in our collective memory, and therefore the canonical beginning of the tour through the camp. . . . In fact, however, the inscribed arch did not have a central position in the history of Auschwitz."[32] Most Jewish prisoners, they show, never went through the gate since they were taken by truck directly to Birkenau to be gassed. The expansion of the camp in 1942, moreover, placed the gate in the interior of the camp, not at its threshold.[33]

4.5 A British soldier clearing corpses at Bergen-Belsen. *Courtesy of Imperial War Museum*

In the pictures, the gate of Auschwitz I is always closed; its warning "Halt" further signals the dangers of opening the door on memory. For the victims, "Arbeit macht frei" remains perhaps the greatest trick of National Socialism, enabling the killers to lure their victims willingly and cooperatively into the camp and later into the gas chamber. It is a lie, but also a diabolical truth: freedom is both the very small possibility of survival through work, and the freedom of death. It is only in retrospect, knowing what lies beyond the closed gate, that one fully appreciates the extent of the trick.

But could "Arbeit macht frei" not also be read, by and for us, in the second generation, as a reference to the tricks played by memory itself, the illusory promise that one could become free if one could only do the work of memory and mourning that would open the gate, allow one to enter back into the past and then, through work, emerge out again into a new freedom? The closed gate would thus be the figure for the ambivalences, the risks of memory and postmemory themselves—"Halt/ Lebensgefahr." The obsessively repeated encounter with this picture thus would seem to repeat the lure of remembrance and its deadly dangers—the promise of freedom and its impossibility. At the same time, its emblematic status has made the gate into a screen memory. For instance, Art Spiegelman in *Maus* draws Vladek's arrival and departure from Auschwitz through the main gate in 1944 and 1945, when the gate was no longer used as a threshold.

For Spiegelman, as for all of us in his generation, the gate is the visual image we share of the arrival in the camp. The artist needs it not only to make the narrative immediate and "authentic": he needs it as a point of access (a gate) for himself and for his postmemorial readers (figures 4.6 and 4.7).[34]

The same could be said of the "Gate of Death" to Birkenau with the multiple tracks leading into it (figure 4.3). Those who read about and study the Holocaust encounter this image obsessively, in every book, on every poster. Like the gate of Auschwitz I, it is the threshold of

4.6 Art Spiegelman, "We knew that from here we will not come out anymore." *From* Maus I: A Survivor's Tale/My Father Bleeds History *by Art Spiegelman, copyright 1986 by Art Spiegelman. Used by permission of Pantheon Books, a division of Random House, Inc.*

IT WAS ALREADY NIGHT, THEY GAVE TO EACH OF US A BLANKET AND A LITTLE BIT FOOD TO CARRY, AND WE WENT OUT FROM AUSCHWITZ, MAYBE THE LAST ONE.

4.7 Art Spiegelman, "And we went out from Auschwitz, maybe the last one." *From* Maus II: A Survivor's Tale/And Here My Troubles Began *by Art Spiegelman, copyright 1992 by Art Spiegelman. Used by permission of Pantheon Books, a division of Random House, Inc.*

remembrance, an invitation to enter and, at the same time, a foreclosure. The electric fences, the towers and lights, the forbidding warning signs—all repeat cultural defenses against recollection, and, especially, against looking beyond the fence, inside the gate of death, at death itself. The postmemorial generation, largely limited to these images, replays this oscillation between opening and closing the door to the memory and the experiences of the victims and survivors.[35] The closed gates and the bright lights are also figures for photography, however—for its frustrating flatness, the inability to transcend the limit of its frame, the partial and superficial view, the lack of illumination it offers, leaving the viewer always at a threshold and withholding entrance.

But when we confront—as we repeatedly do in the texts of Holocaust remembrance—the liberators' pictures of the innumerable bodies being buried or cleared by bulldozers, we come as close as we can in an image to looking into the pits of destruction (figure 4.5). On the one hand, these images are the epitome of dehumanization, the inability, even after the liberation, to give victims an individual human burial. They show, perhaps better than any statistics can, the extent of the destruction, the multiplication of victims that transforms corpses into what the Nazis called "Stücke" (pieces), even by the liberating armies.

They lead us back to the prewar images of individuals, families, and groups, such as the opening image of this chapter (figure 4.1), and as we project these two kinds of images onto each other, seeing them as mutually implying each other, we come to appreciate the extremity of the outrage and the incomprehension with which they leave anyone who looks.[36]

But, on the other hand, can we not see in the pictures of mass graves, too, a figuration of memory and forgetting that might also be involved in their canonization? The earth is open, the wound is open; we stare at the picture in the shock, amazement, and disbelief that Sontag and Kaplan express. This is the image that ruptures all viewing relations. But, at the same time, the opposite is also taking place: the bodies are being buried, the traces are being concealed, forgetting has begun. Every time we look at this image, we repeat the encounter between memory and forgetting, between shock and self-protection. We look into the pit of death, but we know that it is in the process of being covered, just as, in Fink's story, the afternoon snow covered the traces of the crime. The work of postmemory, in fact, is to uncover the pits again, to unearth the layers of forgetting, to go beneath the screen surfaces that disguise the crimes and try to see what these images—the prewar family domestic pictures and the images of destruction—both expose and foreclose.

The bulldozer image disturbs in a different way as well. It inscribes another confrontation, that between the camera and the bulldozer, perhaps mirror images of one another. In this specific context, one could say that these two machines, worked by humans, do a similar job of burial that represents forgetting. That they recall, however obliquely, another machine, the weapon. And that, when it comes to images of genocidal murder, the postmemorial act of looking performs this unwanted and discomforting mutual implication.

The bulldozer image, like the photo in Ida Fink's story, records a fleeting moment, just after and just before—in this case, after killing and before burial. Perhaps the most haunting, arresting moment in Ida Fink's "Traces" is the witness's question, "I wonder who photographed it?"[37] Fink's story reminds us that for photographs associated with genocide, the very fact of their existence may be the most astounding, disturbing, incriminating thing about them. And, she reminds us as well that every image also represents, more or less visibly or readably, the context of its production and a very specific embodied gaze of a photographer—whether perpetrator or liberator—that structures the image and entraps its viewers in a field of broken viewing relations.[38]

These photos—even the images of survivors, even the prewar images—are not about death but about genocidal murder. Even, or perhaps especially, in their endless repetition, they resist the work of mourning. They make it difficult to go back to a moment before death or to recognize survival. They cannot be redeemed by irony, insight, or understanding. They can only be confronted again and again, with the same pain, the same incomprehension, the same distortion of the look, the same mortification. And thus, they no longer represent Nazi genocide but, in their very repetition, they provoke the traumatic effect that this history has had on all who grew up under its shadow.

SCREENS

Those in the postgeneration have had to live with these broken, forestalled, viewing relations. The break preceded us, but each of us relives them when, like Alice Kaplan, we first find those images in a desk drawer or in a book. Through repetition, displacement, and recontextualization, postmemorial viewers attempt to live with, and at the same time to re-envision and redirect, the mortifying gaze of these surviving images.

Commenting on her extensive interviews with children of Holocaust survivors, Nadine Fresco describes their accounts of the silences that separate them from their parents. The stories never get told; instead, symptomatically, they are acted out between parents and children: "the forbidden memory of death manifested itself only in the form of incomprehensible attacks of pain. . . . The silence was all the more implacable in that it was often concealed behind a screen of words, again, always the same words, an unchanging story, a tale repeated over and over again, made up of selections from the war." When Fresco describes what she calls the "black hole" of silence, she insists on the repetition of the words that mask that silence, "again, always the same, unchanging, repeated over and over."[39] The images that are used to memorialize the Holocaust by the postmemorial generation, in their obsessive repetition, constitute a similar screen of unchanging fragments, congealed in a memory with unchanging content. Rather than desensitizing us to the "cut" of recollection, however, they have the effect of cutting and shocking, in the same ways that fragmented and congealed memory fragments reenact the traumatic encounter. The repeated images make us relive the broken looking-relations occasioned by the murderous gaze of National Socialism that will be discussed in greater detail in the next chapter.

Their repetition in books and exhibitions can be seen as a refusal to confront the trauma of the past. In Eric Santner's terms they would thus function as a kind of "Reizschutz"—"a protective shield or psychic skin that normally regulates the flow of stimuli and information across the boundaries of self."[40] As Santner, in his reading of Freud's *Beyond the Pleasure Principle*, insists, the shield that allows individual and collective identities to reconstitute themselves in the wake of trauma has to mobilize a certain "homeopathic procedure," illustrated by the "fort/da" game through which Freud's grandson masters loss: "In a homeopathic procedure the controlled introduction of a negative element—a symbolic, or in medical contexts, real poison—helps to heal a system infected by a similar poisonous substance."[41] But if the "fort/da" game is about integrating trauma and about healing, the repetitions of these images do not have the same effect.

In my reading, repetition is not a homeopathic protective shield that screens out the black hole; it is not an anesthetic, but a traumatic fixation. Hal Foster defines this paradox in his analysis of Andy Warhol's repetitions, which, he argues, are neither restorative nor anesthetizing: "The Warhols not only *re*produce traumatic effects, they also *produce* them. Somehow, in these repetitions, several contradictory things occur at the same time: a warding away of traumatic significance *and* an opening out to it, a defending against traumatic affect *and* a producing of it."[42] It is in this kind of contradictory logic that we can see the closed gates of Auschwitz: the gate is closed, acting as a screen, but it is in itself so real as to disable the screen's protective power. Elaborating on

Foster's analysis, Michael Rothberg has defined this as a form of "traumatic realism": "a realism in which the scars that mark the relationship of discourse to the real are not fetishistically denied, but exposed; a realism in which claims to reference live on, but so does the traumatic extremity that disables realist representation as usual."[43]

The repeated Holocaust photographs connect past and present through the "having-been-there" of the photographic image. They are messengers from a horrific time that is not distant enough. In repeatedly exposing themselves to the same pictures, postmemorial viewers can produce in themselves the effects of traumatic repetition that plague the victims of trauma, even as they attempt to mobilize the protective power of the homeopathic shield. As the images repeat the trauma of looking, they disable, in themselves, any restorative attempts. It is only when they are redeployed, in new texts and new contexts, that they regain a capacity to enable a postmemorial working through. The aesthetic strategies of postmemory are specifically about such an attempted, and yet an always postponed, repositioning and reintegration.

NIGHT AND FOG

I would like to conclude these reflections with an image that illustrates the more enabling functions of repetition and reframing in the workings of affiliative postmemory. Lorie Novak's photograph *Night and Fog* resituates several archival images in a new frame (figure 4.8).[44] The title refers to Alain Resnais's 1956 film and the source of the artist's generational encounter with the documentary images of the Holocaust. The image itself is a composite projection onto a nighttime scene: on the right there is a fragment of Margaret Bourke-White's famous picture of the Buchenwald survivors behind the barbed wire fence, that we already encountered, in Art Spiegelman's drawing, in chapter 1. On the left we can just barely see a hand holding an old, torn photograph. This is a found image from the New York Public Library of someone's relative lost in the concentration camps. Projecting photographs onto trees enables us to see memory as constructed, as cultural rather than natural.

4.8 Lorie Novak, *Night and Fog. Courtesy of Lorie Novak, www.lorienovak.com*

Novak's is a stunning, haunting picture that contains but is not dominated by the repeated trauma fragments of Holocaust imagery. The
hand in Novak's image introduces a viewer, someone who holds, listens,
and responds. That postmemorial artist/viewer can intervene and connect the public and private images that have survived the Shoah, introducing them into a landscape in which they have an afterlife. And although her powerful projectors and her title *Night and Fog* recall the
most fearful moments of the Nazi death machinery, her multiple images,
taken at different moments and brought together here, can succeed in
refocusing our look.

Looking at this image of a projection is very different from watching
the documentary images from the Holocaust. If we recognize its content, however, it is because we have seen those other pictures during
all our lives. But in these projections we can begin to move beyond the

shock of seeing them for the first time, again and again. We can also move out of their obsessive repetition, for they are both familiar and estranged. And thus they begin to reconstitute a viewing relation that cannot be repaired, but that can perhaps be re-envisioned in ways that do not negate the rupture at its source.

5.1 From Jürgen Stroop, *The Warsaw Ghetto Is No More*. *United States Holocaust Memorial Museum, courtesy of Instytut Pamieci Narodowej*

5

NAZI PHOTOGRAPHS IN POST-HOLOCAUST ART

The photograph everyone knows: a boy in a peaked cap and knee-length socks, his hands raised. We do not know when it was taken. During the great extermination, in July or August 1942? Or during the Uprising in the ghetto in 1943? Or perhaps some other time. . . .

It is hard to say if the boy is standing in a courtyard or outside a house entrance in a street. . . . To the right stand four Germans. . . . Two of their faces, three even in good reproductions, are clearly visible. I have pored over that photo for so long and so often that if I were now after 45 years to meet one of those Germans in the street I'd identify him instantly.

One of the Germans holds an automatic pistol under his arm, apparently aiming at the boy's back. . . . To the left there are several women, a few men, and about three children. All with their arms raised. . . . I have counted twenty-three people in this photo, though the figures on the left are so huddled together that I may have miscounted: nineteen Jews and four Germans. . . .

The boy in the center of the picture wears a short raincoat reaching just above his knees. His cap, tilted slightly askew, looks too big for him. Maybe it's his father's or his elder brother's? We have the boy's personal data: Artur Siematek, son of Leon and Sara née Dab, born in Lowicz. Artur is my contemporary: we were both born in 1935. We stand side by side, I in the photo taken on the high platform in Otwock. We may assume that both photographs were taken in the same month, mine a week or so earlier. We even seem to be wearing the same caps. Mine is of a lighter shade and also looks too big for my head. The boy is wearing knee-high socks, I am wearing white ankle socks. On the platform in Otwock I am smiling nicely. The boy's face—the photo was taken by an SS sergeant—betrays nothing.

"You're tired," I say to Artur. "It must be very uncomfortable standing like that with your arms in the air. I know what we'll do. I'll lift my arms up now, and you put yours down. They may not notice. But wait, I've got a better idea. We'll both stand with our arms up."

The above is a passage from Jaroslaw's Rymkiewicz's novel, originally published in Poland in 1988, *The Final Station: Umschlagplatz*.[1] Earlier in the novel, the narrator is perusing his family photo album with his sister:

"Look, that is Swider, in the summer of 1942. That is you on the swing near the house. Here we are standing on the beach by the river. And here I am on the platform at Otwock. Cap and tie. The same white socks. But I can't for the life of me remember the house where we spent our holidays that year."

"Nor can I," says my sister reading the inscription our mother has made on the page with the photo that was taken of me complete with tie, cap, and white socks on the high platform at Otwock. "Church fair in Otwock, July 19, 1942."

"Did you know," I say, "that in the summer of 1942 there was still a ghetto in Otwock?"[2]

If you had to name one picture that signals and evokes the Holocaust in the contemporary cultural imaginary it might well be the picture of the little boy in the Warsaw ghetto with his arms raised (figure 5.1). The pervasive role this photograph has come to play is indeed astounding: it is not an exaggeration to say that, assuming an archetypal role of Jewish (and universal) victimization, the boy in the Warsaw ghetto has become the poster child of the Holocaust.

In Lawrence Langer's terms "the best-known photograph to outlast the catastrophe," it has appeared in films, novels, and poems, and, almost obsessively, on the covers of advertising brochures for Holocaust histories, teaching aids, and popular books.[3] It serves as the cover image not only of such popular publications as *The Jewish Holocaust for Beginners* and the CD-ROM Holocaust history *Lest We Forget*, but also of scholarly texts published in the 1990s and later.[4] Its international reach and recognizability is further emphasized in its prominent place on the cover of Yad Vashem's primary English-language historical booklet *The Holocaust*. The photograph was featured in Alain Resnais's 1956 *Night and Fog* and Ingmar Bergman's 1966 *Persona*, and, in 1990, it became the object of *Tsvi Nussbaum: A Boy from Warsaw*, a documentary examining the contention of Holocaust survivor Tsvi Nussbaum that he is the boy with his hands up. As the opening passage for this chapter shows, it was also the catalyst for Rymkiewicz's novel, and it inspired a number of poets and visual artists, including Yala Korwin, Samuel Bak, and Judy Chicago.

The picture's well-known history, however, mostly remains invisible in its contemporary representations, representations that actually enable viewers to forget or to ignore its troubling source. The picture of the little boy was originally included in the report by Major-General Jürgen Stroop, commander of the operation to liquidate the Warsaw ghetto. Entitled "Es gibt keinen jüdischen Wohnbezirk in Warschau mehr!" ("The Jewish Quarter of Warsaw Is No More!"),[5] the report collected the daily communiqués on the progress of the operation that were teletyped from Warsaw to Krueger, Higher SS and Police Leader East in Cracow. The *Bildbericht* (report in pictures) consisting of 54 photos was added to the communiqués, and the whole was presented to Himmler as a memento. In the image, the young boy stands among a group of Jews herded out of underground bunkers toward the Umschlagplatz, where they would await deportation. Surrounded by soldiers with pointed machine guns, they are photographed in the most vulnerable of poses. This photographic addition to the record of the ghetto's liquidation shows more than the details of the roundup and deportation: it shows the particular ways in which Jews were overpowered and humiliated by their captors. Stroop's caption, rarely, if ever, included in contemporary uses and reproductions, reads: "Mit Gewalt aus Bunkern herausgeholt" ("Removed from the ghetto by force"). This photo thus illustrates well the broken look that shapes photography in the context of an eliminationist racism, a look that Primo Levi tries to understand when he faces a Nazi official during his chemical examination in Auschwitz-Buna "which came as if across the window of an aquarium between two beings who live in different worlds."[6]

The little boy's picture is a perpetrator photograph, taken by perpetrators as an integral part of the machinery of destruction, and it can thus help us to understand the particularities of perpetrator images. But the enormous cultural attraction to it, the obsessive manner in which it has appeared just about everywhere for several decades in the aftermath, enables us to address a different question as well. How can perpetrator images—images shaped by the broken look Levi describes, and evidence of photography's implication in the death machine—have come to play an important, even a prevalent, role in the cultural act of memorializing the victims? How, through what distancing mechanisms, have contemporary artists—even Jewish artists of the second generation—been able to incorporate them so widely into their memorial work?

This chapter concerns the politics of retrospective witnessing that takes the form of appropriating and recontextualizing archival images in post-Shoah memorial works. I argue that if perpetrator images can mediate the visual knowledge of those who were not there, it is only because their contemporary reproductions mobilize some powerful idioms that obscure their devastating history and redirect the genocidal gaze that shaped them. In order to look closely at some of these mitigating idioms, I will examine several specific Nazi photographs and their reproduction by contemporary artists: the little boy image, several images of Einsatzgruppen killings in the East, seen here as reframed by David Levinthal (figure 5.2), and an image of the famous partisan from Minsk, Masha Bruskina walking to her execution, seen here in an installation by Nancy Spero (figure 5.3).[7]

5.2 David Levinthal, from *Mein Kampf (Santa Fe: Twin Palms, 1996). Courtesy of David Levinthal*

jnt
ed
l
n

n

or

Twenty years ago Lev
Arkadyev, a screen writer
working on a film about
the war. saw the photo-
graphs in the minsk Museum
and resolved to identify
the unknown Partisan. He
enlisted Mrs. Dikhyar, then
a reporter for the Soviet
outh radio station "Yun-
ost," and they began a pain
staking investigation.

lo

ed

5.3 Nancy Spero, installation image from *The Torture of Women. Art* © *1996 Estate of Nancy*
Spero/Licensed by VAGA, New York, New York

The re-use of these images in contemporary publications and artistic works serves to illustrate one such mitigating idiom particularly well: the infantilization and feminization of victims and the concomitant hyper-masculinization and thus depersonalization of perpetrators. By making gender a determining if sometimes latent vehicle of remembrance, these artists, however unwittingly, mythologize the images they use, obscure their sources, and thus allow them to become appropriable.

PERPETRATOR IMAGES AND THE NAZI GAZE

Most contemporary viewers confronted with images from the Holocaust do not readily distinguish their source or the context of their production. Indeed, in the vast archive of photographic images that have come down to us from the Holocaust, this information is often difficult to detect. Many images appear in collections with poor labeling, and, when they are reproduced, some are identified by their present owner rather than the date and place of their production. As the previous chapter argued, most contemporary viewers tend to know few images, repeated over and over in different contexts, used more for their symbolic or affective than for their evidentiary or informational power. Moreover, all images associated with the Holocaust—whether they are prewar images of destroyed Jewish communities or images of bulldozers burying bodies at the moment of liberation—are seen through the lens of our knowledge of the total death that divides the people marked for extermination from us as retrospective viewers. It is this knowledge that shapes our viewing, and thus one could say that the photographer's identity is immaterial.

And yet, I want to argue here that the identity of the photographer—perpetrator, victim, bystander, or liberator—is indeed a determining element in the photograph's production, and that, as a result, it engenders distinctive ways of seeing and, indeed, a distinctive textuality. As the previous chapter began to suggest, perpetrator photos are ruled by what we might term a "Nazi gaze" that deeply shatters the visual field and profoundly reorients the basic structures of photographic looking.[8]

There are, of course, many different kinds of perpetrator images, and many different kinds of uses to which they have been or can be put. The

well-documented photographs I am looking at in this chapter—all frontal or side images of victims looking at executioners in which the photographer, the perpetrator, and the spectator share the same space of
looking at the victim—illustrate particularly well the structure of the
genocidal gaze of the Nazi death machine. Thus, in the Warsaw ghetto
image, guns are pointing at the boy from the back and side, even as the
camera records the encounters between perpetrators and victims. The
camera itself embodies the gaze of the perpetrator who stands in a
place identical with the weapon of roundup and execution: it mirrors,
head-on, the most visible soldier's gun.

Theorists of photography have often pointed out the simultaneous
presence of death and life in the photograph: "Photographs state the
innocence, the vulnerability of lives heading toward their own destruction and this link between photography and death haunts all photos of
people," says Susan Sontag in *On Photography*.[9] The indexical quality
of the photo intensifies its status as harbinger of death and, at the same
time, its capacity to signify life. Life is the presence of the object before
the camera; death is the "having-been-there" of the object—the radical
break, the finality introduced by the past tense. The *ça-a-été* of the photograph creates the retrospective scene of looking shared by those who
survive.[10] In its relation to loss and death, photography does not mediate the process of individual and collective memory but brings the past
back in the form of a ghostly revenant, emphasizing, at the same time,
its immutable and irreversible pastness and irretrievability. The encounter with the photograph is the encounter between two presents, one of
which, already past, can be reanimated in the act of looking.

Photographs of total death like perpetrator images redefine what
Susan Sontag describes as the photograph's "posthumous irony." Sontag uses Roman Vishniac's pictures of the vanished world of Eastern
European Jewish life to define this ironic temporality. They are particularly affecting, she argues, because as we look at them we know how soon
these people are going to die.[11] "Strictly speaking," writes Christian
Metz, "the person *who has been photographed*— . . . is dead. . . . The
snapshot, like death, is an instantaneous abduction of the object out of
the world into another world, into another kind of time. . . . The photographic *take* is immediate and definitive, like death. . . . Not by chance,

the photographic art . . . has been frequently compared with shooting, and the camera with a gun."[12]

In the years since Sontag's 1973 book and Metz's 1985 essay, however, the equation between the camera and the gun, and the concomitant view of the photographic gaze as monolithic and potentially lethal has been significantly qualified as theorists have stressed the multiplicity of looks structuring a photographic image.[13] For example, the giant opening image that faces the visitor who enters the permanent exhibition at the United States Holocaust Memorial Museum places the viewer in the position of the unbelieving onlooker or retrospective witness, who confronts the contemporary witnesses and sees both them in the act of looking and what they saw. These multiple and fractured lines of sight among the dead victims, the liberating U.S. Army, and the retrospective visitor confirm some recent work that complicates the assumption that a monocular perspective represented by the camera rules the field of vision, as Metz suggested.

In my own work on the distinction between the familial gaze and look in *Family Frames* I have tried to extricate us from the monocular seeing that conflates the camera with a weapon. Thus I have argued that while the *gaze* is external to human subjects situating them authoritatively in ideology, constituting them in their subjectivity, the *look* is located at a specific point; it is local and contingent, mutual and reversible, traversed by desire and defined by lack. While the look is returned, the gaze turns the subject into a spectacle. "In the scopic field," Jacques Lacan writes, "the gaze is outside, I am looked at, that is to say, I am a picture. . . . What determines me, at the most profound level, in the visible, is the gaze that is outside."[14] But looking and being looked at are interrelated processes; when you look you are also seen; when you are the object of the look you return it, even if only to reflect light back to its source: "things look at me and yet I see them," Lacan says.[15] These individualized local and intersecting looks are exchanged by way of the *screen* that filters vision through the mediations of cultural conventions and codes that make the seen visible. The overarching gaze is mediated by the screen, contested and interrupted by the look. Vision is multiple and power is shared. I believe that we can use photographs to study these complex visual relations. Interpellated by the photograph, its viewers become part of the network of looks exchanged within the image and beyond it. The viewer both participates in and observes the photograph's inscription in the gazes and looks that structure it.

But is this multiplicity of vision sustained in the images of total death that have survived the destruction of the Holocaust and other genocides, like the image of the bodies in the mass grave? In the images of burial and execution, the bulldozer burying the innumerable bodies repeats the act of the gun that has shot those bodies before they are buried, or the gas that has choked them. And the camera recording this violent destruction for posterity cannot stand outside this co-implication. In its staggering multiplication, the triple act of shooting overwhelms all viewing relations.[16]

This can be seen in the images from the mass executions in Russia, Latvia, and Lithuania that depict victims facing the camera moments before they are to be put to death. I am thinking in particular of an image of four women, in their undergarments. In the brutally frontal image, the camera is in the exact same position as the gun and the photographer in the place of the executioner who remains unseen. The victims are already undressed; the graves have been dug. Displayed in their full vulnerability and humiliation they are doubly exposed in their nakedness and their powerlessness. They are shot before they are shot.[17]

How are postmemorial viewers to look at this picture and others like it? Where are the lines of transgenerational identification and empathy? Unbearably, the viewer is positioned in the place identical with the weapon of destruction: our look, like the photographer's, is in the place of the executioner. Steven Spielberg makes that utterly plain when he photographs Amon Goeth's random executions through the viewfinder of his gun in *Schindler's List*. Is it possible to escape the touch of death and the implication in murder that these images perform? To regain a form of witnessing that is not so radically tainted?

Perpetrator images, in particular, are taken by perpetrators for their own consumption. An archive of 38 images from Serbia brings this home with shocking force.

These are pictures of a reprisal action against 20 civilians, gruesomely detailing a roundup, confiscation of valuables, a lineup, the digging of graves, the shootings. The most striking images, however, show

5.4 German soldiers examining photos. Reprisal action, Serbia, 1941. *Courtesy of Etablissement Cinématographique et Photographique des Armées*

soldiers sitting in a field looking intently at photographs (figure 5.4). The pictures they are holding are clearly too large to be images confiscated from the prisoners; they must be images of other *Aktionen* (killing actions) they or others have performed. Or they could be images of German victims, and thus supposed justifications for reprisal actions. How is the act of looking connected to the act of shooting: Is it a form of justification, indoctrination, and instruction, or a retrospective debriefing?[18] No matter. These images illustrate the quality of the perpetrator's look as well as its connection to the perpetrator's deed. When we confront perpetrator images, we cannot look independently of the look of the perpetrator.[19]

The murderous National Socialist gaze that structures these images violates the social viewing relations under which we normally operate. The lethal power of the gaze that acts through the machine gun and the gas chamber, that reduces humans to "pieces" and ashes, creates a visual field in which the look can no longer be returned, multiplied, or displaced. All is touched by the death that is the precondition of the image. When looking and photographing have become coextensive with mechanized mass death, and the subject looking at the camera is also the victim looking at the executioner, those of us left to look at the picture are deeply touched by that death.[20] The Nazi gaze is so all-encompassing that available screens seem to falter, and any possible resistant potential of the look is severely impaired. Viewers find themselves inextricably entwined in a circle from which, even for those of us analyzing the images in the postmemorial generation, it is difficult to find an escape through distanced or ironic insight. Too late to help, utterly impotent, we nevertheless search for ways to take responsibility for what we are seeing, to experience, from a remove, even as we try to redefine, if not repair, these ruptures.[21]

Images connected to mass destruction, whether pictures of executions of even prewar images, inscribe a different temporality than other photographic images. It is not that these women, or these men, were alive when the photo was taken and that we know that they were killed after. The photograph's retrospective irony, whether in Sontag's terms or Barthes's, works in such a way that, as viewers, we reanimate the subjects—in *Camera Lucida*, Barthes's mother or Lewis Payne photographed before his execution—trying to give them life again, to protect them from the death we know must occur, has already occurred. Here is the pathos, the punctum of the picture. But the victims of the Einsatzgruppen were already killed by the murderous Nazi gaze that condemned them without even looking at them. This lethal gaze reflects back on images of European Jews that precede the war, removing from them the loss and nostalgia, the irony and longing, that structure photographs from a bygone era. It is the determining force of the pictures that Jews had to place on the identification cards the Nazis issued and that were marked with an enormous J in gothic script. Those pictures had to show the full face and uncover the left ear as a telltale identity marker. In these documents, identity is identification, visibility, and surveillance, not for life but for the death machine that had already condemned those who were thus marked.

The act of photographing the violent evacuation of the ghetto, and of using these humiliating images to illustrate what came to be known as the "Stroop Report," merely underscores the cruelty and violence perpetrated by the SS. The picture of the Warsaw boy and his compatriots, like all perpetrator images, is deeply implicated in Nazi photographic practices.[22] It is evidence not only of the perpetrator's deed but also of the desire to flaunt and advertise the evidence of that deed. The "Stroop Report," for example, was just that, a letter addressed to Himmler, a gift of victoriously embraced cruelty. The act of photographing the roundup is like the exclamation point in the title of the report "The Jewish Quarter of Warsaw Is No More!" It is a sign of excess, connecting the perpetrator's gaze to the perpetrator's deed. When we as spectators confront perpetrator images, we look at the image as the implied Nazi viewers did, under the sign of that exclamation point. What is often most astounding about perpetrator photographs—and here we must think not only of these images, but of photographs of lynching, torture, and other forms of humiliation—is not what they show but that they even exist.[23]

And yet, if we discuss or reproduce perpetrator images in our retrospective memorial work, we have the burden of acknowledging both the massive genocidal program of which they were a part, and the individual acts of choice and responsibility that enabled the killing machine to function. I believe that this totalized notion of a Nazi gaze, qualified through a recognition of the individual soldier's broken look, helps to define the particular character of perpetrator images. The murderous quality embedded within them remains, even decades years later, dangerously real. Perpetrator images carry this excessive history—this double act of shooting—with them. How then has the picture of the boy in the Warsaw ghetto, among other perpetrator images, been able to assume its pervasive memorializing role? What enables viewers to identify with the boy, to invoke his presence despite the fact that his raised hands, mirroring that exclamation point in the report's title, "The Jewish Quarter of Warsaw Is No More!," become the sign of unredeemable annihilation?

INFANTILIZING/FEMINIZING THE VICTIM

The most common reproductive strategy used by contemporary post-Shoah artists and publishers is cropping, and cropping certainly has attenuating effects. Most reproductions and recontextualizations of the Warsaw boy's picture not only leave out, but actually deny, the original context of its production by focusing on the boy himself, isolating him from the community within which he was embedded and removing the perpetrators from view. They thus universalize the victim as innocent child and, through a false sense of intimacy fostered by the close-up, reduce the viewer to an identificatory look that disables critical faculties. If anyone else is included, it is usually the one soldier standing behind the boy, aiming his gun at the boy's back. This is how, for example, the boy appears in a painting by Rebecca Shope that is on the cover of *The Jewish Holocaust for Beginners*. Victim and perpetrator are enclosed in a large frame; the actual street scene is erased, and, outside of the Warsaw context, all that remains is a mythic encounter between innocence and evil that removes the picture from both its greater and its more specific historical specificity.

Cropping is also a strategy used in a 1995 series of studies, mainly self-portraits, by artist Samuel Bak, a child survivor, that are part of a larger and extremely successful project entitled *Landscapes of Jewish Experience*.[24]

Bak best illustrates the boy's ready availability for viewer projection and identification (figure 5.5). In these images the little boy's face is replaced by a number of other faces, including that of the artist himself. Bak multiplies the image and transposes it into a variety of well-known iconographic motifs, ranging from the crucifixion, to the felled tree of life, to more specific representations of concentration camp life—the striped uniform, the so essential shoes. Like his other images included in this larger series, these "landscapes of Jewish experience" are ruined landscapes, populated only by the most obvious symbols of Jewish life and death—the star, the tree, the candle, the tomb, and, surprisingly, by Christian motifs as well—outspread arms, a cross, and nails. The image is completely decontextualized; perpetrators are invisible, and thus the viewer is sutured into the image through a look of empathic identifica-

5.5 Samuel Bak, Study F, from the exhibition *Landscapes of Jewish Experience*. *Courtesy of Pucker Gallery, www.puckergallery.com*

tion with the boy as archetypal victim. Bak's narrative becomes a mythic narrative of "Jewish experience" rather than the particular narrative of the Warsaw ghetto, or even the Shoah.

Like Rymkiewicz's protagonist and Bak, the Yugoslav writer Aleksandar Tišma, himself a survivor, identifies with the boy: asked by the newspaper *Die Zeit* to send in a photo of himself that holds some particular meaning for him, he sent this picture instead: "There are no photos of me that I connect to an important memory," he writes.[25] "I send you instead the photograph of another that I actually consider as my own. . . . I immediately saw that the boy with his hands up in the right-hand corner of the picture is me. It's not only that he looks like me, but that he expresses the fundamental feelings of my growing up: the impotence in the face of rules, of humanity, of reality. . . . I recognize myself in him, in him alone."[26] Again Tišma emphasizes the general—"impotence in the face of rules"—rather than a more specific history that, after all, he shares with the boy. Identification in itself need not necessarily be a form of decontextualization, but, in these particular cases, the discourse of identification simplifies and distorts, becoming so over-arching as to foreclose a more oblique, critical, or resistant retrospective look.

Bak's dozen or so studies and these other fictional and autobiographical acts of what one might call "transparent" or "projective" identification clarify some of the mediating discourses that have allowed this image to occupy the role of "most famous Holocaust photograph": it is of a child and of a child who performs his innocence by raising his hands, and it is of a child who is not visibly hurt or harmed or suffering. Images of children are so open to projection that they might be able to circumvent even the murderousness of the Nazi gaze. Geoffrey Hartman's suggestion that the image of the boy from Warsaw emblematizes Nazism as the loss of childhood itself underscores the power of the figure this image embodies, the figure of infantilization.[27] As the next chapter will argue in more detail, images of children readily lend themselves to universalization. Less individualized, less marked by the particularities of identity, children invite multiple projections and identifications. Their photographic images, especially when cropped and decontextualized, elicit an affiliative as well as a protective spectatorial look marked by these investments, a look that promotes forgetting, even denial. If a more triangulated and less appropriative encounter with images of children is to be achieved, these images would need to preserve some of their visual layers and their historical specificity.[28]

Judy Chicago's *Holocaust Project* incorporates the boy's cropped picture into a panel entitled *Im/Balance of Power* that illustrates well the gendered dimensions of the victims' infantilization (figure 5.6).[29] Chicago surrounds the boy with other images of hurt or threatened or hungry children.

The boy from Warsaw is just at the center of the scale that will measure a universalized im/balance of power, and he shares the center

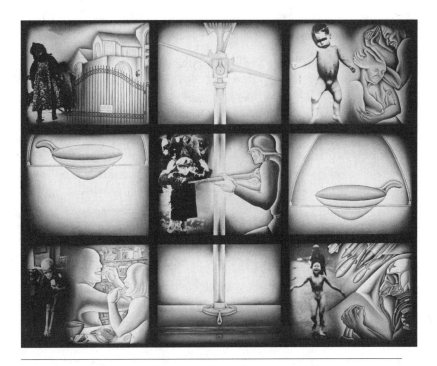

5.6 Judy Chicago, *Im/Balance of Power* (detail) from the exhibition *Holocaust Project: From Darkness into Light*. Sprayed acrylic, oil, and photography on photo linen, 77.25" × 95.25". © *Judy Chicago and Donald Woodman, 1991. Photo © Donald Woodman.*

panel with a painted caricatured Nazi soldier who, in Chicago's reversal, points his enormous gun right at the boy's chest. The boy is the only European child—the starving children in the other panel squares are Asian, African, or Latin American. In the lower right-hand corner, diagonally beneath the Warsaw boy, is the famous photograph of a Vietnamese girl burned by napalm, naked and running; in Chicago's reappropriation, painted bombs point directly at her head. Chicago's crude iconography shows here that infantilization is also, structurally, a figure of feminization: the running girl is overpowered not only by the crassly phallic bombs, but also by a cartoon figuration of a masked soldier who wears a badge marked "AGGRESS. . . ." Similarly, on the back cover of the Yad Vashem brochure, for example, there are three boxes with close-ups: one of the little boy's face, and the faces of two

of the women in the image. If the victim is infantilized, then the perpetrator is hyper-masculinized, represented as the ultimate in phallic,
mechanized, supra-human evil. In inscribing the perpetrator in as exag-
gerated a way as Chicago does, she also points to his absence in the
cropped representations of the boy. In spite of her stated desire to raise
the world's consciousness about the powerlessness and neglect suffered
by today's children, Chicago's panel invites viewers to assume the
subject position of victim, since it is the only position available. In
inscribing themselves only into the place of the victims who are both
infantilized and feminized, viewers are made to participate in the
hyper-masculinization and ultimately depersonalization of perpetrators that allows for an erasure of the agency of perpetration—of the
individual soldier who aims his gun, who takes a picture, who looks at
it afterward. The profound impact that the machinery of destruction
has performed on our very ways of seeing is mitigated in Chicago's
troubling representations. Her naive re-presentation of children's images explains the despair she describes in her journal as she works on
this panel.

But images separated from their original context can certainly function on many different levels. It may thus not be surprising that such a
foundational image of the Holocaust is an image from the Warsaw
ghetto. The name Warsaw is associated with heroism and resistance, and
this boy can thus be both the ultimate victim and the archetypal hero;
he can be feminized by his raised hands and the vulnerability of his
stance in the visual image, even as he is re-masculinized for those who
know of his connection to Warsaw. It is in this way that this image is
reenacted in an Israeli play by Hanokh Levin entitled *HaPatriot*. Here a
little Arab boy, Mahmud, stands, like the boy from Warsaw, with his
hands up, as an Israeli soldier holds a gun to his head. Lahav, the Israeli
character, addresses his mother as he aims the revolver: "He will avenge
your blood and the blood of our murdered family, as then, mother, when
your little brother stood alone in front of the German at night. . . ."[30] In
this complex and politically charged passage, the boy can be both victim and hero, but the gender roles are clearly differentiated: perpetrators, whether Nazi or Israeli, are male, whereas victims, whether Jewish
or Palestinian, are children of grieving mothers. If the memory of the

Holocaust is invoked to shape contemporary politics, it is by relying on familiar gender stereotypes that are facilitated by the use of readily available archetypal imagery.

MEIN KAMPF

This oppositionally gendered politics of representation becomes clearer still in the work of the American artist David Levinthal in his series *Mein Kampf*.[31]

Levinthal is known for his installations of toys photographed with a 20 × 24 Polaroid Land Camera that, when the aperture is wide open, yields glossy, shallow-plane, blurry, and ambiguous images. In photographing toys, Levinthal has dedicated himself precisely to exposing cultural myths and stereotypes. Searching for authentic Nazi toys in amateur shops, Levinthal came upon dolls of Hitler, of Nazi soldiers and Reichsbahn cars. In *Mein Kampf* he was thus able to create a number of reenactments of perpetrator images, some of which remain faithful to their originals, while others are reinterpreted or reimagined.

Most troubling, perhaps, are his reenactments of the frequently reproduced photographs of Einsatzkommando executions in Poland, Russia, Latvia, and Lithuania that show groups of victims, women and men, often undressed, sometimes cradling babies or small children, facing the camera just seconds before they are to be put to death (figures 5.2 and 5.7).[32] In the original photographs, the camera is located in the same place as the executioner, and perpetrators are visible in the image primarily through this disturbing co-implication. The presence of these images on museum walls and in Holocaust textbooks is troubling, especially since in most of these contemporary contexts, the role of photography in the act of genocide remains implicit and unexamined. In the context of the Wehrmacht exhibition, in large part composed of such images, the context is indeed hyper-visible and carefully elucidated, as is the pervasive presence and determinative role of the camera in the process of destruction. The blunt exposure such images receive in the exhibition and their meticulous contextualization offer an important counterpoint to their reappearance in the work of contemporary

5.7 David Levinthal, from *Mein Kampf (Santa Fe: Twin Palms, 1996). Courtesy of David Levinthal*

second-generation artists such as Levinthal. But here they are made more tolerable through various strategies of mythification and mitigation.

If Levinthal's images circumvent the full impact of the Nazi gaze, it seems to be primarily through the minimization offered by the toys and their aestheticization since, in other ways, his recirculation of perpetrator images appears to offer a counter-example to the work of Bak or Chicago. Unlike the writers, artists, and historians using the little boy image, David Levinthal is as interested in perpetrators as he is in victims, and, in reenacting the encounter between victim and executioner, he certainly underscores both the reality of the crime and the excess performed in photographing it. Levinthal's images do not enable us to forget that exclamation point in the title of Stroop's report: in fact, in his re-stagings, soldiers are moved to the front of the image, and their guns, often the only items in clear focus, are pointing right at the victims.

In James Young's reading of *Mein Kampf*, Levinthal's work is significant for post-Holocaust representation because it acknowledges that "when he sets out 'to photograph' the Holocaust, . . . he takes pictures of *his* Holocaust experiences—i.e., recirculated images of the Holocaust."[33] For Levinthal, the pictures are "intentionally ambiguous to draw the viewer in so that you make your own story."[34] If the pictures' composition ensures that this intense imaginary projection on the part of viewers includes the role of the perpetrator as well as the victim, in shooting the pictures, Levinthal himself occupies the place of the Nazi photographers. Similarly, in his title *Mein Kampf* he does not hesitate to claim the most abject space in this representational structure. As Levinthal re-takes the image of the Nazi photographer and reenacts the perpetrator gaze, we as his viewers are invited to stand in the space of the Nazi viewers who were the addressees of the image. That space is disturbing in a number of ways. Looking is necessarily and, I believe intentionally, an act of revictimizing the victims, however miniaturized they are in their doll-like forms. The Nazi toy soldiers, like all such simulacra, are, like Chicago's constructions, masculinized—they are de-individuated, generalized, clichéd amalgamations of body and weapon. The soldiers are seen from the back as, disturbingly, we look over their shoulders. As recirculated toys they can embody the totalizing quality of the Nazi gaze, but they can also mitigate any consciousness we might have of the individual soldier's act of murder.

To stage the victims, Levinthal used naked sex dolls made in Japan for the European market. These busty female dolls with their nipples showing are the perfect demonstration of what happens in the hyperbolic logic of such representations: as the victims are infantilized and feminized, the perpetrators are hyper-masculinized and de-realized. In the encounter of such figures with one another, the radical power difference between them thus becomes eroticized and sexualized. As an alibi, and in response to both James Young's and Art Spiegelman's personal objections to these female dolls, Levinthal maintains that he is only repeating the eroticization of Nazi murder in the popular imagination as seen in films such as *Night Porter, Sophie's Choice, The White Hotel, Schindler's List*.[35]

Levinthal is making us conscious of the uncomfortably tainted position we always occupy when we view perpetrator images. His photographs point out not only the implicit presence and defining role of gender in all of these relationships and positions; they also reveal how gender can serve as a means of forgetting. I would argue that his critique, or his reenactment of the perpetrator-photographer's position—for critique and reenactment are never easily distinguishable—is also a form of obfuscation. If there is blurring in these blurred images, it is the blurring between sexualization and "racialization": to the contemporary postmemorial viewer, like Levinthal, these female victims may have maintained their sexuality, but to the murderers, these Jewish victims were surely no more than vermin, *Stücke*, to be added to the statistics of extermination, indistinguishable by gender, class, age, or other identity markers. David Levinthal's images, in eroticizing the power relationship between perpetrator and victim, is also "deracializing" it. And in subjecting the scene of execution to a pornographic gaze, he moves it into a different register of looking altogether, circumventing the murderousness of the Nazi gaze that shapes the pictures on which his work is based.

Levinthal says—and, surprisingly, Young agrees—that sexual humiliation in the victims' last moments was one of the tactics of the Nazi dehumanization of their victims. Certainly Jewish women were more sexually vulnerable than men, and there was rape and sexual abuse in the ghettos and camps. These are often repressed stories that feminist scholars have only begun to recover. Yet, there is no evidence, in anything that I have read about the Einsatzkommando killings in particular, that the killers in any way recognized the victims' sexuality or that there was anything sexual in these murders. In fact, the opposite seems to have been the case: the victims were dehumanized precisely by being desexualized. Robbed of any subjectivity in the impersonal machine of destruction, they were also robbed of their sexuality. Nazi killers were not deviant sexual perverts but "ordinary men" whose murderous work became routine.[36] In an article titled "Pornographizations of Fascism," the art historian Silke Wenk analyzes the pornographization that characterizes contemporary visualizations of national socialist crimes.[37] She relies on Ruth Klüger's analysis of sentimentality, kitsch, and pornography, which emerge as defenses against the memory of past violence and trauma.[38] For Wenk, sexuality and perversion offer familiar explanatory paradigms, and thus pornography can mitigate the anxiety and discomfort caused by atrocity photos: it is a form of universalization, a transformation of discomfort into cliché. Stereotyped femininity functions as myth or fetish for the threatened retrospective witness.[39] Levinthal's hyper-masculinized and hyper-feminized figures and the pornographic gaze enacted in his images thus allow for a great amount of obfuscation and appropriation, granting the original perpetrator images a disturbing artistic and testimonial afterlife.

BEYOND CLICHÉ

Nancy Spero's installations based on the photographs of the execution of the 17-year-old Russian partisan Masha Bruskina, the heroine of Minsk, offer an alternative use of perpetrator images to this analysis (figures 5.3 and 5.8).

The eight surviving archival photos of Bruskina were taken by a Lithuanian battalion member collaborating with the Germans. On October 26, 1941, Masha Bruskina was one of three communist resisters who were paraded through the streets of Minsk and publicly hanged. The gruesome photos of their humiliation and execution were made public just after the war, but only the two men were identified; the girl carrying signs and executed with the men was denied an identity, and especially a Jewish identity, until 1968, when Russian filmmaker Lev Arkadyev initiated an investigation about the "unknown girl." Eyewitnesses provided detailed descriptions and stories about this Jewish 17-year-old, who lightened her hair and changed her name so that her Jewish identity would not interfere with her resistance work. They not only identified Bruskina, but also told about her remarkable demeanor on the day of her execution.[40]

Spero has included the execution photos in a number of installations that are part of her series *The Torture of Women* or that focus exclusively on the images and the story of Masha Bruskina.[41] The installations are built around the archival perpetrator photos, but here the images are presented through various alienation devices: they are surrounded with text, with other related images, with figures from Spero's large corpus

5.8 Nancy Spero, installation image from *The Torture of Women. Art* © *1996 Estate of Nancy Spero/Licensed by VAGA, New York, New York*

of goddesses and mythological characters. They are cropped, multiplied, reproduced at various angles and in unexpected spaces, such as the bottom or the top of a gallery wall, on the ceiling, in a corner. These strategies prevent the viewer from simply looking at the Nazi image head-on, repeating the spectatorial gaze of the Nazi viewer. Instead, Spero's installations make us conscious of the looks that structure the image itself, of the screens and mediations that separate them from us in the present, of the artist's and our own compromised relation to them. The texts speak explicitly about the photographs, thus removing any simple transparence from them and restoring their original context. Significantly, Spero's photographic intertextuality enables a consciousness on the part of the viewer about the interaction between perpetrators, victims, and bystanders. The bystander testimonies are part of the texts, and the perpetrators are included in the images. The media through which these images have come down to us—newspaper articles, archival collections, documentary films—are explicitly foregrounded. Spero's installations are self-conscious, as well, about the gender dymamics that shape the heroization of Bruskina, about the dynamics of racialization that erased her Jewish identity and about the politics of its reclamation. Masha Bruskina herself, like the sign she carries, becomes a symbol, but Spero needs to redirect the Nazi gaze in her installations and redefine the symbolization to which Bruskina has been subjected. Confronted with Spero's collages and installations, the viewer must read as well as look, thereby extricating herself from any unilateral identification with either victim or perpetrator. In one installation, Spero crops the image slightly, removing one of the men, thus highlighting Masha's heroic role. In another, she superimposes another archival picture, found in the pocket of a member of the Gestapo and showing a naked woman bound with a noose around her neck. Unlike the picture of Masha Bruskina, this is a spare, formally almost classical image that emphasizes the mythification of the female victim or hero, especially when it is placed in relation to Spero's mythic goddesses. This image of a bound woman does reveal the pornographic dimension of the perpetrator/victim relationship, which might seem to corroborate Levinthal's interpretation. Certainly, some Nazi killers did sexualize the act of murder, but while Spero shows this by reproducing an image that is already pornographic, Levinthal adds a pornographic dimension to images that exist in a different register altogether. And by confronting these two images, Spero multiplies feminine roles and complicates gender stereotypes.

In some installations, Spero surrounds these pictures with poems— Bertolt Brecht's ballad about Marie Sanders, who slept with a Jew, a poem by Nelly Sachs, one by Irena Klepfisz. In this way, Spero's representations of Masha Bruskina participate in the mythification and universalization of the resistance hero. She makes clear that surviving archival images cannot evade appropriative discourses of transmission and mediation. Those discourses have now become part of the images themselves, but Spero implicitly acknowledges that fact rather than simply re-enacting it.

Even as she attempts to extricate the girl from Minsk from the Nazi gaze, then, Spero nevertheless inscribes her in other mythic frameworks.

By surrounding her image and story with some of her stock mythological figures, she comments on the monumentality of her own installations, on her own signature and relation to these haunting figures from the past. Masha Bruskina becomes part of the story Spero herself tells about the torture of women, about war and the particular victimization of women in war, and about female resistance. This is also a gendered story that rests on binary oppositions between victims and perpetrators. But, by including text, Spero highlights the historical specificity of Masha Bruskina's life and of her victimization. She allows her to be both individual and symbol.

Spero may be no less appropriative, no less invested than Bak, or Chicago, or Levinthal. But I would say that in her layered images she reveals a greater level of consciousness and responsibility about her role as retrospective witness. Her imaginative and layered aesthetic strategies allow Spero to resist too easy an identification with the female victim or a mere repetition of the perpetrator gaze, and to replace these with an act of denunciation. Spero thus refocuses our look without repairing what has been irrevocably broken. At its best then, her use of Nazi photographs in her memorial artwork would allow us to be conscious of photography's implication in the dynamics of power and powerlessness, seeing and being seen.

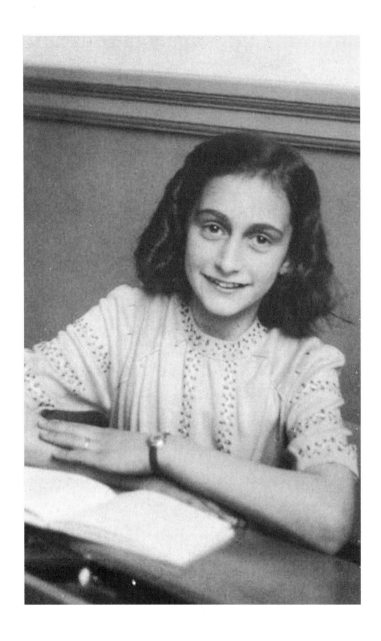

6.1 Anne Frank. © *Anne Frank Fonds-Basel/Anne Frank House/Premium Archive/Getty Images*

6

PROJECTED MEMORY

In my house in Santiago there were certain photographs that kept me good company, that watched over me like a constant presence. There were photographs of my great-grandfather Isidoro, whom we named the chocolate-covered soldier because he was so beautiful and exquisite; also there was a photograph of my aunt Emma who sang arias and spoke French; and there was a small photograph that my grandfather José had given me in the summer of 1970. . . .

Anne Frank's presence in that little photograph was always at my side during my childhood nightmares. I knew that Anne had written a diary and that she had perished in the concentration camps only months before the arrival of the Allied Forces. There was something in her face, in her aspect, and in her age that reminded me of myself. I imagined her playing with my sisters and reading fragments of her diary to us. . . .

I began my dialogue with Anne Frank from a simultaneous desire to remember and to forget. I wanted to know more about that curious girl's face that for so long had occupied a place on the wall of my room. . . . I wanted to speak with Anne Frank from an almost obsessive desire to revive her memory and make her return and enter our daily lives.

This is a passage from the introduction to a book of poems by Marjorie Agosín entitled *Dear Anne Frank* and published in a bilingual edition in 1994.[1] The poet addresses Anne Frank directly, thus hoping to "mak[e] her part of our daily lives."[2] "Dear Anne," the first poem begins, invoking the Anne behind the photograph that "disperses your thirteen shrouded years, your thick bewitching eyebrows" (3). "Is it you in that photo? Is it you in that diary?" (15). Agosín observes, "You seem the mere shadow of a fantasy that names you." This volume of poems written by a Latin-American Jewish woman is inspired and motivated by an encounter with an image that has become generally familiar and well-known, perhaps even as pervasive, in contemporary memory and discussion of the Holocaust, as the image of the boy from Warsaw. In both cases, these are images of children. Indeed, if one had to name the visual images most frequently associated with the memory of the Holocaust, these two would certainly be among them. As images of children, their familiarity and openness to identification allows Agosín to project herself directly into the image and to bring its murdered subject out into her present world with extreme ease.

In this chapter, I continue my discussion of iconic photographs by analyzing the triangulated look with which we engage images of childhood vulnerability in the context of persecution and genocide. But the images discussed here emerge not from perpetrator lenses but from more intimate domestic or institutional visual landscapes—the family and the school.

Past Lives, dated 1987, is the work of the Jewish American artist Lorie Novak (figure 6.2). It is a photograph of a composite projection onto an interior wall: in the foreground is a picture of the children of Izieu— Jewish children hidden in a French children's home in Izieu but found and deported by Klaus Barbie, who was tried in 1987. The photograph of the group of children he sent to be murdered in Auschwitz in 1944 appeared in a *New York Times Magazine* article on the Barbie affair. Novak projects it over a picture of Ethel Rosenberg's face. She, a mother of two young sons, was convicted of atomic espionage and executed by electro-

6.2 Lorie Novak, *Past Lives. Courtesy of Lorie Novak, www.lorienovak.com*

cution along with her husband Julius Rosenberg. In the background of Novak's composite image is a photograph of a smiling woman holding a little girl who clutches her mother's dress and looks like she is about to burst into tears. This is the photographer Lorie Novak as a young child, held by her mother. Novak was born in 1954, a year after the Rosenbergs were executed, and thus this family photo dates from the mid-1950s.

By allowing her own childhood picture literally to be overshadowed by two public images, Novak stages an uneasy confrontation of personal memory with public history. Visually representing, in the 1980s, the memory of growing up in the United States in the 1950s, Novak includes not only family images but also those figures that might have populated her own or her mother's daydreams and nightmares: Ethel Rosenberg, the Jewish mother executed by the state, who, in Novak's terms, looks "hauntingly maternal"[3] but who is incapable of shielding either her children or herself from harm, and the children of Izieu, unprotected child victims of Nazi genocide. Novak is not the contemporary of the children in the image: she is, like Agosín, a member of a second generation, connected to the child victims of the Holocaust through a transgenerational act of adoption and identification. Her mother, though younger, is indeed a contemporary of Ethel Rosenberg. Together they trace the trajectory of memory from one generation to the next.

What drama is being enacted in Novak's *Past Lives*? If it is a drama of childhood fear and the inability to trust, about the desires and disappointments of mother/child relationships, then it is also, clearly, a drama about the power of public history to crowd out personal story, about the shock of the knowledge of *this* history—the Holocaust and the Cold War, state power and individual powerlessness. Lorie, the little girl in the picture is, after all, the only child who looks sad or unhappy: the other children are smiling, confidently looking toward a future they were never to have. The child who lives is crowded out by the children who were killed, by the mother who lives, and by the mother who was executed; her life must take its shape in relation to the murderous breaks in these other, past, lives.

In *Past Lives*, as in others of her projections and installations such as *Night and Fog*, discussed in chapter 4 and in the cover image to this book which also features the children of Izieu, Novak shows us the shadow archive that haunts the intimacy of family pictures: institutional images and public stories of murder, deportation, and execution, as well as the fears and nightmares they engender and from which the circle of family, and the maternal embrace, can shield neither children nor parents.

Space and time are conflated here to reveal memory's material presence. As projected and superimposed camera images, the children of Izieu, Ethel Rosenberg, the young Lorie, and her young mother are *all* ghostly revenants, indexical traces of a past projected into the present, seen in the present as overlays of memory. As her childhood image bleeds into the picture of the murdered children, as the picture of her mother merges with the image of the mother who was executed, Novak enacts a very particular kind of confrontation between the adult artist looking back to her childhood, the child she is in the image, and the victims projected unto these two incarnations of her. This triangulation of looking, figured by the superimposition of images from disparate moments of personal and public history, is in itself an act of memory—not individual but cultural memory. It reveals memory to be an act in the present on the part of a subject who constitutes her/himself by means of a series of identifications across temporal, spatial, and cultural divides. It reveals memory to be cultural, fantasy to be social and political, in the sense that the representation of one girl's childhood includes, as a part of her own experience, the history into which she was born, the figures that inhabited her public life, and perhaps also the life of her imagination. The present self, the artist who constructs the work, encounters in the image the past self and the other selves—the child and maternal victims, related to her through a cultural act of identification and affiliation—that define that past self, shaping her imagination and constituting her memories.[4]

These affiliations mark the subject of these memories as a member of her generation and a witness of her particular historical moment: born after the Second World War, as a Jew, she represents herself as branded by the harrowing memory of Nazi genocide, a memory that gets reinterpreted, repeatedly, throughout the subsequent half-century. Her work, shaped by identification with the victims, invites her viewers to participate with her in a cultural act of remembrance. Photographic projections, as we have seen, make this marking literal and material as the image of Novak's body is inscribed with the story of those other children. Losing their physical boundaries, bodies merge with one another across time and media.

IMAGES OF CHILDREN

I have been haunted by *Past Lives* since the first time I saw it. When I look at it, I see myself both in the sad little girl who is clutching her mother's dress and in the smiling girl who, at the very left of the picture, is half outside its frame, looking to a space beyond. I look at the straight lines of that bare corner wall that encloses the figures like a photographic frame, and at the ghostly figures emerging from its depths and attempting to escape from that frame, and I am propelled right back into my childhood daydreams and nightmares. The dreams and fantasies of a child of survivors of Nazi persecution during the Second World War growing up in Eastern Europe in the 1950s were dominated by The War: Where would I have been, then? How would I have acted? The doorbell rings in the middle of the night, the Gestapo is at the door, what do I do? The imbalance of Novak's image speaks to me forcefully: in remembering my childhood, I too feel as though I were crouching in the corner of a bare room populated by larger-than-life ghosts: my parents' younger selves during the war and children who had to face dangers that I, a child born after, tried hard to imagine. *Past Lives* describes the very quality of my memories of my childhood, memories crowded out by the memories of others: stronger, more weighty ones, more vivid and more real than any scenes I can conjure up from my own child life. Thinking about my childhood, I retrieve their memories more readily than my own—their memories *are* my memories. And yet, unlike Agosín's poems, Novak's layered image also invites us to resist this equation.

In *Past Lives* Novak stages, retrospectively, a moment of knowledge for the Jewish child growing up in the 1950s whose own needs, desires and cares fade out in relation to the stories that surround her, the traumatic memories that preceded her birth but that return to define her life story. Here Novak affiliates, through projection and identification, with the subject position of the child of survivors. But her image also persists and asserts its own presence, as our spectatorial look shifts from one visual place to another, complicating our affiliative trajectories.

The use of familiar public images, whatever their provenance—the boy from Warsaw, Anne Frank, the children of Izieu—enfolds viewers in a postmemorial membrane made of familiar artifacts: viewers will remember seeing these images or others like them before. When Agosín describes Anne Frank's photographic presence in her childhood, her readers will likely remember seeing the same image during theirs: respective memories will trigger one another across subjects and spaces. As readers, we can thus enter the network of looks established in Agosín's poem—we imagine Marjorie looking at Anne's picture, which is looking back at her and at us; at the same time, we look at our own earlier selves looking at Anne's photograph or thinking about her story. The memorial circle is enlarged, allowing for shared memories and shared fantasies. As we look at these images, they look back at us, and, by means of the mutual reflection and projection that characterizes this act of looking, we enter the visual space of postmemory mediated by certain readily available public images of the Holocaust. But is not this familiarity too easy, are not these images too accessible to mark the gravity and the distance of the event from which we must, after all, remain inexorably separate?

Not herself a child of Holocaust survivors, Agosín nevertheless speaks from the position of affiliative postmemory. Inasmuch as they are instruments of memory, camera images, particularly still photographs, expose its resolute but multilayered presentness. As objects of looking they lend themselves, in Kaja Silverman's terms, to either idiopathic or heteropathic identification, to self-sameness or to displacement.[5] Holocaust photographs certainly have the capacity to retain their radical otherness. The challenge for the postmemorial artist is precisely to find the balance that allows the spectator to enter the image and to imagine the disaster, but that simultaneously disallows an overly appropriative identification that would make the distances disappear and thus create too available, too easy an access to this particular past.

The pervasiveness of Anne Frank's image, for example, is of great distress to commentators like Bruno Bettelheim who find it problematic that this young girl's strangely hopeful story should for a generation have constituted the only encounter with the knowledge of the Holocaust, an encounter engendering the type of adolescent identification we see in Marjorie Agosín's book of poems.[6] Anne Frank, Agosín insists, "had a name, had a face, . . . she was not just one more anonymous story among the countless stories of the Holocaust."[7] And Anne Frank continues to function in this way for generations of children who identify with her so unproblematically as to write letters to her for school assignments and friend her on Facebook. Her story persists in serving as the occasion for plays, novels, films, writing competitions that reanimate her as Agosín's poems do, and bring her into the present.

Why are the most powerful and resonant among iconic images after the Holocaust images of children? In fact, of course, we have already encountered a number of vulnerable and impressionable children throughout the pages of this book, from Jacques Austerlitz and Anne Karpff to Richieu and Artie Spiegelman, from the boy in the Warsaw ghetto to Anne Frank and Lorie Novak, from Morrison's, Seiffert's, and Fink's characters to the figures in Bak's and Chicago's paintings and Wolin's and Hasbun's photographs. And, in the following chapters, we will encounter yet other lost children and the complex fantasies they elicit. Culturally, at the end of the twentieth century and the beginning of the twenty-first, the figure of the "child" is an adult construction, the site of adult fantasy, fear, and desire. Our culture has a great deal invested in the children's innocence and vulnerability, and also, at the same time, in their eroticism and knowledge. Less individualized, less marked by the particularities of identity, moreover, children invite multiple projections, and lend themselves to universalization. Their photographic images elicit an affiliative and identificatory as well as a protective spectatorial look marked by these investments. Thus, as Lucy Dawidowicz argues, images of children can bring home the utter sense-lessness of Holocaust destruction:

In the deluded German mind, every Jewish man, woman and child became a panoplied warrior of a vast Satanic fighting machine. The most concrete illustration of this delusion is the now familiar photograph taken from the collection attached to Stroop's report of the Warsaw ghetto uprising. It shows uniformed German SS men holding guns to a group of women and children; in the foreground is a frightened boy of about six, his hands up. This was the face of the enemy.[8]

Children, moreover, were particularly vulnerable in Hitler's Europe: in the entire Nazi-occupied territory of Europe only 11 percent of Jewish children survived, and thus the faces of children signal the unforgiving ferocity of the Nazi death machine.[9] It does not matter whether Anne Frank survived or not for us to feel that vulnerability; with statistics of such enormity, every child whose image we see is, at least metaphorically, one who perished. In the post-Holocaust generation we tend to see every victim as a helpless child, and, as Froma Zeitlin has noted in an article on post-Holocaust literature, we enact a fantasy of rescuing at least one child as an ultimate form of resistance to the totality of genocidal destruction.[10]

THE CHILD WITNESS

To understand the visual encounter with the child victim requires an analysis of the types of identification—idiopathic or heteropathic, based on appropriation or displacement—that shape it. I would like to approach this analysis by way of a very revealing scene from the 1996 film *Hatred* by Australian director Mitzi Goldman.[11] *Hatred* uses interviews, archival footage, and montage shot largely in New York's Harlem, in Germany, and in the Middle East to explore hatred as an emotion. It contains a number of scenes in which Goldman returns with her father to Dessau, the German city from which he fled as a Jew in 1939. Her position as the child of this survivor shapes her inquiry into hatred in numerous ways, but this determining subject position is most clearly revealed in a scene in which the voice-over asks, "What do I know about the Holocaust?"

In this recurring scene a white child (at one time a boy, another time a girl) watches archival film footage of Nazi horror, and in a similar scene a third child, an Asian boy, watches television footage of the Vietnam War (figure 6.3). The archival images projected are, again, overly familiar images seen in many films or displays on the Holocaust and on Vietnam: the records of the Allied soldiers taken on the liberation of the camps and the journalistic footage taken in Vietnam during the war. The voice-over continues: "The horror that was fed to us as children, I buried beneath a tough exterior. It was ancient history, not my life."

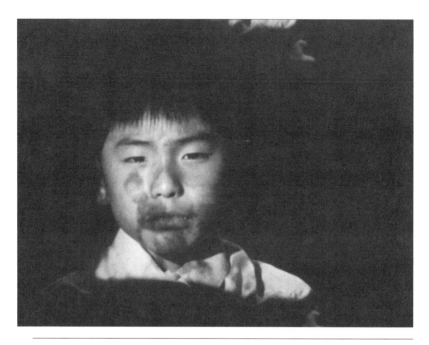

6.3 Film still from Mitzi Goldman, *Hatred* (1996). *Courtesy of Mitzi Goldman*

The three children in Goldman's film are secondary witnesses of horror; they are witnesses not to the event but to its visual documentary records. In Goldman's scene, the child on the screen—the child we see—is not the victim but the witness, looking not at an individualized child victim but at the anonymous victims of the horrors of human brutality and hatred. Still, it seems to me that this representation of the child witness can tell us a great deal about the visual encounter with the child victim. As we see the children watching, it appears to us as if the images are projected right onto their skin, embodying memory and transmitting its bodily wounds.

Strangely, the children are chewing as they watch. Mitzi Goldman has spoken of her strange memories of the Jewish school she attended in Australia, where, on rainy days when they could not go outside at lunchtime, the children were shown films about the Holocaust.[12] The children on the screen feed on images of horror; they have to ingest them with lunch, but, even more graphically, they are marked by them, bodily, as "Jewish" or as "Vietnamese." They watch and, like the film's narrator, they "feed on" images that do and do not impact on their present lives. Looking at the children watching, we see them and the images they see on the same plane; thus the child witness is merged with the victims she or he sees. More than just specularity, looking produces the coalescence of spectator and spectacle; the object of the look is inscribed not only on the retina but on the entire body of the looking subject.

As we look at the face of the child victim, do we not also see there what that child saw? In her poem to the Warsaw boy, Yala Korwin describes this confrontation:

> All the torments of this harassed crowd
> are written on your face.
> In your dark eyes—a vision of horror.
> You have seen death already
> on the ghetto streets, haven't you?[13]

As the child victim merges with the child witness, as we begin to recognize their identity, we ourselves, as spectators looking at the child victim, become witnesses, *child* witnesses, in our own right. Thus we see both from the adult vantage point, retrospective and more knowing, and from the vantage point of the uncomprehending child "grown old with knowledge beyond your years."[14]

It is my argument that the visual encounter and identification with the child victim occurs in a triangular field of looking. The adult viewer sees the child victim through the eyes of his or her own child self. The poet Marjorie Agosín looks at Anne Frank's photo through the adolescent in Chile who had fantasized about conversing with Anne and had asked her to join in her games. The artist Lorie Novak finds the picture of the children of Izieu in the *New York Times*, and she superimposes it on a picture of herself as a child: it is only through that identificatory subject position that she can encounter these children. When the director Mitzi Goldman takes her father back to Dessau, she can do so only by way of her own childhood experience of feeding on images of hatred. The adult viewer who is also an artist shares the child viewing position with her own viewer, who also enters the image in the position of child witness. The present tense of the photograph is a layered present on which several pasts are projected; but at the same time the present never recedes. The adult also encounters the child (the other child and his or her own child self) both as a child, through identification, and from the protective vantage point of the adult looking subject. Identificatory looking and protective looking coexist in uneasy balance.

The split viewing subject that is evoked by the image of the child victim—both adult and child—is emblematic of the subject of memory and of fantasy. In the act of memory as well as the act of fantasy the subject is simultaneously both actor and spectator, both adult and child; we act and, concurrently, we observe ourselves acting.[15] It is a process of projection backward in time, and, in that sense, it is also a process of transformation from adult to child that produces a relationship between children.

But in the particular case of postmemory and "heteropathic recollection," where the subject is not just split between past and present, adult and child, but also between self and other, the layers of recollection and the subjective topography are even more complicated. The adult subject of postmemory encounters the image of the child victim as the child witness, and thus the split subjectivity characterizing the structure of memory is triangulated. Identification is affiliative group or generational identification. The two children whose mutual look defines the field of vision I am trying to map here are linked culturally, and not personally or familially. But that connection is facilitated, if not actually produced, by their mutual status as children and by the child's openness to identification. Through photographic projection, moreover, distances diminish even more and identities blur. When two children "look" at one another in the process of photographic witnessing, the otherness that separates them is diminished to the point where recollection could easily slide into the idiopathic, where displacement risks giving way to interiorization and appropriation. The image of the child, even the image of the child victim of incomprehensible horror, displaces what Silverman calls "the appetite for alterity" with an urge toward identity.[16] This could be the effect of the "it could have been me" created specifically by the present political climate that constructs the child as an unexamined emblem of vulnerability and innocence. Under what circumstances, then, could the image of the child victim preserve its alterity and thus also its power?

(IM)POSSIBLE WITNESSING

In his work on Holocaust memory, Dominick LaCapra has enjoined us to recognize the transferential elements that interfere with efforts at working through this traumatic past: "Acting out may well be necessary and unavoidable in the wake of extreme trauma, especially for victims," LaCapra writes in *Representing the Holocaust*.[17] But for "the interviewer and the analyst" (and, one might add, for the postmemorial generation), LaCapra urges that "one would attempt to put oneself in the other's position without taking the other's place. . . . One component of the process," he suggests, "is the attempt to elaborate a hybridized narrative that does not avoid analysis, . . . it requires the effort to achieve a critical distance on experience."[18]

If the image of the child victim places the artist, the scholar, or the historian into the space of the child witness, then it would seem to impede working-through unless distancing devices are introduced that would discourage or disable appropriative identification. What is disturbing, however, is precisely the obsessive repetition of these images of children—in itself an example of acting out and the compulsion to repeat. The image of the child victim, moreover, facilitates an identification in which the viewer can too easily assume the position of a surrogate victim. Most important, the easy identification with children, their virtually universal availability for projection, risks the blurring of important areas of difference and alterity—context, specificity, responsibility, history. This is especially true of the images I have discussed in this chapter, images of children who are not visibly wounded or in pain. In this light, one might contrast them with the shadow archive of images of emaciated, dirty, visibly suffering children taken in the Warsaw ghetto and elsewhere—images that have never achieved the same kind of visual prominence as the little boy with his hands up, the children of Izieu, or the picture of Anne Frank.

And yet, depending on the context into which they are inscribed and the narrative that they produce, these pictures can be vehicles of a heteropathic memory, they can maintain their alterity and become part of a "hybridized narrative that does not avoid analysis."[19] Clearly, the images' use and meaning vary significantly with the new contexts into which they are inscribed. Thus some of these works rely on specific distancing devices that allow for a triangulated look, for the displacement that qualifies identification. The introduction of the Asian child in the scene from *Hatred* creates a space of reflection, a form of displacement and connection, and thus a mediated identification not necessarily based on ethnic or national identity. Similarly, the inclusion of Ethel Rosenberg's face in *Past Lives* introduces a third term between the child victim and the child witness, and refocuses the attention onto the two adults in the text.

I would like to try to sort out these different forms of identification more closely by way of another image and the context in which it mysteriously appears not once but twice.

Figure 6.4 shows the picture of Holocaust survivor Menachem S., whose testimony was taken at the Yale Fortunoff Video Archive for Holocaust Survivor Testimony by the psychoanalyst Dori Laub. In separate chapters of their coauthored book *Testimony*, Shoshana Felman and Dori Laub refer to Menachem's moving story to illustrate the very different points they each try to make in their essays—Felman to explore how her class received the testimonies they read and watched, Laub to comment on the role of the listener or witness to testimony.[20] Strangely, both reproduce this photograph in their chapters, but neither of them makes even the most cursory reference to it. What is the work performed by this image of the victim child in the work of memory performed by *Testimony*?

At the age of five, Menachem was smuggled out of a detention camp by his parents so that he might survive. In Laub's account, "His mother wrapped him up in a shawl and gave him a passport photograph of herself as a student. She told him to turn to the picture whenever he felt he needed to do so. His parents both promised him that they would come and find him and bring him home after the war."[21] The little boy was sent into the streets alone; he went first to a brothel, where he found

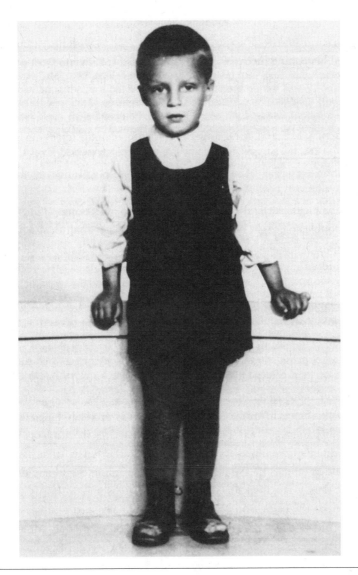

6.4 Menachem S., at the end of 1946 (age 5). *Courtesy of Menachem Stern*

shelter, and later to several Polish families who took him in and helped him to survive. After the war, however, his reunion with his parents destroyed his coping mechanisms. As Laub writes, "His mother does not look like the person in the photograph. His parents have come back as death camp survivors, haggard and emaciated, in striped uniforms, with teeth hanging loose in their gums."[22] The boy falls apart; he calls his parents Mr. and Mrs. and suffers from lifelong terrifying nightmares, and only when he is able to tell his story in the testimonial context after a 35-year silence does he gain some possibility of working though his traumatic past.

Felman cites several of Menachem's own reflections: "'The thing that troubles me right now is the following: if we don't deal with our feelings, if we don't understand our experience, what are we doing to our children? . . . Are we transferring our anxieties, our fears, our problems, to the generations to come? . . . we are talking here not only of *the lost generation* . . . this time we are dealing with *lost generations.*'"[23] For Felman's class "these reflections of the child survivor on the liberating, although frightening effects of his own rebirth to speech in the testimonial process . . . were meant to conclude the course with the very eloquence of life, with a striking, vivid and extreme *real example* of the *liberating, vital function of the testimony.*"[24] Note the repetition of terms like "speech," and "eloquence," for it is precisely language and the ability to speak that gets lost in the class after the students watch Menachem's videotaped account. To address the "crisis" that her class was undergoing as they watched the video testimonies, Felman decides that "what was called for was for me to reassume authority as the teacher of the class, and bring the students back into significance."[25] (Again, note this term and note the strictly differentiated adult/child roles that are assumed). To "bring the students back into significance," Felman gives a half-hour lecture, an address to her class. "I first *reread* to them an excerpt from Celan's 'Bremen Speech' about what happened to the act of speaking, and to language, after the Holocaust." Felman stresses to her students their own "loss of language" in the face of what they were encountering, their feeling that "language was somehow incommensurate with it."[26] She concludes the course with an invitation for students to write their own testimony of the class itself. Citing some of their reflections, she concludes that "the crisis, in effect had been worked through and overcome. . . . The written work the class had finally submitted turned out to be an amazingly articulate, reflective and profound statement of the trauma they had gone through and of the signficance of their own position as a witness."[27] By implication, they have resumed their adult status, in language, in a language commensurate with their experiences. They have been able to work through the trauma, as adults.

Felman's strong insistence on language as *the* means of working through the crisis of witnessing returns me to her inclusion of the child's photograph and her own rather remarkable silence about it. Clearly, this included photo is not the picture that is at the crux of Menachem's story, the ID picture of his mother that he carried with him throughout his years as a hidden child. Menachem went into hiding in 1942 at age 4; the picture is labeled "the end of 1944 (age 5)." It was taken during the war when Menachem was in hiding, when, according to his own narrative, he spent every evening gazing at his mother's photo. In his eyes, in his serious face, we can imagine seeing the reflection of that other, shadow, photograph and the simultaneous loss and presence it signaled. And we can also see, as in the eyes of all child victims, the atrocities the child has already witnessed at the age of five. Perhaps this image is performing the same work in Felman's account that the video testimonies did in her class. In the formulation of one student: "until now and throughout the texts we have been studying . . . we have been talking (to borrow Mallarmé's terms) about the '*testimony of an accident.*' We have been *talking* about the accident—and here all of a sudden *the accident happened* in the class, happened *to* the class. An accident *passed through* the class."[28] In the midst of Felman's own "amazingly articulate, reflective, and profound" analysis in her chapter, the little boy's picture, we might say, is that "accident" that passes through the book, allowing the crisis to be communicated, if on a different register. And, as Laub's own account demonstrates, the image projects the viewer, the subject of "heteropathic" memory, into the position of the child witness and thus into speechlessness.

Laub's own essay, as he explains, "proceeds from my autobiographical awareness as a child survivor."[29] He shares with other child survivors a very peculiar ability to remember: "The events are remembered and seem to have been experienced in a way that was far beyond the capacity of recall in a young child of my age. . . . These memories are like discrete islands of precocious thinking and feel almost like the remembrances of another child, removed yet connected to me in a complex way."[30] The essay indeed goes on to tell the story of another child— Menachem S.—and to discuss his silence, his struggle with witnessing, so as to illustrate a larger point about the impossibility of telling, about the Holocaust as "an event without a witness."[31]

In Laub's essay this same photo is labeled differently: " 'This essay will be based on this enigma of one child's memory of trauma.' "[32] Had we not seen this picture earlier in the book, we would not know that this is not a childhood picture of Laub himself: it is placed in the midst of his own story and not Menachem's at all. In fact, every time I look at the picture and its generalized caption, I have to remind myself that this is not a picture of Dori Laub; it is as if the identities of the two subjects of Laub's essay, Menachem S. and Laub himself, were projected or superimposed onto one another. The essay includes three more photographs: *Menachem S. and his mother, Krakow, 1940*; *Menachem S., 1942*; and *Colonel Dr. Menachem S., 1988*. The fact that the first image carries no name reinforces this blurring of identities between Dori Laub and Menachem S.

Laub's argument in his essay rests on another picture, the ID picture of the mother, in Laub's reading the necessary witness who allowed the five-year-old boy to survive by standing in as a listener to his story. In the essay itself, however, the 1944 picture of the child victim Menachem S. is playing that very same role: it is the silent witness that enables the analyst Dori Laub to perform his articulate analysis but that, with the child's serious and sad eyes, undercuts that wisdom, providing in the essay a space in which to experience uncomprehending speechlessness in the midst of articulate analysis. This photograph, we might argue, is the ground of indirect and paradoxical witnessing in this "event without a witness."

In the ways in which it is reproduced, repeated, and not discussed in the pages of *Testimony*, this image of the boy Menachem S. maintains its alterity, an alterity from which both Felman and Laub quite resolutely try to dissociate themselves in the very space of their identification. In the particular context in which they place it, in the distancing discourse of scholarly discussion in which they embed it, the image of the child victim stands in for all that cannot be—and perhaps should not be—worked through. This image *is* the accident that happened in the midst of all the talking and writing that can only screen its effect. It is the *other child*, in his irreducible otherness, the one who has not yet translated, who might never be able to translate, memory into speech. A reminder of unspeakability, a vehicle of infantilization, it may well be the best medium of postmemory and heteropathic identification, of cultural memorialization of a past whose vivid pain is receding more and more into distance. In his own analysis of working-through, Saul Friedlander explains why: "In fact, the numbing or distancing effect of intellectual work on the *Shoah* is unavoidable and necessary; the recurrence of strong emotional impact is also often unforseeable and necessary. . . . But neither the protective numbing nor the disruptive emotion is entirely accessible to consciousness."[33] As my reading of Felman and Laub's texts suggests, in the right intertextual context, in the hybrid text, the image of the child victim can produce the disruptive emotion that prevents too easy a resolution of the work of mourning.[34]

TWO ENDINGS

In a later scene from Mitzi Goldman's *Hatred*, an Israeli colonel (not Menachem S.) tells of a moment after his unit leveled a Palestinian household suspected of harboring terrorists. "Of course we had to destroy it," he says. When they are done, a little girl in a pink skirt walks out of the rubble, holding a doll. He describes her in such detail that we can visualize her face and dress and posture. "As a human being," the colonel concludes, "you see a small child and you think she can be your child. You cannot afford not to be a human being first." With his response—not identificatory, but protective—he elicits our sympathy, based on a shared humanity, on a universal urge to care for the vulnerable child. Using the child as an alibi, however, also enables the colonel to erase his responsibility for the massacre that just occurred. He projects the image of the child between himself as agent and us as viewers, and it is the child that absorbs our attention. The image of the child can screen out context, specificity, responsibility, and agency. This scene contains all that is problematic about the pervasive use of the image of the child victim.

In her discussion of heteropathic memory, Kaja Silverman quotes a scene from Chris Marker's film *Sans Soleil*: "Who says that time heals all wounds? It would be better to say that time heals everything except wounds. With time the hurt of separation loses its real limits, with time the desired body will soon disappear, and if the desired body has already ceased to exist for the other then what remains is a wound, disembodied."[35] Silverman adds: "If to remember is to provide the disembodied 'wound' with a psychic residence, then to remember other people's memories is to be wounded by their wounds."[36] In the conclusion to his first essay in *Testimony*, Dori Laub speaks of the "hazards of listening"[37] to the story of survivors, of becoming a secondary witness or the subject of heteropathic recollection. Those of us in the generation of postmemory watch survivors rebuild their lives, we watch them amass fortunes and erect castles. "Yet," writes Laub, "in the center of this massive dedicated effort remains a danger, a nightmare, a fragility, a woundedness that defies all healing."[38] The image of the child witness, an image on which, figuratively at least, he projects his own childhood image, produces this woundedness in his writing and in our reading. It is a measure of the massive effort in which, as a culture, we have been engaged during the last 70 years—to attempt, however unsuccessfully, to rebuild a world so massively destroyed without, however, denying the destruction or healing its wounds or using it as an alibi for further violence. The image of the child victim, which is also the image of the child witness, provides the disembodied wound of Holocaust destruction with a residence.

1.1 *In the Palm of a Hand. Courtesy of the photographer, Leo Spitzer*

7

TESTIMONIAL OBJECTS

(WITH LEO SPITZER)

Between 1942 and 1944 Mina Pächter and several of her women neighbors interned in the Terezín (Theresienstadt) camp undertook a remarkable project: together they reconstructed from memory and wrote down in German on small scraps of paper the meal recipes they had routinely prepared in prewar times. Even while they themselves were barely surviving on potato peels, dry bread, and thin soup, they devoted their energy recalling recipes for potato and meat dumplings, stuffed goose neck, and Gulasch with Nockerl, for candied fruits, fruit rice, baked matzohs, plum strudel, and Dobosch Torte. Many of them had inherited these recipes from their mothers, and, in writing them down, they used them not only to remember happier times, or to whet their mouths through recollection, but—more important—as a bequest addressed to future generations of women. Before her death in Terezín in 1944, Mina Pächter entrusted the assembled recipes to a friend, Arthur Buxbaum, asking him to send them to her daughter in Palestine if he should somehow survive. Arthur Buxbaum did survive, but it took 25 years and several other intermediaries for the mother's package to reach her daughter, Anny Stern, who had since moved to the United States. Another 20 years later, in 1996, the recipes were published in the original German and in English translation, in a book edited by Cara De Silva and entitled *In Memory's Kitchen: A Legacy from the Women of Terezín.*[1]

Nowadays, more than 65 years after the end of the Second World War, children of victims and survivors of the Holocaust, dispersed throughout the world, are still discovering legacies such as the recipe book from Terezín among their parents' possessions, and are still trying to scrutinize the objects, images and stories that have been bequeathed to them—directly or indirectly—for clues to an opaque and haunting past. Such "testimonial objects" carry memory traces from the past, to be sure, but they also embody the very process of its transmission. They testify to the historical contexts and the daily qualities of the past moments in which they were produced and, also, to the ways in which material objects carry memory traces from one generation to the next.

In Memory's Kitchen, for example, carries powerful personal, historical, cultural, and symbolic meanings that far exceed its deceptively ordinary contents, drawn from the domestic everyday world of its authors. We cannot cook from the recipes in this volume—most of them leave out ingredients or steps, or they reflect wartime rationing by calling for make-do substitutes (for butter or coffee, for example) or by making eggs optional. But we can certainly use them to try to imagine a will to survive, and the determined commitment to community and collaboration that produced this extraordinary book. For persons familiar with the history of the Terezín ghetto, moreover, the recipe collection becomes a testament to the power of memory and continuity in the face of brutality and dehumanization.[2] Evoking shared trans-cultural associations of food and cooking with home and domesticity, the recipe writers also, paradoxically, enable us to imagine hunger and food deprivation through the moving and extraordinarily detailed fantasies of cooking and eating that their fragmentary efforts reveal. The recipe collection testifies to the women's desire to preserve something of their past world, even as that world was being assaulted, and it attests to their own recognition of the value of what they had to offer, as a community of women—the knowledge of food preparation.

As a book of recipes, created and exchanged among women, and bequeathed from mother to daughter, *In Memory's Kitchen* thus invites us to think quite pointedly about how acts of transfer may be gendered and engender feminist readings. The recipes embody and perpetuate women's cultural traditions and practices both in their content and in the commentary that accompanies some of them—one, for example, is annotated as "Torte (sehr gut)" ("Torte [very good]"). But in a book about food created in a concentration camp, considerations of gender can also quickly disappear from view as we bear in mind the Nazi will to exterminate all Jews, and to destroy even the memory of their ever having existed. A reading of *In Memory's Kitchen*, therefore, also illustrates some of the hesitations about using gender as an analytic category in relation to the Holocaust that we have seen in previous chapters: the fear of thereby detracting attention from the racializing categorizations that marked entire groups for persecution and extermination. If those targeted for extermination were utterly dehumanized and stripped of subjectivity by their oppressors, were they not also degendered? Gender, in circumstances of such extreme dehumanization, may well be an immaterial, even offensive, category. Hunger and thus food, after all, is an ever-present concern of every Holocaust victim. It is a persistent topic in every testimony and every memoir, regardless of the victim's gender and other identity markers. This extends even to accounts of food preparation, which, perhaps in less sophisticated form, preoccupied male as well as female prisoners throughout Nazi ghettos and camps.[3] At the same time, the book of recipes from Terezín does raise significant historical questions about the role of gender then, in the ghettos and camps, and representational questions about its role now, in our understanding of those experiences. As we have seen in previous chapters, gendered tropes often mediate the transmission of traumatic remembrance in expected and unexpected ways. A feminist reading and a reading of gender constitute, at the very least, compensatory, reparative acts. In fact, as our reading of a second book will show, we are interested in looking at gender precisely when it recedes to the background, when it appears to be elusive or even invisible. It is in this context that gender itself becomes a point of memory offering insights into how memory functions and is transmitted.[4]

The recipes from Terezín were collected by one woman, ostensibly for her daughter. But, as a project, the recipe collection unites a larger community of women in an act of collective resistance, and as such it is directed not just to Anny Stern, but to her generation of daughters and sons, enabling them to experience some of what their mothers lived during the war. As a collective work, it also invites broader forms of affiliation and attachment within and across generations. The second book, from the Romanian camp of Vapniarka is also the result of a collaborative act of resistance among the prisoners. Passed down from father to son, in this case, it also testifies to more expansive forms of affiliation in times of extremity and thus, like *In Memory's Kitchen*, provokes and clarifies the workings of affiliative postmemory.

THE SECOND BOOK

This little book (figure 7.1) came to us through the family archive of a cousin, David Kessler, the son of Arthur Kessler, a medical doctor who, along with a group of others accused of communist or anti-government activities during the early war years, had been deported in 1942 from the city of Cernăuți to the Vapniarka concentration camp in what was then referred to as Transnistria (figure 7.2).[5] When Arthur Kessler was diagnosed with Alzheimer's disease in Tel Aviv in the early 1990s, his son David inherited a number of boxes containing documents and memorabilia from his father's experiences in Vapniarka in 1942 and 1943. In subsequent years, David Kessler, now an engineer in Rochester, New York, spent much of his free time sorting and cataloging the items that would teach him about events his father had mentioned only rarely, and that father and son could no longer discuss during their regular visits over the last decade of Arthur Kessler's life. Vapniarka was a camp run by the Romanians (allied with the Germans) for political prisoners, communists, and other dissidents, most of them Jews, and it was a camp that housed not only men but also women and some children. The Kessler family archive has been invaluable to us in our research into the painful history of the virtually unknown and highly unusual Vapniarka camp and the deliberately induced lathyrism, a disease that maimed or killed many of its inmates.

Throughout his childhood and youth, the camp's existence had been constituted for David through his father's fractured stories, through his

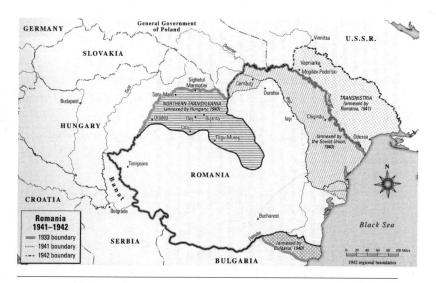

7.2 Map of Romania and Transnistria showing Vapniarka. *From Radu Ioanid,* The Holocaust in Romania: The Destruction of Jews and Gypsies Under the Antonescu Regime, 1940–1944 *(Chicago: Ivan R. Dee, 2000)*

encounters with other camp survivors, and through silences, whispers, and the power of his own fantasies and nightmares.

He told us:

> I knew about this mysterious place called Transnistria and that there is some place called Vapniarka there, that it was a camp. But nothing specific. You could not not hear about it. There was a string of people coming to our house on crutches. I knew the people, we were surrounded by them. They had special cars, built especially for them. My dad took care of them. It was all part of my surroundings. And my father would say in German, "There are some things children should be spared knowing. One day the story will be told." . . . In my imagination it was someplace over there that doesn't exist any more. It was always in black and white of course, very unreal, it belonged to the old old past, it had to do with old people.[6]

Now that his father could not transmit that story directly, David was left with the testimonial objects in the boxes labeled "Vapniarka": a photograph of a model of the camp, built by an inmate after the war and exhibited at the Kibbutz Lohamei Hagetaot museum in Israel; a lengthy typed memoir in German that his father had written during the 1950s and 1960s but that David was unable to read because the language they shared in Israel was Hebrew; some published and unpublished accounts of the camp; a vast correspondence that included numerous requests for Dr. Kessler to certify his patients' camp-related ill health before various reparations boards. The boxes also contained carefully filed copies of the medical articles Arthur Kessler had published about lathyrism, the debilitating paralysis Vapniarka inmates contracted from the toxic *lathyrus sativus* chickling peas that were the substance of their diet—from peas fed to them, but not to the camp guards and officers.[7] In addition, David found a series of original woodcuts by Moshe Leibl, a camp inmate, depicting scenes from the camp (figure 7.3), and a number of small handmade metal memorabilia: a key chain and shoehorn marked with a capital V, a bracelet charm featuring a pin and miniature crutch, and a medallion of a running man casting

7.3 *Entrance to Vapniarka.* Drawing by Leibl and Ilie. *Courtesy of the Kessler family archive*

away his crutches. The most compelling of these is a tiny book, less than one inch long and about a half-inch wide (figure 7.1).

Vapniarka, like Terezín, was a camp where the prisoners occasionally had some amount of autonomy, and during these times, artists there were able to produce remarkable work. The little book and the metal-work memorabilia in the Kessler family archive, as well as the woodcuts and drawings by various artists, attest to the lively cultural and artistic life that was thriving in the camp even at its worst moments. In his Vapniarka memoir *Finsternis* (*Darkness*), Matei Gall evokes the determination with which artists created their works in the camp:

> One day I saw a man who held a nail in his hand and tried to flatten it, to refigure it so as to create a kind of chisel; this seemed unusual if not somewhat suspicious. I continued to observe him. From somewhere—may be from a fence, or from his bunk, I don't know—he got a piece of rotting wood; he looked at it, tried to make it smooth, found a place in the courtyard of the lager and started working on that piece of wood, to chisel it. . . . A few days later the men who unloaded coal at the railway station brought him something he mixed to create a kind of ink. Now he had color! With a brush made out of some remnants of rags he began to color his piece of wood and he pressed the damp surface onto a sheet of paper. The carving became a work of art: in front of me I saw an engraving that represented our pavilion. It is only then that I learned that this carver was a well-known and talented artist, a master of wood-cuts, engravings, and lithography who had worked at a number of magazines.[8]

We know from the Vapniarka memoirs and testimonies that in 1943, toward the end of Arthur Kessler's internment in the camp, under a more lenient camp commander, inmates invented ways to pass a few of their evening hours through various entertainments and cultural activities. This was possible because of the unusual organization of the Vapniarka camp, the absence of Kapos, the prisoners' own initiative in running certain aspects of camp life, and the experience of a number of them in clandestine activity from their work in the communist underground.

The professional artists, musicians, theatrical persons, and scholars interned in the camp narrated stories, recited poetry, gave lectures on topics such as Marxism, fascism, the cause of the war, the history of Jewish resistance against the Romans. They performed music, dance pieces, theatrical sketches. They composed and made up songs in German and Romanian, a number about the very place where they were imprisoned. Matei Gall writes that "In Vapniarka I heard [Schiller's "Ode to Joy"] for the first time, and I was deeply moved, even though it was sung without orchestral accompaniment."[9] And, perhaps most tangible and potentially accessible from the perspective of memory transfer across generations, they produced woodcuts and drawings, reflecting their physical surroundings and camp life—works of impressive quality and superb testimonial value.

Together with the drawings and woodcuts, the little Vapniarka book enables us to imagine the elaborate cultural activities in the concentration camp and their function as forms of communal spiritual resistance against both the dehumanization imposed by the jailors and the despair produced by the spread of an incurable disease.

The little book fits easily into the palm of a hand. Bound in leather and held together by a fancifully tied but simple rope, it immediately betrays its handmade origin. Elegant raised lettering graces the cover: "Causa . . . Vapniarka, 194 . . ."—the last number is missing, the writing or decorations at the top impossible to make out, the word "Causa" (spelled with an "s") making little sense in Romanian. The title page, in purple lettering in Romanian, is less a title than a dedication: "To doctor Arthur Kessler, a sign of gratitude from his patients." Its forty pages contain a series of scenes and anecdotes of camp life, expressed, in graphic form, by seven different artists: each begins with a signature page, followed by several pages of storyboard drawings, a few with labels, one page of writing. We know that the majority of the seven artists are male, but some signed only a last name and thus their gender is ambiguous. More than the question of the signature, however, the little book raises a more fundamental question about the readability of gender in this account of poison, disease, starvation, and resistance.

The little book David Kessler found in his father's Vapniarka archive has a great deal in common with the recipe collection from Terezín.

Both books were hand-sewn and fashioned out of scarce scrap paper; collectively made in the camp in communal acts of defiance and resistance, they constitute unconventional collective memoirs marked by the bodily imprints of their authors; both were assembled as gifts. Although, unlike Mina Pächter, Arthur Kessler survived and would have been able to tell his story to his son, the transmission of the full story of Vapniarka was also broken, delayed by a half century (the only three published Vapniarka memoirs appeared in the late 1980s and 1990s). Both books, moreover, were structured in response to rigid formal limitations—the recipe format, the tiny rectangular page—and they thus conceal as much as they reveal, requiring us to read the spaces between the frames, to read for silence and absence as well as presence, employing Roland Barthes's "insistent gaze."[10] Both texts emerged out of moments of extremity and provoke us to think about how individuals live their historical moment, how the same moment can be lived differently by different people. In surviving the artists to be read by us, now, the two texts also embody the temporal incongruity that Barthes identified in the punctum of time. They demand a form of reading capable of juxtaposing the meanings they may have held then with the ones they hold for us now. And, like the book from Terezín, the little book from Vapniarka is intensely preoccupied with food—not as a source of fond memories of home, but as the cause of a crippling and deadly disease.

Arthur Kessler's memoir describes the moment when he received the little book and other gifts—just before the camp was dissolved toward the end of 1943, when the war on the eastern front had begun to turn against the Germans and their Romanian allies and the prisoners were relocated to other camps and ghettos in Transnistria. Kessler left in the first group of a hundred inmates. "The patients feel that changes are under way; they are grateful to us as physicians and turn up later with expressions of thanks and small handmade symbolic presents . . . testaments to their artistic talents."[11]

For Dr. Kessler, the little book was no doubt a sign of gratitude, a form of recognition of his remarkable work as a physician who diagnosed the lathyrism disease brought on by the inmates' food and who spared no effort in trying to get the authorities to change the camp diet.

The book was a gift that shows, as he writes, not just the patients' talents for drawing, but also their ingenuity in finding the materials, their skill in bookmaking, their resilience and collaboration. It is a testament to him as well as to his fellow inmates—to their relationships and sense of community—a message of good wishes for freedom, health, and a safe journey.

But the book was certainly also intended to be a souvenir containing scenes and anecdotes of camp life in graphic form: the barbed-wire compound, the buildings, the bunks, mealtimes, men and women on crutches. Souvenirs authenticate the past; they trigger memories and connect them indexically to a particular place and time. They also help to recall shared experiences and fleeting friendships. Some of the pages in the little book are thus located and dated "Vapniarca, 1943"; and each series of drawings is also signed and personalized, as though to say: "Remember me?" "Remember what we lived through together?" And as a souvenir, the book is also a testament to a faith in the future—to a time yet to come when the camp experience will be recalled. It is thus an expression of reassurance—of a will to survive.

There is no doubt that Arthur Kessler and his fellow survivors would have found meanings in this little book that for us now, looking at it in the present, remain obscure. There may be messages, references to specific incidents that we are unable to decode. For us, in the context of our second- and third-generation remembrance, the little book is less a souvenir or gift than an invaluable record—a testimonial object, a point of memory. Read in conjunction with other now available sources for its visual account of small details of the camp itself and of camp experiences, it transmits much of what the Romanian authorities meant to commit to oblivion when they dissolved Vapniarka—all that today, in the now-Ukrainian town of Vapniarka, and on the site of the camp itself, is largely erased and forgotten. Concerning gender relations and differences, for example, it illustrates that in this camp, unlike in other better-known camps, men, women, and children were among the internees and they shared some of the same spaces. It displays the inmates' primary preoccupations, with food, water, the crippling malady—as well as with freedom and the possibilities of attaining it. It confirms that the prisoners clearly came to understand the connection between food and disease and that both women and men suffered from the paralysis. But both Arthur Kessler's and Nathan Simon's account of the spread of the disease agree that, proportionately, women contracted lathyrism at a lower rate and suffered fewer fatalities from it than did men. Their explanation is that women consumed smaller portions of the toxic pea soup.

The book, of course, testifies to Arthur Kessler's important role in the camp, depicting him in a number of the drawings as a competent and respected doctor. But it also reveals contemporary prejudices and highlights details obscured in subsequent memoirs. In one of the sequences, for instance, we see a woman working along with Dr. Kessler, either as a fellow doctor or as a nurse. We know from Arthur Kessler's memoir and other sources that there were more than 20 doctors in the camp, and that one, Dora Bercovici, was a woman who headed the nursing staff that the prisoners had organized. Written accounts of Vapniarka, including Kessler's very detailed narrative, mention Bercovici in passing, but give her little of the recognition for battling the lathyrism epidemic that in the opinion of Polya Dubs, a woman survivor who had worked with her, she rightfully deserves.[12] However slightly, a feminist reading of the little book and other sources does help us to redress this inequity. Dubs's testimony and some of the camp drawings that have survived underscore the traditional gender differences that were operative in Vapniarka: women did not work outside the camp but tended to stay in the one camp building that was assigned to them and their children; they worked as nurses and cleaning staff, and they prepared food.

In looking for confirmation and elaboration of some of these differences in the little book, a detailed scrutiny of the way human figures are represented by its artists can prove instructive. Is gender clearly recognizable in these figures, and if so, are there instances when they are particularized and explicitly gendered, and others when gender and other forms of particularity disappear from view? Are any patterns detectable? Such a close reading does immediately reveal that the little book offers us more than the historical information it contains or the scenes it narrates—scenes that all seem to tell the same story, through the same bare-bones, minimalist plot, repeated seven times, with slight variations. What is most strikingly apparent is not uniformity at all but minute and larger-scale differentiation—the stamp of individuality, of voice, tone, and modulation that each of the miniature graphic accounts is able to convey.

The first artist, Romășcanu, for example, uses purple ink and closely drawn grids to frame his pictures tightly (figure 7.4).[13] Through the grids, as through windows, we can make out images of daily life that seem to provide regularity, perhaps even comfort: several scenes of nursing, close human contact, cooking and food. Still, these scenes are mediated, almost inaccessible. We have to peer around the backs of the

7.4 Romășcanu illustrations. *Courtesy of the Kessler family archive*

figures that obstruct the access to the interior spaces, allowing only partial views. The train in the last frame of this sequence, marked *spre libertate* ("toward freedom"), may be traversing a railroad crossing, but it is still encased by the claustrophobic grid. Freedom may be hoped for. But it has certainly not been reached.

Preceding the departure, there is a scene of farewell between a male doctor and a woman standing below him, with her back to the viewer. She is looking right, toward the train. His look is kind, paternal; hers, however, is in no way submissive, despite her smaller stature and the lower positioning of her figure. But with her back to us, she seems bodily to enact the inaccessibility of these images and the privacy they seem to wish to preserve. Questions emerge: were these first drawings in the little book done by a female artist (the artist's signature contains no first name)? Or did a male artist draw them, sketching a woman to figure mystery and opacity? These questions stimulate us to think about gender as not only a factor in everyday life or a historical category, but also as a vehicle of representation.

When we view the second artist, Ghiță Wolff's images, all the framing inhibiting our vision is gone (figure 7.5). These drawings appear joyful, childlike, revealing a seemingly unbounded (or indomitable) life within. Here the same everyday scenes of outdoor camp existence take place under a smiling sun, and they seem to reflect a brighter, perhaps more optimistic, consciousness. Gender is clearly marked in some of them: the first includes men, women, and children, but the next two only men. Yet in the ensuing sketches gender is illegible. The figures, whether lying in their bunks or in the infirmary, are of indeterminate sex. Indeed, in the last image of Wolff's sequence—a drawing that appears to dissolve even the boundaries set by the book page—a small stick figure walks out through the camp gate toward us, raising her (or his) arms on the road to freedom. The individual is "liber," free. But this fantasy of liberation from ruthless confinement appears to transcend gender or other markers of social difference.

All allusion to liberty disappears in the next three segments. The third artist, "Avadani," is the most cryptic (figure 7.6). The stick figures here are initially simpler and more basic than Wolff's, but they evolve, becoming more complex, less skeletal, as the illness seems to advance.

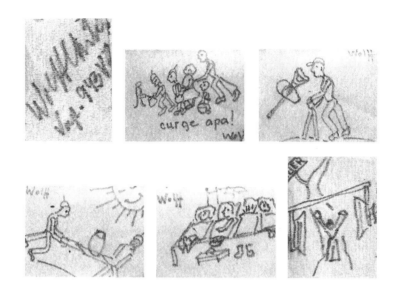

7.5 Ghiţă Wolff's illustrations. *Courtesy of the Kessler family archive*

Even here, however, gender is not clearly marked until the fourth panel. In this one, a more substantial figure (a doctor perhaps? Dr. Kessler?) stands before a pot of food, possibly coming to the conclusion that we now know was made: that the toxic contents of the inmates' diet induced their increasingly debilitating, frequently fatal paralysis. Or is the figure, here and in the final sequence, not meant to be an inmate at all, but a camp guard, more "fleshed out," perhaps, because he enjoys a nontoxic, chicken-in-the-pot meal? Certainly, a context is missing in these sketches: their figures, almost entirely unmoored, are not identifiable or located in a specific moment or place.

And yet the panel in the little book that follows "Avadani's" enigmatic contribution—the only page of writing within it besides the cover page—contains a powerful allusion to place in the form of a proverb: "Omul sfinţeste locul; Locul sfinţeste omul—Wapniarca" ("Man sanctifies the place; the place sanctifies man—Wapniarca"). Read as a proverb, applied to a concentration camp in which inmates were being slowly poisoned by the officials imprisoning them, its words are ironic, if not sarcastic, to say the least. But as an insertion within an artist's book

7.6 "Avadani's" illustrations and the proverb. *Courtesy of the Kessler family archive*

praising the efforts and accomplishments of Dr. Kessler, it must certainly also be read more straightforwardly—as a tribute to the honor he bestowed on the place (and on his fellow inmates) with his presence. Like so much else transmitted in such testimonial objects, the page's meanings are layered and not at all mutually exclusive. The generic universal *omul* (man), moreover, like the incongruous genre of the proverb, is related to some of the universalizing gestures we find in the drawings—if, indeed, it makes sense to say that the artists are universalizing the figures when they make gender invisible. Or are they perhaps just erasing particularity in the way that a proverb comes to stand in for and reduce a wealth of experience to a formula that, no matter how à propos, is always inadequate?

Jeşive's watercolors, which come after the proverb, stand out among all the drawings for their visual complexity (figure 7.7). They require that we turn the pages sideways at times, since some are horizontal and others vertical. Although all depict exterior scenes, they offer no allusion to freedom. These stark scenes of disease and forced labor—performed by clearly male and also by some more ambiguous unmarked

7.1 Jeşive's illustrations. *Courtesy of the Kessler family archive*

figures—stand in sharp contrast to the beauty of their pastel depiction, as they most poignantly illustrate the stubborn persistence of the imagination amid pain and persecution. Jeşive's colors perform an escape into beauty, even as they refuse to represent the dream of escape that is present in the form of trains or open gates in virtually all the other drawings.

In Mărculescu's images, which follow and which project a very different view of exteriority, the shaded ink drawings seem dark and sinister in comparison to Jeşive's pastels (figure 7.8). In them, each figure is situated in front of a barbed-wire fence or a massive building, or both. Here the only escape is through the imagination: the first panel shows a man, perhaps the artist himself, drawing, and the last shows isolated figures in their bunks (or, ill, in the infirmary), alone with their thoughts and their dreams. The first three panels depict men, but the last two, representing extreme imprisonment and extreme privacy and interiority, are more ambiguous, echoing a pattern we've perceived before.

7.8 Mărculescu's illustrations. *Courtesy of the Kessler family archive*

The last two sequences in the little book are briefer, as though the artists were running out of space. "DB' "s dynamic stick figures—male, it would seem—give a foreshortened, minimal history of the Vapniarka inmate experience, in four panels (figure 7.9). A figure walks through the open gateway of the camp energetically, with a walking stick, carrying a bundle on his back. This is the moment of arrival at the camp. But the disease cripples him, and we see him on crutches in front of a barbed-wire fence. He is not alone: in the next panel, three figures stand with arms interlocked in front of this fence, in a gesture of defiant resistance. And in the last panel by DB, the now seemingly empowered figure runs out through the same camp gateway, his arms raised in triumph.

The book ends with a sequence of drawings by Gavriel Cohen, one of the talented artists who also produced a number of additional pencil and pen-and-ink sketches of life at the Vapniarka camp (figure 7.10). Here he sketches a double-page scene in accurate perspective of what must have been the interior of the infirmary. A doctor or nurse is tending to a patient reclining on a bunk. Another patient lies on another bunk, a crutch by the side, in a position suggesting resignation, if not

7.9 The DB sequence. *Courtesy of the Kessler family archive*

7.10 The Gavriel Cohen sequence. *Courtesy of the Kessler family archive*

despair. Gender is blurred in these sketches, secondary to the disease and affliction that are foregrounded. In this light, the final panel of the series, and of the book itself—of a moving train with a giant question mark above it—takes on a layered meaning. Certainly, it too echoes the yearnings for departure and freedom expressed by the previous artists. But the unknown destination implied by the mark can also be read as a final entreaty to the departing Dr. Kessler. When he leaves, what will happen to the patients left behind?

Although they tell nearly identical plots, the drawings in the little book have vastly divergent emotional colorings. Like the recipes from Terezín, and like witnesses in oral testimony, they expose more than they say, and they do so through mode, shading, and tone. In proportion to the book's small size, each of these differentiations, including gender, becomes hugely meaningful. As Barthes suggests in his elaboration of the punctum, in each of the artistic representations in the little book, one aspect of an image, one detail, can make everything else recede from view. And yet, as we have also seen, the testimonial impact of the little book—for Arthur Kessler at the time when he received it, and for us now—greatly exceeds the sum of its parts and, of course, its miniature form.

How can we understand the book's miniaturization, its most distinctive feature? Certainly the materials—leather, paper, string, pens, and watercolors—must have been difficult to come by, and the miniature form, in all likelihood, attests to their scarcity. It would also have been easier for Arthur Kessler to hide such a minute object when he left the camp for unknown further destinations in Transnistria. Gaston Bachelard, who has written eloquently about the miniature, provides us with an insightful observation that is applicable to this little book. He recounts a passage by Hermann Hesse, originally published in *Fontaine*, a French literary journal published in Algiers during the Second World War, that describes a prisoner who paints a landscape on the wall of his cell showing a miniature train entering a tunnel. When his jailors come for him, the prisoner in Hesse's story writes: "I made myself very tiny, entered into my picture and climbed into the little train, which started moving, then disappeared into the darkness of the tunnel. For a few seconds longer a bit of smoke could be seen coming out of the round hole. Then this smoke blew away, and with it the picture, and with the picture my person."[14] This passage vividly highlights the deep connection between miniaturization, confinement, and power. The miniature offers the powerless the fantasy of hiding, of escape, and of a victory over the powerful jailors. The escape is possible only through wit, imagination, and fantasy, as legendary small figures like Tom Thumb have demonstrated again and again. One could argue that as a fantasy of the disempowered, the miniature is marked by gender. Feminized and infantilized by their jailors, male prisoners engage in fantasies of escape, expressed within and through the miniature, instead of armed combat, a traditionally more masculine response.

Susan Stewart writes that the miniature is a "metaphor for the interior space and time of the bourgeois subject," while the gigantic is a metaphor for "the abstract authority of the state and the collective, public, life."[15] Even though it was collectively made, we can see the little Vapniarka book as an expression of the subjective interiority that is most assaulted and threatened by confinement in a concentration camp—an interiority that is not subsumed but that is nurtured by the community in which it is able to survive. But the book is also a remnant, and a reminder, of resilience and persistence against all odds. Each miniature drawing in stick-figure form represents individualized experiences of unprecedented suffering and survival, even as it underscores the inadequacy of this or any other idiom for its expression. Whatever the practical reasons for the book's miniature status, they need to be supplemented with an understanding that by giving Arthur Kessler this tiny object, the patients were giving him the most precious gift they could bestow—the small bit of privacy and interiority, of depth and subjectivity, they had been able to preserve. Handmade, jointly conceived and constructed, yet individually imagined, the miniature object they are endowing to him—and through him and his son, to us as well—contains not only their signature but also their bodily marking. Through this multiple act of transfer, the miniature appears as the small core of privacy, a shared privacy in this case, that defies smothering by the deadly authority of the state.

Along with other surviving Vapniarka drawings and woodcuts, the little book enables us to imagine the elaborate cultural activities of the Vapniarka camp and their function as forms of spiritual resistance against the dehumanization imposed by the jailors and the despair produced by the spread of an incurable disease. In this way, again, the little book is related to the recipe book from Terezín. In Terezín, where art was sanctioned and even coerced for use in Nazi propaganda efforts, the recipe book, generated by the women as a clandestine project, reflected a refusal and a resistant challenge to the purposes of the Nazi authority.

Additionally, the Vapniarka book's tiny size specifically relates to, and provides a graphic analog for, another incident of miniaturization discussed in several of the Vapniarka memoirs: the elaborate communal letters the inmates composed and smuggled to the outside world. Here is Matei Gall's account:

> What are our letters like? An ordinary sheet of paper was folded so as to produce 24 squares of one centimeter each. Every square was numbered front and back, each one of us received a code number

that corresponded both to the number on one of the squares and to the number of our respective family. I for example had the correspondence number 14. Once the courier arrived safely with the folded and well-hidden sheet of paper, the letter was cut into the respective squares and everyone received the correct message.[16]

Arthur Kessler, upon receiving the little book as a gift, would no doubt have recalled the miniaturized form of letter writing in which he also participated. For us, as well, its reduced dimension enables us to better visualize those collective letters and the calculated process of producing them. This ability to make us imagine the camp's lively cultural activity, or the practice of smuggling letters, makes the little book and its drawings into points of memory that pierce through the temporal and experiential layers separating us from the past.

But, as we have already seen, more is at stake in the miniature form. The little book's size reflects the minimalism of the master plot that we find in the seven narratives. Perhaps, paradoxically, it is only through minimalism and miniaturization that the prisoners could express the enormity of their experience. As with the recipes from Terezín, it is literally only by going off the scale in the other direction that we can begin to imagine the numbers, the totality of devastation, the shattering of individuality and collectivity that was the Holocaust. As we look at the recipes and the drawings in the little book, we can imagine how Anny Stern might have read the book her mother transmitted to her, how she might have tried to find hidden messages, accounts, and explanations, meanings that exceed the recipe form. We can try to imagine receiving a one-centimeter letter from a relative in Vapniarka, as Judith Kessler, Arthur's wife, did: how minimal the messages must have been and how rich and multivalent they must have become in the act of her probing readings. The recipes from Terezín, and the little book from Vapniarka elicit similarly meticulous and multiple readings from us. There is so little space that every line, every word counts as a possible clue. In such a context, minute marks and variations, virtually invisible, become hyper-visible, disproportionately enormous.

A similar oscillation between invisibility and hyper-visibility marks the question of gender in relation to the genocide: its seeming irrelevance makes it all the more relevant and significant. Like a figure/ground pattern, or like the oscillation between stick figures and fleshed-out drawings, it emerges as significant, tangible, only to recede again, making space for other concerns. The recipes from Terezín and the drawings from Vapniarka thus become more than microcosms and emblems of the camps in which they were produced—they are emblems for the very process of reading gender within the context of the catastrophe. As points of memory, they have indeed provoked a piercing insight that traverses time and space—the incongruity of gender and the Holocaust, its oscillation between foreground and background, its legibility and illegibility.

The miniature, Stewart writes further, contains the daydream that "the world of things can open itself to reveal a secret life . . . a life within life."[17] But this tiny memory-book, a remnant that has now survived the death of those who could have told us more about it, does not reveal its secrets easily. It took bright lights, magnifying glasses, and a great deal of persistence for us to decode even its cover—and yes, once we succeeded, it did reveal a secret life. It turns out that the word "Causa," which is part of the book's title, was not meant to be Romanian at all, for it became apparent to us that, before some of the letters had faded, the cover title actually read "Dr. Honoris Causa, Vapniarca, 1943" (figure 7.11).

Once the cover became legible, it became hyper-visible, exposing the depths of irony and incongruity structuring this gift. Indeed, the irony revealed is particularly evident to us who dwell in academia. With this gift, patients were bestowing on Arthur Kessler an *honorary doctorate from their concentration camp*! Once we decode the cover, the book's intent as gift and souvenir is thus superseded by its function as an award of honor—as a kind of ironic certificate of merit embellished by a loopy ribbon made of ordinary string. But that honor does not contain any grand official diploma. It contains, instead, in graphic form, small individual accounts of the patients' encounters with Dr. Kessler. The miniature form, juxtaposed with the grand title, underscores the incongruity of producing art in a concentration camp, of finding kindness, goodness, and friendship in the midst of deprivation and suffering. That juxtaposition, once we are able to make it visible, is indeed poignant. The punc-

7.11 Dr. Honoris Causa, Vapniarca, 1943. *Courtesy of the photographer, Leo Spitzer*

tum here is not in the details, but precisely in this incongruity that echoes others—the incongruity of asserting humanity in the face of starvation and dehumanization, of figuring hunger through dreams of food, of reading gender in the context of dehumanization.

But in holding this testimonial object from Vapniarka in the palm of a hand, and reading its images with an insistent gaze, we can do even more. We can remember those who created and crafted its contents, and we can highlight and try to further transmit their courage, their resilience, and their collaborative determination. And yet only if we acknowledge the distance that separates us from them, the layers of meaning and the multiple frames of interpretation that the intervening years have introduced and that have influenced our reading, can we hope to receive from them the testimonies and the testaments they may have wished to transmit.

III.

CONNECTIVE
HISTORIES

8.1 Bracha Lichtenberg-Ettinger, image no. 5 from the exhibition *Mamalangue—Borderline Conditions and Pathological Narcissism*. *Courtesy of Bracha Lichtenberg-Ettinger*

8

OBJECTS OF RETURN

Edek resumed his digging. He dug and he dug. Half of the outhouse's foundation now seemed to be exposed. Edek got down on
his knees, and dug a hole at the base of the foundations. Suddenly
he stiffened.

"I think I did find something." Everyone crowded in. . . .

He reached under the foundation and dug around with his fin-
gers. He was lying stretched out on the ground.

"I got it," Edek said breathlessly. He pulled out a small object,
and began removing the dirt from its surface. The old man and
woman tried to get closer.

"What has he got? What has he got?" the old woman said. . . .

Edek got up. He had cleaned up the object. Ruth could see it. It
was a small, rusty, flat tin. "I did find it," Edek said, and smiled.

Lily Brett, *Too Many Men*

At the end of Lily Brett's 1999 novel, *Too Many Men*, Edek and his
Australian-born daughter Ruth return one more time to Kamedulska
Street in Lódz where Edek had grown up as a small boy and young man

in the 1920s and 1930s. They had already been there several times and, each time, had discovered additional objects that provided clues to Edek's and his family's past. Ruth had gone there by herself to buy, for inordinate sums of money, her grandmother's tea service and other personal items that the old couple living in Edek's former apartment brought out for her in a slow and emotionally tortuous process of extortion. But after traveling on from Lódz to Kraków and then to Auschwitz, where Edek and his wife Rooshka had survived the war, Edek insisted on returning to Lódz and to Kamedulska Street once more to retrieve an additional item of immense personal value. "Did they find gold?" the neighbors kept asking, but the old couple had already searched every inch of ground and come up empty. To his great joy, Edek does find the precious object buried in the ground: it is "a small, rusty, flat tin."[1]

It isn't until later, at their hotel, that Edek opens the small tin. Ruth "could feel the dread in her mouth, in her throat, in her lungs, and in her stomach. . . . The tin held only one thing. Edek removed the object from the tin. It was a photograph. A small photograph. . . . It was a photograph of her mother. . . . Rooshka was holding a small baby. The small baby was Ruth. . . . 'It does look like you,' Edek said. 'But it is not you.' Ruth felt sick."[2] Edek then proceeds to tell Ruth a story concerning her parents that she had never heard before. After liberation, Edek and Rooshka had found each other again and had had a baby boy in the German displaced persons (DP) camp Feldafing. The baby had been born with a heart problem that required a kind of care that these stateless Auschwitz survivors were not in a position to provide. At the advice of their doctor, they made the excruciating decision to give him up to a wealthy German couple for adoption. Before giving him away, Edek had taken a photograph of the baby. Rooshka, however, "'was angry. She did say that if we are going to give him away, he will be out of our lives, so why should we pretend with a photograph that he is part of us. . . . Mum did tell me to throw away the photograph. But I did not want to throw it away'" (524). Edek gave the photo to his cousin Herschel who was going back to Kamedulska Street, which, he believed, "'was still more his home than the barracks'" (525). Herschel took the photo with him and, discovering that this could, in fact, never again be his home, buried it in the yard under the outhouse before returning to the DP camp.

Too Many Men belongs to a genre of Holocaust narrative that has been increasingly prevalent in recent years: the *narrative of return*, in which a Holocaust survivor, accompanied by an adult child, returns to his or her former home in Eastern Europe, or in which children of survivors return to find their parents' former homes, to "walk where they once walked." Memoirs by these children of survivors dominate this narrative genre, but *Too Many Men* provides a rich fictional example and the chance to discuss the characteristics of return plots that are generally punctuated by images and objects that mediate acts of return.[3]

Narratives of return are quest plots holding out, and forever frustrating, the promise of revelation and recovery; thus Edek's discovery of the metal tin and the baby's photograph offers a rare epiphanic instant in this genre. And yet, characteristically perhaps, this moment of disclosure and satisfaction serves only to raise another set of questions that defer any possibility of narrative closure. Why, when Edek's baby was born after liberation, in Germany, was his photo taken back to Lódz, to Kamedulska Street, to be buried there? And why does Edek spend such enormous sums of money and effort to go back to his former home one more time to search for and to retrieve the photograph? If the photo is so important to him, why does he not dig for it on his first visit? Why, in fact, does he wait? Narratives of return, like *Too Many Men*, abound in implausible plot details such as these. What, actually, does Ruth find out about her parents and about herself when her father succeeds in unearthing the photo of her lost brother? What can these moments of narrative fracture and incongruity tell us about the needs and impulses that engender return in different generations and about the scenarios of inter-generational transmission performed in and by acts of return?

In this chapter, I want to read Brett's novel alongside two other works that clarify the incongruities, the implausibilities and impossibilities, and the fractured shapes characterizing the impulse to return and its narrative and visual enactments: Palestinian writer Ghassan Kanafani's 1969 novella *Return to Haifa*, a work that deals not with the Holocaust but with the Nakba, and the Eurydice series of Bracha

Lichtenberg-Ettinger, an Israeli visual artist who is the daughter of Holocaust survivors. These three works enable us to look, in particular, at the role that objects (photographs, domestic interiors, household objects, items of clothing) play in return stories, marking their sites of implausibility and incommensurability.[4] Such testimonial objects, lost and again found, structure plots of return: they can embody memory and thus trigger affect shared across generations. But as heavily symbolic and over-determined sites of contestation, they can also mediate the political, economic, and juridical claims of dispossession and recovery that often motivate return stories.

Read together, these three works stage the impulse to return as a fractured encounter between generations, between cultures, and between mutually imbricated histories occurring in a layered present. From Australia, New York, and Israel to Poland and back, from the West Bank to Haifa, from a layered present to a complicated past, return is desired as much as it is impossible. In focusing on an emblematic figure we have encountered in previous chapters, the figure of the lost child, these works expose the deepest layers of the contradictory psychology of return and the depths of dispossession that reach beyond specific historical circumstances. How can divergent histories that expose children to danger and abandonment be thought together, without flattening or blurring the differences between them? Perhaps in a feminist, *connective* reading that moves between global and intimate concerns by attending precisely to the intimate details, the connective tissues and membranes, that animate each case even while enabling the discovery of shared motivations and shared tropes. Such a feminist reading, as I see it, pays attention to the political dimensions of the familial and domestic, and to the gender and power dynamics of contested histories. It foregrounds affect and embodiment and a concern for justice and acts of repair. It is *connective* rather than *comparative* in that it eschews any implications that catastrophic histories are comparable, and it thus avoids the competition over suffering that comparative approaches can, at their worst, engender.

In Kanafani's text, a Palestinian couple drives from Ramallah to the house in Haifa that they were forced to leave in 1948. It is June 1967, twenty years later, and Said S. and Safiya join many of their neighbors and friends curious to revisit the homes that they had left behind and that they were allowed to visit after the Israeli annexation of the West Bank and the opening of the borders. As they approach Haifa, Said S. "felt sorrow mounting from inside him. . . . No, the memory did not come back to him little by little, but filled the whole inside of his head, as the walls of stone collapsed and piled on top of each other. Things and events came suddenly, beginning to disintegrate and filling his body."[5] Return to place literally loosens the defensive walls against the sorrow of loss that refugees build up over decades and that they pass down to their children. Just as Ruth responds to the photograph in *Too Many Men*, so Said S. and Safiya respond viscerally, with trembling, tears, sweat, and overpowering physical feelings of torment. As the couple approaches their former house, the streets they cross, the smells of the landscape, the topography of the city all trigger bodily responses that are not exactly memories, but reenactments and reincarnations of the events of the day in 1948 when they left their home. The past overpowers the present, "suddenly, cutting like a knife"[6] and we are with Said S. in 1948 as he desperately attempts to get back to his wife through the bullets and confusion on the city streets; we also see her haste to get to him, and her inability to fight her way back through the flood of refugees to the house where her baby Khaldun remains asleep in his crib, tragically left behind. Later that day, offshore, as the boats took them away from Haifa, "they were incapable of feeling anything" (107). The loss is so overwhelming that for twenty years, Khaldun remains a family secret: Khaldun's name is rarely pronounced in their house, and then only in a whisper. Their two younger children do not know about their lost brother. And even as they drive toward Haifa together in 1967, neither Said S. nor Safiya, who talk about everything else during the journey, "had uttered a syllable about the matter that had brought them there" (100). On the surface, the trip is about seeing their house again—as they say, "just to see it" (108).

Both these fictional works represent refugees' and exiles' reencounter with the material textures of their daily lives in the past.[7] "Habit," Paul Connerton writes in *How Societies Remember*, "is a knowledge and a remembering in the hands and in the body, and in the cultivation of habit it is our body which 'understands.' "[8] In returning to the spaces and objects of the past, displaced people can remember the embodied practices and the incorporated knowledge they associate with home. When Said S. slows his car "before reaching the turn which he knew to be hidden at the foot of the hill," when he "looked at all the little things which he knew would frighten him or make him lose his balance: the bell, the copper door knocker, the pencil scribblings on the wall, the electricity box, the four steps broken in the middle, the fine curved railing which your hand slipped along" (111), he reanimates deep habits and sense memories. Ordinary objects mediate the memory of returnees through the particular embodied practices that they reelicit. And these embodied practices can also revive the affect of the past, overlaid with the shadows of loss and dispossession.

Said S. and Safiyah notice every detail of the house, comparing and contrasting the present with the past "like someone who had just awoken from a long period of unconsciousness" (112). Much remained exactly the same: the picture of Jerusalem on one wall, the small Persian carpet on the other. The glass vase on the table had been replaced with a wooden one, but the peacock feathers inside it were still the same, though of the seven feathers that had been there, only five remained. Both wanted to know what happened to the other two.

Somehow, those two missing feathers become signifiers of the incommensurability of return—a measure of the time that had passed and the life lived by other people and other bodies in the same space and among the same objects. Emerging from this bodily reimmersion in his former home, Said S. begins to realize that, for years, other feet have shuffled down the long hallway, and others have eaten at his table: "How very strange! Three pairs of eyes all looking at the same things . . . and how differently everyone sees them!"(113). In Kanafani's novella, the third pair of eyes belong to Miriam, the wife of the deceased Evrat Kushen, both Holocaust survivors who had been given the house by the Jewish Agency only a few days after Said S. and Safiya left it.[9] " 'And with the house, he was given a child, five months old!,' " Miriam tells the stunned Said S. and Safiya as they sit in the living room that all three of them consider their own" (120). Miriam also tells them how she had been ready to return to the Italian DP camp to which they had been sent after the war because of the disturbing scene she had witnessed during those days in 1948: Jewish soldiers throwing a dead Arab child, covered with blood, into a truck "as if he were a piece of wood" (119). When they adopted the baby, Evrat Kushen hoped that his wife would be able to heal from the shock of that vision.

As Said S. and Safiya discuss whether to wait for the boy who had been raised by his Jewish parents as Dov, or whether to leave immediately, accepting the fact that their son had irrevocably been taken from them, they surprisingly equate their child with the house that had been, and was now no longer, theirs. Both house and child are invested with agency and power—to accept or to deny their former owners/parents. As Said S. tells Safiya, " 'Don't you have those same awful feelings which came over me while I was driving the car through the streets of Haifa? I felt that I knew it and that it had denied me. The same feelings came over me when I was in the house here. This is our house. Can you imagine that? Can you imagine that it would deny us?' " (123). What could figure the enormity of their dispossession as powerfully as the loss of a child, or a child's refusal to recognize his parents? When Khaldun/Dov finally appears on the scene, he is wearing an Israeli uniform.

Although, in Kanafani's novella, the lost child structures the story of return, the novella's plot does not fully motivate the loss of Khaldun: we are told that Safiya tried, desperately, to return to the house to fetch her baby, but how, we cannot help but wonder, could she have left him there in the first place? This narrative implausibility is compounded by other textual incongruities, most notably Dov's revelation that "they" (his parents) only told him "three of four years ago" (131) that he was not their biological son, even though he said earlier that "my father was killed in Sinai eleven years ago."[10] Is this temporal disjunction a mistake on Kanafani's part, or an indication of the son's very belated acceptance of his adoption? These implausible elements of the story and the questions they raise produce moments of fracture in which different plot possibilities are overlaid on one another with no possible resolution. They can be motivated only on the level of fantasy and symbol—as the measures of a failed maternity and paternity in a time of historical extremity, and as emblems of the radical dispossession that is the result of Israeli occupation.

For Said S. and Safiya, as for Edek and Rooshka in *Too Many Men*, the lost child remains a shameful and well-kept secret, haunting and layering the present. When Edek regrets giving his baby up for adoption and worries that he had made the wrong decision, Ruth attempts to alleviate her father's guilt by insisting, "You did nothing wrong."[11] Here, also, extreme historical circumstances fracture family life and disable parental nurturance. Just as Said S. and Safiya need to return to their former home and to reencounter the objects that trigger body memories and with them the emotions of inconsolable loss they had so long suppressed, so Edek needs to find the photograph of his baby son if he is to tell the story to his daughter. More than objects of intimacy—Ruth's grandmother's tea service, or her grandfather's overcoat and the photographs that are in one of its pockets—the photo of the lost child figures the expulsion from home and the impossibility of return. In the narrative, we need to wait for its revelatory power; we need to witness the progressive discovery Edek and, with him, Ruth undergo. Suspense, partial disclosures, and delayed revelations structure the plot: several scenes of digging have to precede the unearthing of the small tin can. In both texts, the loss of the child, associated with guilt and shame, is deeply suppressed. It can be brought into the open and confronted only gradually, by crossing immense temporal and spatial divides.

For Edek, the photograph becomes the medium of a narrative shared across generations. Ruth wonders why her parents had never told her about her baby brother and insists that this is *her* story as much as it is her mother's and father's: "It was impossible to grow up unaffected. The things that happened to you and to Mum became part of my life. Not the original experiences, but the effects of the experiences."[12] It is these effects that motivate Ruth's journey to Poland, her need to imagine her parents' lives, her tireless search for every object and every detail of their past. They propel her repeated returns to Kamedulska Street, and her need to go there with her father. And, through a process of unconscious transmission of affect, they motivate a recurrent nightmare that plagues Ruth throughout her trip to Poland, before she ever sees the photo or learns about her lost brother:

> She had had one of her recurring nightmares. The worst one, the one in which she was a mother. The children were almost always

babies. . . . In these dreams she lost her babies or starved them. She misplaced them. Left them on trains or buses. . . . The abandonment in her dreams was never intentional. She simply forgot that she had given birth to and brought home a baby. When in her dreams she realized what she had done, she was mortified.[13]

How does the act of returning to place and how do the objects found there inflect the process of affective transmission that so profoundly shapes the postmemory of children of exiles and refugees?

RETURNING BODIES

In *Der lange Schatten der Vergangenheit* (*The Long Shadow of the Past*), Aleida Assmann reflects on the role of objects and places as triggers of body or sense memory.[14] Invoking the German reflexive formulation of "ich erinnere mich" (it is reflexive also in French, "je me souviens"), she distinguishes what she calls the verbal and declarative, active "ich-Gedächtnis" (I-memory) from the more passive "mich-Gedächtnis" (me-memory), which appeals to the body and the senses rather than to language or reason. Assmann's "mich-Gedächtnis" is the site of involuntary memory that is often activated and mediated by the encounter with objects and places from the past.[15] Scholars of memory sites like James Young and Andreas Huyssen have been skeptical of what they deem a sentimental Romantic notion that endows objects and places with aura or with memory. In response, Assmann specifies that, though objects and places do not themselves carry qualities of past lives, they do hold whatever we ourselves project onto them or invest them with. When we leave them behind we bring something of that investment along, but part of it also remains there, embedded in the object or the place itself. Assmann uses the metaphor of the classical Greek legal concept of the *symbolon* to conceptualize this. To draw up a legal contract, a symbolic object was broken in half, and one of those halves was given to each of the parties involved. When the two parties brought the two halves together at a future time and they fit, their identity and the legal force of the contract could be ratified. Return journeys *can* have the *effect* of such a reconnection of severed parts, and, if this indeed happens, they can release latent, repressed, or dissociated memories—memories that, metaphorically speaking, remained behind, concealed within the object. And, in so doing, they can cause them to surface and become reembodied. Objects and places, therefore, Assmann argues, can function as triggers of remembrance that connect us, bodily and thus also emotionally, with the object world we inhabit.[16] In her formulation, the "mich-Gedächtnis" functions as a system of potential resonances, of chords that, in the right circumstances—during journeys of return, for example—can be made to reverberate.

But can the metaphor of the *symbolon* cover cases of massive historic fractures, such as the ones introduced by the Shoah and the Nakba? Would not contracts lose their legal force in such cases, so much so that the pieces would no longer be expected to fit together again? Worn away not only by time but also by a traumatic history of displacement, forgetting and erasure, places change and objects are used by other, perhaps hostile owners, over time coming merely to approximate the spaces and objects that were left behind. Cups and plates chip, peacock feathers disappear, wooden vases replace glass ones, keys to houses, obsessively kept in exile, no longer open doors. "Home" becomes a place of no return.

And yet embodied journeys of return, corporeal encounters with place, do have the capacity to create sparks of connection that activate remembrance and thus reactivate the trauma of loss. In the register of the more passive "mich-Gedächtnis," or the "repertoire," they may not release full accounts of the past, but they can bring back its gestures and its affects. Perhaps the sparks created when the two parts of a severed power line touch ever so briefly constitute a more apt image for this than the ancient *symbolon* cut in half. The intense bodily responses to the visits of return that we see in both these novels testify to the power of these sparks of reconnection that increase expectation and thus also intensify frustration.

The powerful body memory engendered by return is compounded in these narratives by the trope of the lost child that clarifies the enormity of the stakes involved. In the face of expulsion and expropriation—

especially childhood expulsion—home and identity are in themselves implausible and objects remain alienating and strange.

GENERATIONS AND SURROGATIONS

The impossibility of return is intensified if descendants who were never there earlier return to the sites of trauma. Can they even attempt to put the pieces together, to create the spark? Or are the point of connection and the physical contact with objects lost with the survivor generation? What if several generations pass? What if traces are *deliberately* erased and forgetting is *imposed* on those who are abducted or expelled, as Saidiya Hartman asks in her moving memoir of "return" to the slave routes of Ghana, tellingly entitled *Lose Your Mother*?[17] If her narrative, like other second and subsequent generational stories of "return" to places not visited before, attempts to reclaim some form of memory or connection to the objects and places of the past, it is only while making evident the irreparability of the breach. Narrative incongruity in fictional accounts may well serve the purpose of signaling the fractures underlying both home and return in the autobiographical and fictional accounts of postmemorial generations that have inherited immeasurable loss. And images, objects, and places function as sites where these implausibilities manifest themselves.

In *Too Many Men*, Ruth says to Edek that "so much of what happened in your life became part of my life."[18] Along with stories, behaviors, and symptoms, parents do transmit to their children aspects of their relationship to places and objects from the past. Ruth had wanted to visit Poland the first time "just to see that her mother and father came from somewhere. To see the bricks and the mortar. The second time was an attempt to be less overwhelmed than she was the first time. To try and not to cry all day and night. . . . And now she was here to walk on this earth with her father."[19] He identifies places and objects, gives her information, but also, together, they are able to relive the most difficult and painful moments of his past—to transmit and to receive the sparks of reconnection. These are often provocative and disturbing, as when Said S. and Safiya confront Dov with the reality of his double identity, or when Ruth cannot evade the running mental dialogue with Rudolf Hoess, the commandant of Auschwitz whose voice, implausibly again, addresses and argues with her as soon as she arrives in Poland, from the dead, or, as he presents it, from "Zweites Himmel Lager," second heaven camp, as part of his own rehabilitation program.

This need on the part of the child born after the war, and after the moment of expulsion and expropriation, to visit the places from which her parents were evicted provides another explanation for cousin Herschel's return and the burial of the baby's photograph in Lódz in *Too Many Men*. It comes from a yearning to find a world *before* the loss has occurred, before the Rudolf Hoesses dominate the scene—from a need for an irrecoverable lost innocence that descendants of survivors imagine and project.

With the small tin and the photo inside it, Edek is unearthing more than his repressed feelings of loss. He is demonstrating to Ruth her own surrogate role: she is not the first child to "return" "home" to Lódz; the baby had already come back before she did, albeit in the guise of a photo. As Joseph Roach argues in *Cities of the Dead*, cultural memory of loss works through a genealogical network of relations we might think of as surrogation: memory is repetition but always with some change, reincarnation but with a difference.[20] Those of us living in the present do not take the place of the dead but live among or alongside them. In encountering the baby's photo, Ruth comes to understand her role as surrogate. The lost brother's photo is literally dug up from under the foundation of the house. His image, *like* and also *unlike* her, emerges as the fantasmatic figure shared by all children of survivors who tend to think of themselves as "memorial candles"—stand-ins for another lost child who become responsible for perpetuating remembrance, for combating forgetting, for speaking in two overlapping voices.[21]

The structure of surrogation functions even more literally in Kanafani's text. The children Said S. and Safiya have after losing Khaldun are called Khalid and Khalida. These children do not know about their brother. And yet, on some level, they may have learned that, in the familial economy of loss, they are taking his place. At the end of the novel, Said S. emotionally authorizes Khalid to take up arms for Palestine, to win back the home from which they were evicted. Mythically, brother will fight against brother.

Connecting these two texts, however, shows how differently memory can function in the different contexts in which journeys of return take place. When Edek returns to Kamedulska Street, the old couple residing there worry that he plans to reclaim his property. Nothing could be further from his intentions: Edek and Ruth are there to find the past, not the present. Even though Edek enjoys the food of his youth and feels at home in his language, he is uninterested in Poland, cannot wait to leave it. Ruth could not imagine living there: her project is one of mourning and psychic repair, not recuperation. Bringing her grandmother's tea service to New York promises to reconnect some of the disparate parts of her life, to find continuity with a severed past—not to bring it into the present. But Hoess's constant whisper, overlaid onto her musings about her parents' and grandparents' world of before, shows her how much the past and also the future are dominated and overshadowed by the incontrovertible fact of the genocide. No revelation or recovery can heal the breach.

In Kanafani's text, we see an entirely different economy at work. " 'You can stay for a while in our house,' " Said S. says to Miriam and to Dov as he leaves. It is *his* house, and he imagines that his son Khalid will help recover it. Khalid had wanted to join the *fedayeen*, to become a guerilla and sacrifice his life for the struggle, but his father and mother had been opposed. Now, driving back to Ramallah, Said S. hopes that his son has left while they were away. Memory serves a future of armed struggle and resistance here, not one of mourning or melancholy. And in a context in which the conflict continues and resolution cannot yet be envisioned, return serves the cause of legal and moral claims of recovery.

But the fantasmatic structure of surrogation functions in a more disturbing and open-ended fashion as well. In both texts, the lost child's survival is, for a while at least, submerged in ambiguity. Said S. and Safiya do not know whether they will find Khaldun when they return to Haifa. Ruth harbors fantasies of searching for and finding her lost brother, and, in fact, the novel, implausibly again, holds out that possibility: a German woman Ruth meets on her trip tells her about a young

Christian German man named Gerhard who looks exactly like her and who, though a gentile, identifies profoundly with Jews. At the end of the novel, Ruth, in a fantasy of recovering her lost brother, sets out to search for Gerhard. Could the lost child, then, function in these texts according to the logic of the uncanny—as the embodiment of childhood innocence and hope, of the belief in a future, irrevocably lost with war and dispossession? In this schema, surrogation would work backward toward a primordial past, rather than forward into the future, and Edek, as well as Said S., would be finding not their sons but their own childhood selves—lost, unprotected, neglected, forgotten, repressed, but returning, perpetually and uncannily, to haunt a tainted present and to hold out the vision of an alternative ethical and affective future.

VISUAL RETURNS

I turn now to a third body of works that exhibit a visual aesthetics of return characterized by fracture, overlay, and superimposition. The works by Bracha Lichtenberg-Ettinger, a second-generation Lacanian psychoanalyst and feminist visual artist, allow us to measure the political and psychic implications of the repetitions and irresolutions of return.

In her Eurydice series, produced between 1990 and 2001, Ettinger goes back to a street in Lódz at a moment "before" the Shoah.

A 1937 street photograph of Ettinger's parents from the Polish city of Lódz has become an obsessive image that recurs throughout her visual work in many iterations (figure 8.2). In the image, her young parents are walking smilingly and energetically down a street in their town, exuding comfort and safety. They are happy to look and be looked at, to display and perform their sense of belonging in this city and its urban spaces. In a label on her Web site, the artist informs viewers that, unlike her parents, the friend walking on the street with them was later killed by the Nazis. The image of her young parents taken before her own birth appears in Ettinger's *Mamalangue* superimposed onto another image, a washed-out photograph of her own childhood face (figure 8.1).

The child's smile is covered, almost erased, by the mother's smiling figure. The pre-war stroll through the city, the couple walking toward a

8.2 Street photo, Lódz, 1937. *Courtesy of Bracha Lichtenberg-Ettinger*

future they could not yet imagine, bleeds into the face of the child who grew up in a distant place, dominated by stories and histories that preceded her birth. Here, in overlay fashion, are the past and the present, two worlds that the postwar child longs to bridge: the world her parents once knew—where the Holocaust had not yet happened—and her own world, "after Auschwitz." In projecting her own face onto and into the spaces of the past, Ettinger absorbs some of the embodied practices of that past moment, enacting a kind of return journey in photographic mode. This journey is characterized by structures of superimposition and overlay similar to those in Brett's and Kanafani's fictions. Past and present coexist in layered fashion, and their interaction is dominated by objects that provoke deep body memory and the affects it triggers.

Thus, in Ettinger's composite images, the Lódz street photo of her parents, and the image of her childhood face, are often juxtaposed, overlaid, or blended with yet a third image—a disturbing, well-known photograph of a group of naked Jewish women, some holding children, herded to their execution by Einsatzgruppen in Poland. This image, no doubt taken by one of the Nazi photographers who accompanied the Einsatzgruppen and thus structured by the perpetrator gaze, serves as the basis for Ettinger's Eurydice series.[22] This is not a space to which one would want to return; it is the antithesis of "home."

For her artwork, Ettinger made reproductions of various details of the Einsatzgruppen photo, which she then ran through a photocopier, enlarged, cut into strips, mounted on walls, and tinted with India ink and purple paint to a point where all details are washed out or made virtually invisible (figures 8.3 and 8.4). The juxtapositions of the Lódz and Einsatzgruppen photos—one taken by a prewar street photographer, a fellow citizen, the other snapped and shaped by the annihilating Nazi gaze conflating the camera with the gun—illustrate the child's deep fear of parental impotence in a time of extremity that dominates all the texts under discussion. They illustrate the underside of return, the fear that violence will be repeated, that, as in Eurydice's backward look, return will prove to be deadly. As objects coming out of the past, the layered images contain and activate those fears, and Ettinger mobilizes them in

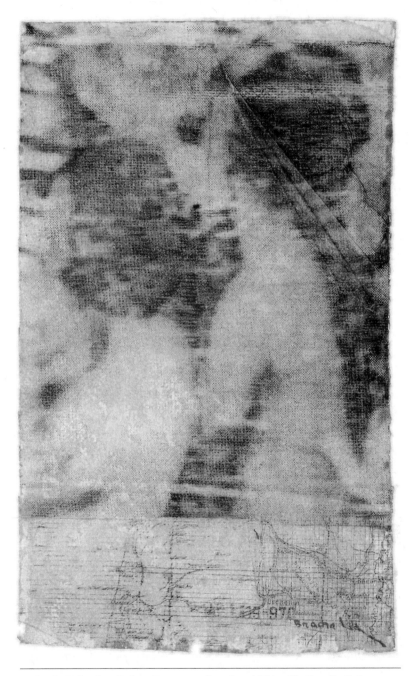

8.3 Bracha Lichtenberg-Ettinger, image no. 2 from the exhibition *The Eurydice Series*.
Courtesy of Bracha Lichtenberg-Ettinger

her superimpositions, revealing the shadow archives that haunt domestic images and objects from before.

The women walking toward their death, holding their babies, suffer the ultimate failure of parental care: they cannot protect their children, or themselves, from annihilation. They are witnesses and victims of the ultimate breach of a social contract in which adults are supposed to protect infants, rather than murder them. In these composite images, the artist, as child, becomes the surrogate of the dead baby; the infant held by the mother in the picture becomes, by implication, her own phantom sibling or her fragile child self—the emblem of the unconscious nightmares plaguing the postgeneration.

In the Eurydice images, the photos from "before" cannot be separated from the photos taken "during" and "after" the destruction. As a child born after the war—a child who might easily never have been born at all had her parents' fates taken a slightly different turn—Ettinger is unable to return to the spaces from "before" without the superimposed, layered, screen image of the atrocity "during." The prewar photo from the family album—from the seemingly protected intimate and embodied space of the family and its repertoires—cannot be insulated from the collective, anonymous images in the killing fields, and the child born after the war is inevitably haunted by the phantom sibling. The two kinds of images, and the three temporalities, are inextricably linked. In this way, Ettinger's juxtapositions forge a powerful anti-nostalgic idiom for the postmemorial subject. Return, even metaphoric return, cannot jump over the breach of expulsion, expropriation, and murder.

In foregrounding and recasting Eurydice into the maternal figure who lost her child, Ettinger, moreover, is reframing the father/son and father/daughter perspectives presented in Kanafani's and Brett's fictional works. Ettinger's Eurydice is the maternal figure who returns from Hades having witnessed the loss of her child. In her powerful reading of the Eurydice series, Griselda Pollock sees Eurydice as the woman precariously alive "between two deaths"[23]: for the women in the ravine, this is the brief moment between being shot by the camera and by the gun. Eurydice's story is no doubt the prototypical narrative of impossible return. For Pollock, however, Ettinger, the daughter artist, is reframing the Orphic gaze of no return, in favor of an aesthetic of what Ettinger calls "wit(h)ness" and "co-affectivity."[24] In subjecting her original images to technologies of mechanical reproduction, in degrading, recycling, reproducing, and painting over them, Ettinger underscores the distance and anonymity of the camera gaze. But, at the same time, she allows all of these images to invade, inhabit, and haunt her, and she therefore inscribes them with her own very invested act of looking, exposing, in the images, her own desires, fears, and nightmares. In Pollock's reading, the purple paint is a physical touch that marks the images with "the color of grief."[25]

But more still is at stake in a few of the images from this series that include yet one more level of superimposition.

The grid visible in some of the images (figures 8.3 and 8.5) is of a First World War map of Palestine, and of aerial views of Palestinian spaces taken by German warplanes during the First World War when Palestine was occupied by the British. Ettinger, born in Israel after the Second World War, has inherited other traces of loss—traces of Palestinian spaces that she maps onto the spaces of Polish streets before the war.

These competing spaces and temporalities become part of a multi-layered psychic grid, unconsciously transmitted, merging geography and history, and challenging any clear chronology or topography of return. The views are aerial shots taken by military airplanes. In including them in her own family image, Ettinger dramatizes, in a closer and more intimate manner, the irreconcilable stakes of memory and return. The spectral unconscious optics that emerge in her composite images blend the spaces of the individual journey of return with a larger global awareness of contested space and competing geopolitical interests.[26] Hers is an enlarged map that incorporates the losses of the Shoah into a broader intertwined psychology and geography of irrecoverable loss. The illegibility of her works, moreover, and the multiple generations they have undergone in the process of copying and reproduction, signal the loss of materiality of the objects and images, as well as the multiple expulsions they survived in faded, and sometimes unrecognizable, form.

8.4 Bracha Lichtenberg-Ettinger, image no. 5 from the exhibition *The Eurydice Series*. *Courtesy of Bracha Lichtenberg-Ettinger*

8.5 Bracha Lichtenberg-Ettinger, image no. 37 from the exhibition *The Eurydice Series*.
Courtesy of Bracha Lichtenberg-Ettinger

SEQUELLAE

Ettinger's layered compositions use the image of the fractured family and the lost or murdered child in the service of a political reading in which the structure of surrogation produces a layered memory that can recall and call attention to multiple losses across unbridgeable divides. The figure of the lost child and the textual implausibilities it engenders complicate and subvert the temporal and emotional trajectories of return narratives. A spectral figure that cannot be neatly integrated into the plot, it haunts the return story sprouting into series, subplots, projections, overlays, and sequels.

Just as the return plot of *Too Many Men* is punctured by the voice and implausible subplot of Rudolf Hoess, the primary plot of *Return to Haifa* is also interrupted by a long subplot. Said S. tells Safiya about a neighbor, Faris al Labda, who went back to his old home in Jaffa to find the picture of his martyred brother Badr still hanging in the house they had left. The picture inspires the brother who finds it and the Israeli Arab family who has been living in the house to take up arms for Palestine.

Both texts have also sprouted sequels. Brett's sequel to *Too Many Men*, the 2006 *You've Gotta Have Balls*, renamed *Uncomfortably Close* in the paperback edition, takes Ruth and her father back to New York. Kanafani, killed in an Israeli reprisal raid in 1972, could not, of course, write a sequel to *Return to Haifa*, but several adaptations and sequels have appeared in Israel, producing overlay reinterpretations of the original. These Israeli rewritings and stage adaptations use Kanafani's text in the service of fantasies of peace and reconciliation, covering over the breaches and angers that shape the original. Most notable is Iraqi-Israeli novelist Sami Michael's 2005 novel *Doves in Trafalgar*—a work that did not initially acknowledge its debt to Kanafani and that features the two mothers in the narrative. Michael's novel ends with the son Zeev's dream of "a federation between two nations . . . with two flags and one common currency."[27] The 2008 theater production of *Return to Haifa* by Boaz Gaon staged on the occasion of Israel's 60th anniversary in Tel Aviv, and more recently in Washington, D.C., "wanted to offer an opening for something else to happen."[28] Gaon claims to find in the novella "a moment of grace where perhaps they could become one family."[29]

In contrast to these recent rewritings, I have read return stories precisely for the breaks and incongruities that foreclose reconciliation. Ettinger's series conform to this structure of irresolution. The Eurydice series returns to the same images and the same themes obsessively, again and again. But this is not an art of endless melancholy and perpetual return. I prefer to see the different images in the series, the recurring dreams and nightmares, the multiple plots and subplots in the novels, as versions, or approximations—drafts of a narrative in process, subject to re-vision. It is an open-ended narrative that embraces the need for return and for repair, even as it accepts its implausibility.

And I Still See Their Faces
Images of Polish Jews

FUNDACJA SHALOM

Fotografia Żydów polskich

I ciągle widzę ich twarze

9.1 Book cover. *From Golda Tencer and Anna Bikont, eds.,* And I Still See Their Faces: Images of Polish Jews *(Warsaw: Shalom Foundation, 1998)*

9

POSTMEMORY'S ARCHIVAL TURN

I am the wrong generation to let it go.

—Edmund de Waal, *The Hare with Amber Eyes*

In 2004, the art historian Hal Foster famously identified an "archival impulse" at work internationally in contemporary art practices.[1] Archival artists, Foster writes, aim to critique the archive, understood in Michel Foucault's terms as the set of hegemonic rules that determine how a culture selects, orders, and preserves the past. Connecting various randomly found decontextualized images and objects to one another, artists construct installations that function as private counter-archives that emerge from daily life or popular culture. Foster discusses artists like Tacita Dean, Thomas Hirschhorn, and Sam Durant in relation to precursors like Gerhard Richter, Robert Rauschenberg, and Richard Prince, and even pre–Second World War artists like John Heartfield, Kurt Schwitters, and Alexander Rodchenko. Their "will to connect what cannot be connected,"[2] Foster argues, responds to feelings of radical disconnection characterizing postmodernity. Foster finds that the arbitrary private archives these artists assemble have both utopian and paranoid dimensions, and he speculates that both "emerge out of a similar sense of failure in cultural memory."[3] This dissatisfaction leads artists to envision alternative pasts or futures, proposing "new orders of affective association" characterized either by fantasy and hope or by fear and disillusionment.[4]

In this chapter, I follow a related archival impulse characteristic of the aesthetic and ethical practices of postmemory, practices that situate themselves in the specific aftermath of historical catastrophe. Unlike the work Foster discusses, however, the aftermath projects I discuss have, in the last two decades, aimed to reclaim historical specificity and context, rather than jettisoning these in a familiar postmodern move. In a consciously reparative move, they assemble collections that function as correctives and additions, rather than counters, to the historical archive, attempting to undo the ruptures caused by war and genocide.

During the period of the 1990s that Foster follows, a period of intense political as well as technological changes, the material qualities of the images and objects that are thus obsessively collected and reassembled come into sharp relief with ever-greater ease of digitization and Web-based dissemination. I am interested in the postmemorial archival practices that emerge from this moment and that, in their particular forms of *assembling, arranging,* and *display,* have taken the form of *albums* that exhibit and underscore some of these material qualities.[5] The album as a medium has been fundamental to the ways in which the events of the Holocaust and of other twentieth-century historical catastrophes have come down to us. But what transformations does the album undergo in the age of digital archival domiciliation and consignation?[6] And what postmemorial practices, what alternate histories, are enabled by the tremendous capacities offered by the World Wide Web as an archival space?

The devastation of the Holocaust immediately spurred the urge not just to document the destruction, but to collect and reassemble any possible aspect of the world that was lost. Archival projects continue to abound to this day, assembling and cataloging documents, images, objects, and individual and group testimonies in traditional and new libraries, archives, and museums sponsored by state and private institutions. Within and against these archives, albums have played a significant role. We need only think of the prominence granted to Nazi albums like the notorious "Stroop Report" discussed in chapter 5, the *Auschwitz*

Album, the various ghetto albums assembled by Wehrmacht soldiers and Nazi officials, the albums of individual soldiers from the Eastern Front that were so widely used in the Wehrmacht exhibition, and the recently discovered group album of the Nazi leadership in Auschwitz, to name only a few. Equally significant are the numerous albums collected, arranged, and disseminated in various media in the aftermath by survivors and descendants, by historians and archivists eager not so much to account for the destruction as to remember and to reanimate the lives of those who were murdered. Important examples include Serge Klarsfeld's *French Children of the Holocaust*, albums like *The Children of Izieu*, *Image Before My Eyes*, Yaffa Eliach's *Tower of Faces*, and a project by the Polish stage actress Golda Tencer, *And I Still See Their Faces: Images of Polish Jews* (figure 9.1).

In this chapter, I analyze the archival impulses of postmemory by way of a close look at two representative projects dedicated to commemorating victims of genocidal destruction in two very different historical contexts. Both of these, *And I Still See Their Faces: Images of Polish Jews*, by Tencer, and *Kurdistan: In the Shadow of History* (figure 9.2), by the American photojournalist and artist Susan Meiselas, date from the early 1990s. Both projects have assembled large collections of images and stories on behalf of lost communities of Polish Jews and of Kurds, and both collections have been published as books, traveled as exhibitions, and been installed as active Web sites by their creators. In arranging their archives in the form of albums, these projects have invented similar forms through which to tell and to disseminate alternative histories. Margaret Olin suggests, "Any gathering of photographs is a community. The handling of photographs always took part in imagining a nation, especially a diaspora."[7] It is in this spirit that these artists assume the work of collectors, archivists, and curators, revealing the archive as a site of creative artistic production rather than mere reproduction.

Tencer and Meiselas engage in critical as well as reparative memorial and postmemorial practices for two different vulnerable diasporic communities. In placing *And I Still See Their Faces* and *Kurdistan* alongside each other, however, I certainly do not wish to compare the massive human and cultural losses that spawned them. Thinking them in relation is a form of connective memory work that, unlike the installations Foster discusses, attempts to connect disparate histories with the aim not of blurring their specificities, but of discovering shared aesthetic and political strategies, affects and effects—elements of what we might think of as a global space of remembrance with intersecting histories. At the same time, each of these projects itself engages in connective memorial and political strategies that expose unexpected submerged local histories.

What is more, the shift to the digital links and relates all content, however disparate, along the multiple interconnected pathways of the Internet. A reflection on the practices of comparative and connective memory work and the qualities and textures it assumes in the digital becomes even more vital.[8]

TWO ALBUMS

"I am an actress of the Polish theater. I was born after the War," writes Golda Tencer in the preface to *And I Still See Their Faces*.[9] In 1994, Tencer and the Shalom Foundation she founded in Warsaw sent a widespread appeal to her Polish compatriots and to émigrés and refugees abroad to help save the memory of the extinguished world of Polish Jews. Photographs, she correctly surmised, are ubiquitous objects of gift, souvenir, and exchange, and she imagined that many had survived their subjects in the albums, drawers, and attics of the neighbors, classmates, friends, coworkers, and rescuers of Polish Jews or of their relatives living abroad. "From all over Poland, the smallest villages and towns, as well as from abroad: Israel, Canada, Italy, USA, Argentina, these gifts of the heart" flowed in, she writes.[10] And each image was accompanied by a story: "I am in possession of a photograph of a woman of Jewish nationality with a small child. They both fled from the ghetto in Lowicz, she stayed for the night with us and she left me this photograph" (6). "When we looked through my wife's family album, we found a picture of a Jewish family pasted there. After we removed it, on

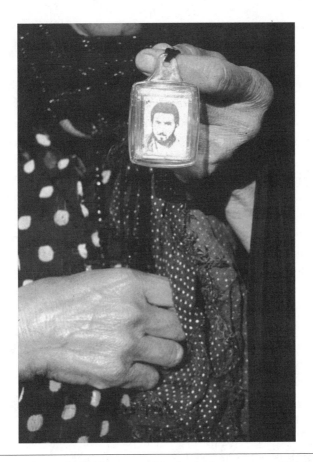

9.2 Susan Meiselas, Mother holding a memorial to her dead son, cemetery of Sulaimania, Iraq, 1992; installation image from *Kurdistan: In the Shadow of History. Courtesy of Susan Meiselas/Magnum*

the reverse, we found a note with the year 1914" (10). "Her name was Taube, or Tauber, or may be Tauberg. I remember the name from stories told by my mother. Regina was a very good friend from a home-tailoring or a lace-making course. She had seven children" (19).

An internationally known photojournalist working with the Magnum photographic agency, Susan Meiselas decided to document the aftermath of the Gulf War and the 1988 Anfal campaign across Kurdish villages in northern Iraq in which Saddam Hussein authorized the use of poison gas. Having read about the flight of the Kurds from the regions under attack in 1991, she joined the Middle East Watch team of Human Rights Watch and worked with forensic anthropologists to construct an unassailable accusation of genocide. She photographed mass graves, mourning relatives, decimated villages, fragments of clothing and household items. Soon, however, Meiselas said in an interview, "I began to notice people holding on to photographs of the disappeared. They were wearing the photographs."[11] People showed her the photos they had in their possession as a way of telling her their history. And Meiselas became obsessed. Struck by the power of photos to perform memory, Meiselas began collecting photographs rather than merely taking them. She took photos of people's photos, and she tried to gather the stories around them: who took them, who was depicted in them, why they were taken and saved. Working before the arrival of digital technology, Meiselas took along a Polaroid camera that processed positive/negative film, and thus she was able to reproduce the originals rather than taking them away with her. The positive prints enabled people to see what they were contributing, and the prints thus became a "public reference set."[12] "I traveled around with a suitcase, collecting everything I could find."[13] And, though not biographically or culturally connected to Kurdish communities, she understood the vulnerability of people who, until recently, had the status only of a threatened minority in several nation states. Thus she took on the construction of what one participant called "our collective family album."[14] "An accessible repository of Kurdish images," Meiselas realized, "is impossible anywhere in the Middle East. It is no accident that the Kurds do not have a national archive."[15]

In enlarging and supplementing a limited cultural and historical archive with intimate, personal, and familial documents, both Tencer and Meiselas aim to reclaim lost worlds, but with a critical distance. Albums tend to be created at times of transition; they mark stages, high points in a lifetime. Weddings, graduations, significant birthdays are moments that merit the collection of materials and the backward-looking glance of the album. As communal albums, the two postmemorial projects under discussion mark urgent moments of historical transition, not only for individuals and families, but also for groups and communities. Thus they attempt to reconstruct, through photographs and through stories, violently destroyed worlds and communities whose very records were targeted for erasure, and whose survivors are dispersed throughout the world. Clearly, albums dedicated to them also have to reflect these ruptures and erasures, as well as acts of resistance and the will to cultural survival.

In this fashion, Tencer and Meiselas personalize the archive, presenting collected materials in open-ended, hybrid, and multiply interconnected fashion. At the same time, they also extend and transform key functions of the album by politicizing it. The traditional album, particularly the family photo album, though fragmented, multiple, and porous, still tends to support dominant familial and communal ideologies instead of questioning them. Tencer and Meiselas do the opposite—they shift accepted views and hegemonic narratives and are able to open up previously unseen, unexpected or suppressed stories and memories. In addition to reassembling objects from a lost world, both these projects also reflect on them as media of history, calling attention to the fragile materiality of the collected images and texts, as well as to their existence and survival—to their personal, social, and political roles and effects in space and over time. And they enable us to reflect on the shifts in media, from the analog to the digital, and on the possibilities and limitations, the gains and losses, involved in the radical technological transformations that have challenged the album form itself.

TELLING HISTORY THROUGH PHOTOS

"Can you tell history through photos?" Susan Meiselas has asked.[16] Albums indeed create the space for historical narratives. Physical family albums tend to reflect the moment of their construction. They are time-bound documents that tell a particular story about the family, one that is handed down from generation to generation. Often they are assembled and annotated by one family member who imposes his or her vision on the album's contents. Of course, the narrative within the album can change, and albums are sometimes reshaped to reflect broken marriages, family deaths, moves, and displacements. They can be arranged

9.3 Image 304, Deborah Goldstein-Rosen. *From Golda Tencer and Anna Bikont, eds.*, And I Still See Their Faces: Images of Polish Jews *(Warsaw: Shalom Foundation, 1998)*

chronologically, thematically, by the size of the image, by family member, or even randomly, but the arrangement always reflects a process of selection and classification. Mostly, their contents are finite and their narrative and organization in some sense coherent and at least provisionally complete.

Golda Tencer explicitly introduces *And I Still See Their Faces* as an "album," and, indeed, it conforms to the qualities of the genre. Consisting of six sections, it is organized thematically and generically by type of photo. Numerous photographic genres are represented: studio portraits of families and individuals, and of children; street photographs and images of houses and shops; school and youth group pictures; pictures of demonstrations, of army units, of town officials and charity organizations, of weddings and wedding anniversary celebrations in urban and village settings. There are also some landscape pictures, such as a rare color image of the Warsaw ghetto in flames. And, in the album's last section, entitled "For Everyone to See," there are wartime images from various ghettos and camps, including Auschwitz. Here many of the pictures' very existence and survival are utterly improbable. Zahava Bromberg, for example, writes about a small, triangular, almost illegible portrait of her mother (figure 9.3): "I carried this photograph of my mama through two selections by Dr. Mengele at Auschwitz. Once, I held it in my mouth, the second time, I taped it with a bandage to the bottom of my foot. I was 14 years old."[17]

Although a number of pictures stand out for their aesthetic qualities, most are conventional and generic. It is the text that accompanies them, in the form of either a label or an adjacent block of type that distinguishes these pictures from similar ones of the same historical period. The touching, often devastating stories contained in the text underscore the retrospective irony of photographs that survive lives that were violently cut short. As Tencer writes: "Those in the photographs do not know yet that soon their houses will be deserted, the streets of their towns covered with the black snow of fluff from slit eiderdowns. . . . All that will remain after them, when the biblical names have left in cattle cars—could be put in a drawer, hidden in the attic, buried in junk."[18] As an album, *And I Still See Their Faces* is structured by this ironic retrospection—Barthes's punctum of time, the discrepancy between what the viewer knows and what the subject of the photograph cannot yet have known.[19] Since most of these photographs emerge from prewar domestic and institutional settings, the album's gaze, one the viewer is invited to share, is an elegiac and nostalgic one, mourning a destroyed world. But it also engages the viewer in the archival impulse—both the obsessive practice of collecting and multiplying and the more contemplative urge to peer inside the images and find out more about the particular life stories they indexically call forth. And as some of these stories of survival unfold, in however fragmentary fashion, they provide surprising correctives to received histories. Unexpectedly, in many of the cases, Poles emerge as rescuers and witnesses, holders of Jewish memory.

Like Tencer, Susan Meiselas also becomes immersed in a passionate practice of archival collecting, attempting to assemble and identify everything she can find relating to the lost Kurdish history she works to recuperate. At the same time, she is deeply engaged in current struggles for forms of reparative justice and looks to a future of Kurdish survival. Indeed, the *Kurdistan* project is itself part of a juridical claim on behalf of the Kurdish community. In order to undertake it, however, Meiselas had to assemble images and fragments from a great variety of archives and sources.

As a traveler among Kurds, Meiselas began to think about other travelers like herself who had taken images of Kurds away with them, and she started to look for those photographic records in various archives in the West. The search was difficult, since terms like "Kurd" or "Kurdistan" tended not to be part of the acquisition or catalog information. Instead, photos of Kurds most often appear under a number of different archival categories—national origin, ethnic type, or the name of the photographer who took the picture. Meiselas had to accept that "most of the images and written artifacts about the Kurds that survive, survive in the West," and thus she sees her project to "re-create the Kurds' encounter with the West" as one of the only ways to reconstruct a history that many Kurds now living in Turkey, or Iraq, or the former Soviet Union do not themselves know and that was most appropriate for her, as a foreigner, to make.[20]

The history Meiselas relates through photographs and stories is a fragmentary one. As a book, *Kurdistan* feels more like a composite historical text and visual history beginning with the earliest photographic records than like a family and communal album. Its organization is sweepingly chronological, creating parallel narratives of the different regional Kurdish communities. It includes several introductory historical essays (translated at the end of the volume into Turkish and Sorani) as well as numerous documents and facsimiles. Early chapters consist primarily of images and documents from colonial archives and the albums of Western travelers, anthropologists, missionaries, journalists, and diplomats. But, where possible, they also include pictures from local studios and private family albums (figure 9.4). Later chapters feature more informal group photos from Kurdish communities, as well as images taken by journalists and photographers covering Kurdish official histories in Turkey, Iraq, Russia, and Yerevan and donated by families when they saw the images Meiselas had repatriated from the West. The end of *Kurdistan* is devoted to pictures taken by photojournalists in the aftermath of the chemical attacks against the Kurds by Saddam Hussein's regime, images of wounded bodies, exhumations, mourning, but also of legal depositions, protests, and other acts of resistance. As Margaret Olin has written, "The book is a sustained testament to the power of photographs to create national history."[21]

9.4 Saring Mahmoud with his family, undated. *Courtesy of Akim Saringovich Farizian*
Courtesy of Susan Meiselas

THE LIMITS OF THE ALBUM

One of the most distinctive aspects of the traditional album is its materiality and its tactility. Albums are usually larger in format than books; they often have special paper, transparent protective sheets, photo corners, or other means of affixing images and text. The two albums under discussion here, collecting copies of copies, often digitized ones, in mediated fashion, have certainly lost many of these material qualities.

And I Still See Their Faces is oversized in format, like a large photo album. Its paper is glossy, and the images and blocks of text are carefully laid out on its pages. Reading it and looking at it, turning the pages, conforms to the experience of leafing through a photo album. We take the time to view a particularly striking image; we skip over another. On some pages, the text dominates; others are entirely composed of black-and-white or sepia-colored photographs.

Surprisingly, the collection seems to vary remarkably little between its book and exhibit and even its Web-based forms. Certainly a gallery exhibit elicits a different embodied trajectory and a different confrontation with images that are blown up to large size. Shuttling back and forth between reading the labels on the walls and looking at the images is not the same as turning the pages of an album or a book. But, in this case, the exhibition and the book have similar linear organizational structures and suggest similar trajectories in which the images remain distant, opaque and unapproachable. It is thanks only to the accompanying stories of how they circulated and survived and how they were collected that they are brought into the present.

In recent years, however, these archival images of Polish Jews have acquired a renewed material life on the streets of today's Warsaw, where they have become elements of the urban landscape (figure 9.5). They

9.5 Isaac Bashevis Singer festival, Warsaw Cemetery. *Courtesy of the photographer Barbara Kirshenblatt-Gimblett*

are regularly used by Golda Tencer herself as part of an open-air stage set in Warsaw for the annual Isaac Bashevis Singer festival staged by the Yiddish theater she runs. Even after the close of the festival the photos remain up, like a set that has not been struck, as haunting reminders of destroyed lives, in the very urban spaces from which many of their subjects were dispersed or deported or where they were murdered. These pictures have also been integrated into impromptu memorials and shrines at the Warsaw Jewish cemetery, acquiring there a different depth, dimensionality, and social function than a book or gallery installation would allow.

Kurdistan has also been part of a number of exhibitions, and Meiselas has been pointedly interested in finding ways to acknowledge the materiality and the social role of the images and objects she has collected, and to make palpable the "sense of time at work on what survives" by alternating warm and cool pages in the book, and reproducing edges, scratches, and broken glass plates (figure 9.6).[22] "I emphasize the photograph as object, as artifact, once held, now torn and stained,"

9.6 Susan Meiselas, installation image from *Kurdistan: In the Shadow of History. Courtesy of Susan Meiselas*

she writes.[23] Displaying original, sometimes torn and charred images and objects in glass cases and on walls, the *Kurdistan* exhibits bring this materiality back. Pictures of people holding or wearing photos of themselves or family members, including pictures of their hands, underscore the tactility of the collected objects and elicit the haptic desires of the visitors. These displays exceed the representational qualities of the images in favor of their testimonial and social value: as testimonial objects they become documents of everyday life, bearing witness to acts of embodied communal exchange in which they played a significant material role. They can hint at the qualities of familial and communal lives, and they testify as well to the cultural encounters that have produced and preserved some of them: encounters with colonizers, missionaries, journalists, and anthropologists, and with archivists and collectors like Meiselas.

Exhibits are fleeting events, however, and if *Kurdistan*, like *And I Still See Their Faces*, will continue to have a life, it will be on the World Wide Web. The Web offers expanded archival capabilities of domiciliation, consignment, and display. Unlike *Aka Kurdistan*, however, the *And I Still See Their Faces* Web site maintains the linear progression of the book and does not make any attempt to use the multiple possibilities offered by the Internet by introducing additional links or alternate trajectories.[24] In contrast, spurred as an Internet site by the publication of the book in 1997, *Aka Kurdistan* is a dynamic network consisting of a series of chronologically, spatially, and linguistically interconnected and linked digital pathways that convey a tremendous amount of cultural and historical information.[25] Mobilizing the capabilities of the Web as a collective repository of images and texts deriving from official and personal archives, it is indeed, as its subtitle indicates, a "place for collective memory and cultural exchange." *Aka Kurdistan* includes several different entry points inviting Web users to explore a recent story and to follow a map and timeline to find photographs and stories from Kurds and Westerners about Kurdistan's history and culture; to identify unidentified images and submit images for identification by others; and to add stories and images. Submissions initially by Kurdish communities in the diaspora and by archivists who had access to lesser-known collections, and later by individuals, researchers, and scholars, can be made digitally, and thus the collection continues to grow and to change. Still, as a Web 1.0 archive, it is curated by one webmaster, Susan Meiselas herself, and it is she who ultimately selects materials to be included. But, Meiselas explains,

> It was an open submission process, most often a picture sent first, then followed with email exchanges to contextualize it with a story. The contributor was then asked to identify the preferred "prototype format" for their story and approved the design and edit, as well as placement, geographically and within the timeline. Email however is not the same as sitting in someone's backyard talking; we found it a tedious, slow process.[26]

The submitted images and stories that emerge from Kurdish sources enhance the personal and familial dimensions of the project. "I was born in 1979 in Iran close to the Iraqi border," Bakhtiar tells us through an interviewer who submitted Bakhtiar's images to the Web site, for example. "Because my father was politically active, we had to flee. This was the first of the 28 moves I've been through." Bakhtiar's, like most other submissions to *Aka Kurdistan*, is arranged like an album page, with images, labels, descriptive text. On the bottom of each page, the timeline continues horizontally, moving through more than a century from before 1900 to 2000 and beyond. Individual stories are thus inserted into a linear history that anchors them in space and time.

What is gained and what is lost as the material album, or the exhibition, becomes a digital site? On the one hand, the ease with which information can be disseminated, accessed, and replicated on the Web and the ever-expanding content of any particular digital archive provide the possibility of reaching a greater audience around the world than do the analog sources from which digital sites derive. The Web allows any archival project to greatly surpass private, familial, or public albums or collections in amount of content and number of potential viewers and users. And yet digital materials, often compressed, enlarged, or cropped, lack the smells, scale, and tactile materiality not only of the "actual," but also of the analog "originals" from which most of them were generated in the process of digitization and dissemination. They are neither testimonial objects *from the past* like their analog sources, nor do they carry traces of human touch from the time between the analog's production and the moment of digitization. What is more, they largely miss the *context* in which the analog originals were first collected and displayed in family albums and in private and communal archives. In Svetlana Boym's terms, scanned or digital materials lose the "patina of history, and everything has the same digital texture."[27] They lose even the idea of "generations" of copy or reproduction.

With the move to Web 2.0, moreover, interactivity increases, and users are able to transform the sites to which they can contribute without curatorial control. Creators and collectors relinquish more and more agency. I would say that this constitutes a move beyond the album to other media of social networking and different technologies of collection, arrangement, and display. On the one hand, this increased participation, already announced in the requests for images and identifications on *Aka Kurdistan,* draws visitors into the site in a form of communal engagement that does more than merely to contribute *content*. It fosters a sense of community and a stake in history through a material embodied participation in the form of clicking, scanning, uploading, and typing, through the acts of research, identification, and storytelling and the forms of sociality and responsibility these foster. But, the openness of the Internet introduces possibilities of interaction that are a lot less benign. *Aka Kurdistan*, for example, was the victim of aggressive hacking by Turkish nationalists who protested the very existence of Kurds, and who actually destroyed files and parts of the site, "leaving their own visual signature of domination."[28]

But what do these changes mean for the historical mission of postmemorial archives? How is affect elicited and transmitted in the digital? Anthropologist Elizabeth Edwards has said that, in *Kurdistan*, "photographs present not only access to a historical reality, but to an affective 'historical poetics.' "[29] The line between the material and the virtual is dissolving as each of these albums and collections continues to assume different forms in different and, I would argue, mutually reinforcing media that enable, for better or worse, archival practices with ever greater openness and participation. And thus the images and objects themselves circulate and continue to "develop" in what Jeff Wall has termed "liquid time," immersed, as they are, in what he calls the "incalculable."[30] At the same time, as photographs, they are also "dry," as a result of the optical photographic apparatus associated with modern vision and its evidentiary power.[31] One image—yet another mother/child image, echoing the others discussed throughout these pages—can illustrate this duality.

ALTERNATIVE HISTORIES AND COUNTER-MEMORIES

Image 124 of *And I Still See Their Faces* shows a smiling young woman, crouching down to hold up a small, well-dressed baby who looks off to the side with a half-smile (figure 9.7). It's a conventional image, taken outdoors in summer: the woman is wearing a summer dress and sandals. Like all the surrounding pictures of family groups with children, this one is poignant and moving—a mother and child looking toward life but facing the imminent genocidal destruction of their entire community. The accompanying narrative is long and striking. It does more than to identify the two subjects of the image as "Cypora Zonshtajn (née Jablon) and her daughter Rachela, born in Sieldce in September of 1941." It tells an elaborate story of rescue and enduring friendship and care, with many specific details of names and dates. And it tells it in the first person of Zofia Olzakowska Glazerowa from Warsaw, who donated the photo. Parts of the story are familiar—the formation of the Sieldce ghetto in 1942, the deportation of the Jews to Treblinka, Cypora's handing over of her child to a non-Jewish friend Sabina Zawadzka. In her brief text, Zofia writes how she took Rachela from Sabina to her sister's, where she was raised with her young nephew; how Rachela, after the war, was taken to her uncle in Israel and raised in a kibbutz. Zofia does not explain her relationship to Cypora, nor does she say what happened to the young woman in the photo. The photo raises many more questions than the brief box of text is able to answer: how did these Jews come by film, and how were they able to get their pictures developed in the deadly summer of 1942, for one? And what happened to Cypora?

9.7 Image 124, Cypora and Rachela. *From Golda Tencer and Anna Bikont, eds.,* And I Still See Their Faces: Images of Polish Jews *(Warsaw: Shalom Foundation, 1998)*

I managed to find out more about this picture from a colleague, Judith Greenberg, a cousin of Cypora and Rachela's in the United States who is currently writing a book about them. Cypora, it turns out, took her own life rather than be deported. Her husband was in the Jewish police, a fact that may offer the explanation for the possibility of taking and developing photographs during this time. Cypora left her young daughter with her school friends Sabina and Zofia, who rescued her and continued to care for her throughout her life. Cypora gave a brief diary and three pho-

tos to a compatriot who ended up jumping from a train and who brought
these objects to Zofia. The back of each of the photos, dating from the
same day as this one, carries a hand-written message addressed to the
baby daughter: "This is your mother who could not raise you," she
wrote on the back of one of them. "I wish you would never feel that I
am not with you and that you will not feel abandoned by me. I wish
that life brings you happiness as you are on your own and for you to be
proud of yourself. That is what I wish for you. Your poor mother."

When Judith Greenberg recently visited Zofia Glazerowa in Warsaw,
she found numerous additional photographs of Cypora in Zofia's
albums—school photos, photos of outings, of birthday and garden
parties. As girls they were tied by a strong friendship. As adults, Zofia
and their other non-Jewish girlfriends became the collective caretakers
of Cypora's child. In the assimilated Jewish community in which Cypora lived, such deep friendships and expanded communities were common. Each of the photos in each of these albums carries such a story,
but the brief labels in the books and exhibits cannot begin to give a
sense of the layers of loss and interrelation that enabled the images to
be included in the collection.

In *And I Still See Their Faces*, Poles become the holders of Jewish
memory. Tencer tells an unexpected story of contact and interaction.
The "I" in the title is Polish, not Jewish; the "their" refers to the Jews.
As the collector, Tencer can inhabit both of these positions. The "still"
indicates the continuity of memory. Donors, Tencer lets us know, relinquish their photos with affection and attention, eager to honor the
memory of their neighbors, schoolmates, or co-workers, and to memorialize these relationships. "This album," Golda Tencer writes,

> has been created by people who kept these photographs during the
> time of the war and then for half a century longer, waiting for some-
> one to collect them. They adopted them, accepted them in their
> families. "I am sending you two photographs of Jews, father's
> friends. Mother was hiding them during the occupation, and after
> the war she pasted them into the album. I am sure you will take good
> care of them. Sorry for the delay, but I had to talk to them a little so
> that I could part with them warmly and without sorrow."[32]

Like Zofia, most of those who donated pictures must have others in their collections, waiting for appropriate repositories to which to donate them, though soon, with subsequent generations, the memorial links identifying these images and objects will certainly be lost. And along with every image we do have, we must imagine thousands of others that were lost or destroyed.

Through Tencer's activist mediation, we find a counter-history to the traditional understanding of Polish collaboration, of pogroms perpetrated by neighbors that continued after the war, and of contemporary anti-Semitism.[33] This album does not deny that history, but it supplements it with evidence of neighbors and friends who act as keepers of each other's memories.

Meiselas, like Tencer, faces images of death and violent destruction, and she nevertheless finds affirmative moments of life. Shifting a received historical narrative is an element of a practice of repair. The story Meiselas tells is also one of contact and interaction. The available archives on Kurdish history are both in Kurdish villages and in the West. One *can* tell the history of the colonized through the archives of the colonizer, native history through the archives of archaeologists and explorers, *Kurdistan* suggests. And as one tells that history, deepening it by inviting the involvement of contemporary viewers, in new media and older ones, one becomes implicated in the relationships that shape the past and are transmitted into the present and the future. At their best, new media can rebuild some of the communal contexts from which these images were abstracted and resituate individuals within their lost communities, if only in virtual space. Interactive sites like *Aka Kurdistan* actively invite such deepening and individualization.

As collective communal projects, *And I Still See Their Faces* and *Kurdistan* enable us to look at structures of affiliation and transmission that exceed the family, even as they highlight, and are able to critique, the enduring power of familial tropes. In addition, Tencer and Meiselas engage not only extrafamilial but also intergroup and transnational structures of contact and attachment, revealing the work of postmemorial practices in vastly different historical contexts. The idea and practice of placing stories, individuals, and groups into a relationship of adjacence and proximity is itself an important component of both these two inherently diasporic projects and an aspect of the counter-memories that they are attempting to activate. I believe that such an emphasis on connective histories maps a future for memory studies beyond discrete historical events like the Holocaust, to transnational interconnections and intersections in a global space of remembrance.

"I WOULD KNOW HER EVERYWHERE"

Archival practices invariably rely on documents, objects, and images that survive the ravages of time and the destruction wrought by violent histories. Even as we amass and display these in albums and private or public collections, in exhibits or on Web sites, we cannot disguise the lost and shadow archives, and the absences, that haunt all that we are able to collect. How can our albums and archives gesture toward what has been lost and forgotten, toward the many lives that remain obscured, unknown, and unthought? As we have seen throughout these pages, the relentless obsessive searches characterizing postmemory, and the inevitable disappointments that follow, enable us to conjure images that cannot be found, marks that are invisible. We fill the emptiness through our performative practices of desire.

In an opposite move, however, silence, absence, and emptiness are also always present, and often central to the work of postmemory. Art Spiegelman figures lost objects as familial when he fills an entire page with the dejected figure of his father surrounded by drawn photographs that he remembers only distantly because they were destroyed, along with the relatives depicted in them.[34] Like the hole at the center of Tatana Kellner's *Fifty Years of Silence*, some of these photos themselves contain holes and gaps, as though family members had been cut out after divorces or breakups. Or is it that Vladek fails to remember their names or their faces as the normal vagaries of family relations are compounded by violent exclusion and removal?

Going further, Régine Robin ends her story collection *L'Immense fatigue des pierres* (*The Immense Weariness of Stones*) with a final chapter consisting of nothing more than a series of 51 empty picture frames.[35] These refer not only to the family members who were killed in the Holocaust or who were forgotten by the little girl who survived in hiding. They are also representations of the loss of their very traces, in photographs and on the surfaces of objects they once held in their hands. Such are the gaps around which our archives are constructed, and the challenge is not to fill the space with projections that would allow these gaps to be screened or disguised.

It is in this spirit that I would like to conclude with a remarkable story from Patricia Williams's *The Rooster's Egg* about how, through visual representation, gaps and silences—signifiers of a violent erasure of subjectivity and humanity—can themselves become the connective tissue conjoining diverse memory communities:

> Many years ago, a friend invited me to her home for dinner. As it turned out, her husband was a survivor of Auschwitz. He had been an artist before he was captured by the Nazis, and, while he had made his living in an entirely different way since coming to the United States, his wife told me that he still painted as a hobby. She took me to their garage and showed me the immense collection of his work. There he had stored paintings that probably numbered in the hundreds—circus-bright landscapes with vivid colors and lush, exquisitely detailed vegetation. Yet in every last one of them there was a space of completely bare canvas, an empty patch in the shape of a human being. "He never finishes anything," my friend whispered, but I could hardly hear her, for I had never seen such a complete representation of the suppression of personality, the erasure of humanity that the Holocaust exacted.
>
> A few weeks after this, my sister sent me a microfiche copy of the property listing from the National Archives documenting the existence of our enslaved great-great-grandmother. The night after I received my sister's letter, I dreamed that I was looking at my friend's husband's paintings, all those vivid landscapes with the bare body-shapes and suddenly my great-great-grandmother appeared in the middle of each and every one of them. Suddenly she filled in all the empty spaces, and I looked into her face with the supernatural stillness of deep recollection. From that moment, I knew exactly who she was—every pore, every hair, every angle of her face. I would know her everywhere.[36]

This passage goes a long way toward exemplifying the feminist practice of postmemory I have been trying to trace in these chapters. It is a story about how the mark of memory gets erased to make space so that, generations later, it may again be found and affiliatively readopted across lines of difference. It is a story of a bold and risky and courageous feminist act of embracing a connective politics across the differences of gender, history, and generation. And it is a great-great-granddaughter's story shaped by the anxious desire for a mutual recognition constitutive of memory and identity.

The National Archives contain property listings on microfiche, and it is in these impersonal inscriptions that descendants can find evidence of the existence of those whose names figure only as objects of property, in Williams's own terms. But postmemory is subject to dreams and desires that can shape an alternate archive. In projecting the great-great-grandmother's face into the empty spaces of the lush landscape paintings made by her friend, Patricia Williams repairs the cold impersonality of the archive. The paintings, or their ekphrastic evocation by way of the artist's impatient wife, enable this connective identification through the space they leave for others—but only for those who are interpellated by them. Is that emptiness in the shape of a human being a mark of violent erasure, or of the hospitality of the artist whose work is open to other past or future histories? The white spot left blank by the male Holocaust survivor enables the great-great-granddaughter of slaves to look at and to know her slave great-great-grandmother profoundly, with the "supernatural stillness of deep recollection." Shared dreams and nightmares form a shadow archive that fills the empty space of the picture. Thus, in a brief virtual encounter, a past life reemerges from the hole in the center, to be re-embodied in the present, for the future.

NOTES

INTRODUCTION

1. Eva Hoffman, *After Such Knowledge*, xv.
2. Ibid., 203.
3. On the notion of generation, see esp. Sigrid Weigel, " 'Generation' as a Symbolic Form," and Susan Rubin Suleiman, "The 1.5 Generation."
4. Susan Sontag, *Regarding the Pain of Others*.
5. "Roundtable Discussion," in Berel Lang, *Writing and the Holocaust*, 273.
6. Theodor W. Adorno, *Prisms*, 34.
7. Diana Taylor, *The Archive and the Repertoire*.
8. Andreas Huyssen, *Present Pasts*, 6. For a critical take on the current surfeit of memory, see esp. Huyssen, *Present Pasts*, and Régine Robin, *La Mémoire saturée*.
9. Arlene Stein dates the "second generation movement" back to a 1975 conversation among a small group of children of survivors published in *Response* magazine and reprinted in Lucy Y. Steinitz and David M. Szonyi, eds., *Living After the Holocaust*. It was also in 1975 that psychotherapists Eva Fogelman and Bella Savran organized the first support group of children of Holocaust survivors in the United States. (Arlene Stein, "Feminism, Therapeutic Culture, and the Holocaust in the United States.") By 1979 Helen Epstein had already published her influential *Children of the Holocaust*.

10. Epstein, *Children of the Holocaust*; Hoffman, *After Such Knowledge*; Leslie Morris, "Postmemory, Postmemoir"; Anne Karpf, *The War After*; Thane Rosenbaum, *Second Hand Smoke*; Mikael Levin, *War Story*; Christian Boltanski, *Lessons of Darkness*; Lisa Appignanesi, *Losing the Dead*; Irene Lilienheim Angelico, dir., *Dark Lullabies*, 1985; Edward Mason, dir., *Breaking the Silence*, 1984; Tatana Kellner, *B 11226: Fifty Years of Silence* (artist book) and *71125: Fifty Years of Silence* (artist book); Irene Kacandes, *Daddy's War*; Julia Epstein and Lorie Hope Lefkowitz, eds., *Shaping Losses*; Dina Wardi, *Memorial Candles*; Aaron Hass, *In the Shadow of the Holocaust*.

11. Ellen Fine, "The Absent Memory"; Nadine Fresco, "Remembering the Unknown"; Henri Raczymow, "Memory Shot Through with Holes"; Froma Zeitlin, "The Vicarious Witness"; James Young, "Toward a Received History of the Holocaust"; Celia Lury, *Prosthetic Culture*; Alison Landsberg, *Prosthetic Memory*; Gabriele Schwab, *Haunting Legacies*.

12. Hoffman, *After Such Knowledge*, 187.

13. On autobiographical reading, see Susan Rubin Suleiman, "War Memories." In her *Trespassing Through Shadows*, art historian Andrea Liss uses the term "postmemories" in a more circumscribed way to describe the effects that some of the most difficult Holocaust photographs have had on what she terms the "post-Auschwitz generation."

14. Rosalind Morris, "Post-it to the Future: After Lyotard," paper presented at "The Politics of 'Post,'" in the Keywords Interdisciplinary Conversation Series at the Center for the Critical Analysis of Social Difference, Columbia University, April 21, 2011.

15. The childhood or adolescent encounter with images of horror, and *Night and Fog* in particular, haunt many of us in the second generation. See, for example, the account of Gabriele Schwab in *Haunting Legacies*, 11; see also my discussion of Alice Kaplan in chap. 4 and Mitzi Goldman in chap. 6.

16. Saul Friedlander, ed., *Probing the Limits of Representation*.

17. Cynthia Ozick, *The Shawl*.

18. Marianne Hirsch and Leo Spitzer, "Gendered Translations."

19. Interestingly, Susannah Radstone and Bill Schwarz's ambitious collection, *Memory: Histories, Theories, Debates*, also names a number of male figures (Nora, Proust, Bergson, Halbwachs, Freud, Kracauer, Benjamin, Adorno, and Deleuze) as foundational to modern conceptions of memory. Most of these figures are Jews, a fact that the editors mentioned to me in conversation but on which they do not comment in their introduction.

20. Marianne Hirsch and Valerie Smith, "Feminism and Cultural Memory," 4, 5. In her sociological work with children of Holocaust survivors, Arlene Stein connects the "second-generation movement" to feminism and the therapeutic culture of the 1980s. Sensitive to critiques of the embrace of victimhood that

characterizes some second-generation writing, Stein and many of the second-generation feminists she interviews see their memory work as pedagogical, compensatory, reparative, and activist. (Arlene Stein, "Feminism, Therapeutic Culture, and the Holocaust in the United States.")

21. For feminist approaches to the Holocaust focusing on women and on more general issues of gender and memory and representation, see, among others, Judith Tydor Baumel, *Double Jeopardy;* Elizabeth Baer and Myrna Goldenberg, eds., *Experience and Expression;* Julia Epstein and Lori Hope Lefkowitz, eds., *Shaping Losses;* Claire Kahane, "Dark Mirrors"; Lillian Kremer, *Women's Holocaust Writing;* Dalia Ofer and Lenore J. Weitzman, eds., *Women in the Holocaust* (New Haven: Yale University Press, 1998); Joan Ringelheim, "The Unethical and the Unspeakable" and "Thoughts About Women and the Holocaust"; and Carol Rittner and John Roth, *Different Voices.* This extensive work has not yet reversed the dominance of male writers and masculine narratives about the Holocaust; see, for example, Ruth Franklin's *A Thousand Darknesses,* which discusses the work of ten classic male writers ranging from Borowski to Schlink. For queer approaches to memory studies, see esp. Ann Cvetkovich, *An Archive of Feelings;* David L. Eng, *The Feeling of Kinship;* and Judith Halberstam, "Like a Pelican in the Wilderness" (book in progress).

22. Claire Kahane, "Dark Mirrors," 162.

23. For an analysis of TRC testimony and its aftereffects, inspired by scholarly work on Holocaust memory, see Heidi Peta Grunebaum, *Memorializing the Past.*

24. Gary Weissman, *Fantasies of Witnessing.*

25. Ruth Franklin, "Identity Theft."

26. Melvin Jules Bukiet, *Nothing Makes You Free;* Alan L. Berger, *Children of Job.*

27. Among others, I would name Eva Hoffman, Ellen Fine, Nadine Fresco, Erin McGlothlin, Efraim Sicher, Froma Zeitlin, James Young, Brett Kaplan, Emily Miller Budick, Sara Horowitz, Pascale Bos, Irene Kacandes, Annelies Schulte Norholt, Arlene Stein, and Gabriele Schwab, as well as psychoanalytic work by Dan Bar-On, Yael Danieli, Nannette Auerhahn and Dori Laub, Martin S. Bergmann and Milton E. Jucovy, Eva Fogelman, and Dina Wardi.

28. See, among others, Amy Hungerford, *The Holocaust of Texts;* Ruth Leys, *Trauma;* Walter Benn Michaels, "'You who never was there.'" Related critiques of victim culture are equally prevalent in feminist work, of course. See, for example, Martha Minow, "Surviving Victim Talk," *UCLA Law Review* 40 (1992–93): 1411–45; Lauren Berlant, *The Queen of America Goes to Washington City: Essays on Sex and Citizenship* (Durham: Duke University Press, 1997); Wendy Brown, "Resisting Left Melancholy," *Boundary 2,* 26, no. 3 (Autumn 1999): 19–27.

29. Daniel Levy and Natan Sznaider, *The Holocaust and Memory in the Global Age*, 4. See Andreas Huyssen, "Transnationale Verwertungen von Holokaust und Kolonialismus." See also the connective work of Naomi Mandel, *Against the Unspeakable*.

30. Michael Rothberg, *Multidirectional Memory*; Schwab, *Haunting Legacies*, 30. Recent historical work also places the Holocaust within the context of other related histories. See esp. Timothy Snyder, *Bloodlands*. On the dangers and risks of exclusivist approaches to Holocaust memory, see Marianne Hirsch and Leo Spitzer, "Holocaust Studies/Memory Studies." Carol A. Kidron's analysis of second-generation support groups in Israel, including her argument that these groups perform the functions and follow the practices of traditional liturgical memory work to preserve a uniquely Jewish memory, goes very much against the grain of the more broadly affiliative, connective, and secular approach to postmemory I attempt in this book. See Carol A. Kidron, "In Pursuit of Jewish Paradigms of Memory," and a series of responses to Kidron in *Dapim* (2010).

31. Andrew Hoskins, "7/7 and Connective Memory," 272. See also Andrew Hoskins, "Digital Network Memory;" J. Van Dijck, "Flickr and the Culture of Connectivity."

32. Eve Kosofsky Sedgwick, *Touching Feeling*.

1. THE GENERATION OF POSTMEMORY

1. Art Spiegelman, *The First Maus* (1972), first published in *Funny Aminals*, reprinted in Art Spiegelman, *Meta Maus*, 105.

2. Art Spiegelman, *Maus I: A Survivor's Tale: My Father Bleeds History*.

3. Paul Connerton, *How Societies Remember*. Gary Weissman objects specifically to the "memory" in my formulation of postmemory, arguing that "no degree of power or monumentality can transform one person's lived memories into another's." (*Fantasies of Witnessing*, 17.) Both Weissman and Ernst van Alphen refer back to Helen Epstein's 1979 *Children of the Holocaust* to locate the beginnings of the current use of the notion of "memory" in the late 1980s and 1990s: in contrast, they indicate, Epstein had described the "children of the Holocaust" as "possessed by a *history* they had never lived," and she did not use the term "second generation," which, van Alphen observes, implies too close a continuity between generations that are, precisely, *separated* by the trauma of the Holocaust. Epstein spoke of the "sons and daughters of survivors." Objecting to the term "memory" from a semiotic perspective, van Alphen firmly asserts that trauma cannot be transmitted between generations: "The normal trajectory of memory is fundamentally indexical," he argues. "There is continuity between the event and its memory.

And this continuity has an unambiguous direction: the event is the beginning, the memory is the result. . . . In the case of the children of survivors, the indexical relationship that defines memory has never existed. Their relationship to the past events is based on fundamentally different semiotic principles." (*Art in Mind*, 485, 486.)

4. Eva Hoffman, *After Such Knowledge*, 6, 9.
5. Ibid., 126.
6. Maurice Halbwachs, *On Collective Memory*.
7. Jan Assmann, *Das kulturelle Gedächtnis*. Assmann uses the term "kulturelles Gedächtnis" ("cultural memory") to refer to "Kultur"—an institutionalized hegemonic archival memory. In contrast, the Anglo-American meaning of "cultural memory" refers to the social memory of a specific group or subculture.
8. Aleida Assmann, "Re-framing Memory."
9. Ibid., 36.
10. Ibid., 40.
11. Ibid., 39.
12. Hoffman, *After Such Knowledge*, 193. When I referred to myself as a "child of survivors" in my writings on memory and postmemory, for example, it never occurred to me that my readers would assume, as Gary Weissman has done, that they were Auschwitz survivors. (Weissman, *Fantasies of Witnessing*, 16, 17.)
13. For a series of distinctions between familial and nonfamilial aspects of postmemory and for a strictly literal interpretation of the second generation, see Pascale Bos, "Positionality and Postmemory in Scholarship on the Holocaust." In *Haunting Legacies*, Gabriele Schwab relies on Nicolas Abraham and Maria Torok's suggestive notion of the crypt to explain the intergenerational transmission of trauma from a psychoanalytic perspective. I have always seen the crypt as an inherently familial structure of transfer, but Schwab usefully defines "collective, communal and national crypts" that ensue from historical traumas. (*Haunting Legacies*; see esp. chap. 2.)
14. On the familial gaze, see Marianne Hirsch, *Family Frames*.
15. Geoffrey H. Hartman, *The Longest Shadow*, 9; Ross Chambers, *Untimely Interventions*, 199ff.
16. See chap. 6 for a theorization of nonappropriative identification based on Kaja Silverman's distinction between idiopathic and heteropathic identification.
17. Hoffman, *After Such Knowledge*, 187 (emphasis added).
18. It is useful, in this regard, to recall Edward Said's distinction between vertical *filiation* and horizontal *affiliation*, a structure that acknowledges the breaks in authorial transmission that challenge authority and direct transfer. (Edward W. Said, *The World, the Text, and the Critic*.) While Said sees a linear

progression from filiation to affiliation, however, Anne McClintock complicates what she calls this "linear thrust" to argue that "the anachronistic, filiative image of family was projected onto emerging affiliative institutions as their shadowy naturalized shape" (*Imperial Leather*, 45).

19. On the relationship of photography and death, see esp. Susan Sontag, *On Photography*, and Roland Barthes, *Camera Lucida*.

20. C. S. Peirce, *Peirce on Signs: Writings on Semiotic by Charles Sanders Peirce* (Chapel Hill: University of North Carolina Press, 1991).

21. Certainly witness testimony is an equally pervasive genre transmitting the memory of the Holocaust. But I would argue that the technology of photography, with its semiotic principles, makes it at once a more powerful and a more problematic vehicle for the generations after. The technologies recording witness testimony, the tape recorder and the video camera, share the promises and the frustrations embodied by the still camera and the photographic images that are its products.

22. Barthes, *Camera Lucida*, 80. See my *Family Frames* for a reading of these photographs in *Maus*.

23. Georges Didi-Huberman, *Images in Spite of All*, 32ff.

24. For the relationship of visuality to trauma, see esp. Ulrich Baer, *Spectral Evidence*; Jill Bennett, *Empathic Vision*; Shelley Hornstein and Florence Jacobowitz, eds., *Image and Remembrance*; Barbie Zelizer, ed., *Visual Culture and the Holocaust*; Bernd Hüppauf, "Emptying the Gaze"; and van Alphen, *Art in Mind*.

25. For a discussion of this aspect of photography and postmemory, see Silke Horstkotte, "Literarische Subjektivität und die Figur des Transgenerationellen in Marcel Beyers *Spione* und Rachel Seifferts *The Dark Room*."

26. Connerton, *How Societies Remember*.

27. Bennett, *Empathic Vision*, 36.

28. Aby Warburg, "The Absorption of the Expressive Values of the Past."

29. Georges Didi-Huberman, "Artistic Survival."

30. For a critical discussion of the trope of maternal loss and mother-child separation in Holocaust remembrance, see Claire Kahane, "Dark Mirrors."

31. Andreas Huyssen, *Present Pasts*, 135.

32. W. G. Sebald, *Austerlitz*, 72.

33. On transposition, see Judith Kestenberg, "A Metapsychological Assessment Based on an Analysis of a Survivor's Child."

34. Sebald, *Austerlitz*, 245.

35. Ibid., 251.

36. Ibid.

37. See chap. 6 for a discussion of the Nazi gaze.

38. Sebald, *Austerlitz*, 251.

39. Barthes, *Camera Lucida*, 53.

40. Margaret Olin, *Touching Photographs*, 60.
41. But Olin is also mistaken, as Nancy K. Miller pointed out to me in conversation: the English translation leaves out the more specific description in the French where the necklace is described as being "*au ras du cou*" ("at the neckline") rather than long and hanging down as in the image of the "two grandmothers." See Roland Barthes, *La Chambre claire: Note sur la photographie* (Paris: Gallimard, 1980), 87.
42. Walter Benjamin, "A Short History of Photography," 206.
43. Olin, *Touching Photographs*, 62.
44. Ibid., 68.
45. Ibid., 69.
46. Sebald, *Austerlitz*, 245.
47. Ibid., 183.
48. Ibid., 183, 184.
49. Ibid., 185.
50. Ibid.
51. Sebald, *Austerlitz*, 182.
52. Sigmund Freud, "Family Romances" ["Der Familienroman der Neurotiker"] (1908), in *The Standard Edition of the Complete Works of Sigmund Freud*, ed. James Strachey, 24 vols. (London: Hogarth, 1953), 9, 238–39.
53. See chap. 8 for a discussion of other accounts of the quest for this pre-Holocaust world.
54. Sebald, *Austerlitz*, 184.
55. Ibid., 182–83.

2. WHAT'S WRONG WITH THIS PICTURE?

1. On street photographs, esp. from Czernowitz/Cernăuți, see Marianne Hirsch and Leo Spitzer, "Incongruous Images," and the response by Geoffrey Batchen, "Seeing and Saying: A Response to 'Incongruous Images,'" *History and Theory* 48 (December 2009), 26–33.
2. For the Holocaust in Czernowitz/Cernăuți and the deportations to Transnistria, see Matatias Carp, *Holocaust in Rumania: Facts and Documents on the Annihilation of Rumania's Jews—1940–1944* (Budapest: Primor, 1994); Florence Heyman, *Le Crépuscule des Lieux*; Marianne Hirsch and Leo Spitzer, *Ghosts of Home*; Radu Ioanid, *The Holocaust in Romania: The Destruction of Jews and Gypsies Under the Antonescu Regime, 1940–1944* (Chicago: Ivan R. Dee, in assoc. with the United States Holocaust Memorial Museum, Washington, D.C., 2000).
3. Ulrich Baer, *Spectral Evidence*, 2.
4. Ibid., 181.

5. Roland Barthes, *Camera Lucida*. Barthes's compelling discussion of the relationship of photography to death has inspired much of the vast literature on visuality, photography, and the Holocaust, and on the transmission of affect in the act of memory. See esp. Shelley Hornstein and Florence Jacobowitz, eds., *Image and Remembrance*; Baer, *Spectral Evidence*; Barbie Zelizer, *Remembering to Forget*; Barbie Zelizer, ed., *Visual Culture and the Holocaust*; Bernd Hüppauf, "Emptying the Gaze"; Ernst Van Alphen, *Caught by History* and *Art in Mind*.

6. Among the numerous insightful discussions of Barthes's notion of the punctum, see Jean-Michel Rabaté, *Writing the Image After Roland Barthes*; Jacques Derrida, *The Work of Mourning*; Margaret Olin, *Touching Photographs*; Jay Prosser, *Light in the Dark Room*; Michael Fried, "Barthes's Punctum."

7. Barthes, *Camera Lucida*, 44. See my discussion of the necklace in Chapter 1.

8. For a feminist reading of *Camera Lucida*, focusing on Barthes's discussion of the detail, see Naomi Schor, *Reading in Detail*. On the relationship of photography to death and to the mother, see esp. Lawrence D. Kritzman, "Roland Barthes: The Discourse of Desire and the Question of Gender"; Peggy Phelan, "Francesca Woodman's Photography"; Amelia Jones, "The 'Eternal Return'"; and Jane Gallop and Dick Blau, *Living with His Camera*.

9. Barthes, *Camera Lucida*, 96.

10. Ibid.

11. Michael André Bernstein, *Foregone Conclusions*, 16.

12. We are grateful to Susan Winnett for suggesting the Seiffert novel to us. For a reading of Seiffert and postmemory, see Silke Horstkotte, "Literarische Subjektivität und die Figur des Transgenerationellen in Marcel Beyers *Spione* und Rachel Seifferts *The Dark Room*."

13. Rachel Seiffert, *The Dark Room*, 27.

14. Ibid., 28.

15. For a discussion of such display photos, see Cornelia Brink, *Ikonen der Vernichtung*, 82–99.

16. See Muriel Hasbun, *Saints and Shadows*, www.zonezero.com/exposiciones /fotografos/muriel2/default.html. For other examples of Muriel Hasbun's artistic work, see *Memento: Muriel Hasbun's Photographs*, www.corcoran .org/exhibitions/Exhib_current.asp?Exhib_ID=106, and "Protegida: Auvergne-Ave Maria," www.barnard.edu/sfonline/cf/hasbun.htm.

17. Transcript of soundtrack in Hasbun's installation *Triptychon: Protegida: Auvergne- Hélène*.

18. Andrea Liss, *Trespassing Through Shadows*, 86.

19. For a discussion of such illicit structures of identification, see Susannah Radstone, "Social Bonds and Psychical Order," and Karyn Ball, "Unspeakable Differences, Unseen Pleasures."

20. Barthes, *Camera Lucida*, 96.

21. Eve Kosofsky Sedgwick, *Touching Feeling*, 123–51.
22. Ibid., 128–29, 146–51.
23. Muriel Hasbun, e-mail communication with the authors, April 19, 2004.
24. Ibid.

3. MARKED BY MEMORY

1. Toni Morrison, *Beloved*, 61.
2. Roberta Culbertson, "Embodied Memory, Transcendence, and Telling," 170.
3. Charlotte Delbo, *Days and Memory*; Jill Bennett, "The Aesthetics of Sense-Memory," 92.
4. Morrison, *Beloved*, 316.
5. Gayatri C. Spivak, "Acting Bits/Identity Talk," 169.
6. Ibid.
7. The relationship of *Beloved* to the memory of the Holocaust has been a matter of extensive critical discussion, esp. in relation to Morrison's dedication to the "Sixty Million and More," since Stanley Crouch's devastating review of the novel, "Aunt Medea," in *New Republic* (October 19, 1987: 38–43). For more productive engagements of African American and Jewish memory in readings of *Beloved*, see, e.g., Emily Miller Budick, *Blacks and Jews in Literary Conversation* (New York: Cambridge University Press, 1998) and Eric J. Sundquist, *Strangers in the Land: Blacks, Jews, Post-Holocaust America* (Cambridge: Harvard University Press, 2009). In my own reading in this chapter, *Beloved* functions as a theoretical text that illuminates how the bodily mark of trauma can be transmitted between mothers and daughters. But it also functions as a text open to a *connective* approach to the subject of memory and postmemory, as elaborated more fully in chapters 8 and 9.
8. See Juliet Mitchell's *Mad Men and Medusas* for a model of recognition as a fundamental element of subject-formation that, when breached, can cause trauma. See esp. her chapter 9, "Trauma."
9. See Mitchell, *Mad Men and Medusas*. Mitchell goes so far as to suggest that "an actual trauma in one generation may not be induced until the next" (280).
10. See Delbo, *Days and Memory*; Dominick LaCapra, *Writing History, Writing Trauma*; Mitchell, *Mad Men and Medusas*; Bessel A. van der Kolk and Onno van der Hart, "The Intrusive Past"; Nicolas Abraham and Maria Torok, *The Shell and the Kernel*.
11. On reenactment in the work of post-Holocaust artists, see Ernst van Alphen, *Caught by History*.
12. Judith Kestenberg, "A Metapsychological Assessment Based on an Analysis of a Survivor's Child," 148, 149.

13. Ibid., 141.
14. Morrison, *Beloved*, 36.
15. Ibid., 47.
16. Anne Karpf, *The War After*, 102, 103, 106.
17. Karpf, *The War After*, 126.
18. Ibid. For a discussion of the recent prevalence of memorial tattoos, and 9/11 tattoos in particular, see Jane Caplan, " 'Indelible Memories.' " See also Jane Caplan, *Written on the Body*.
19. Kestenberg, "A Metapsychological Assessment," 156, 150.
20. Karpf, *The War After*, 253.
21. Eve Kosofsky Sedgwick, *Epistemology of the Closet*, 59–63.
22. Kaja Silverman, *The Threshold of the Visible World*, 185. Silverman borrows the term coined in Max Scheler, *The Nature of Sympathy*. Psychoanalytic theories of identification tend to stress its incorporative, appropriative logic based on idealization of the other. See in particular Diana Fuss's helpful discussion in her *Identification Papers*. I appreciate Silverman's effort to theorize identification at a distance, but what I find particularly helpful is her alignment, through the theorization of the look, of the structure of identification with the structure of memory, a process whereby we can "remember," through seeing, the memory of another.
23. Silverman, *Threshold of the Visible World*, 185.
24. For Silverman's discussion of Barthes's terms, see her *Threshold of the Visible World*, 181–85.
25. Silverman, *Threshold of the Visible World*, 181.
26. Kosofsky Sedgwick, *Epistemology of the Closet*, 61.
27. The following discussion of Tatana Kellner's work is in part based on an article with a different focus that I cowrote with Susan Suleiman. See Marianne Hirsch and Susan Suleiman, "Material Memory." I am grateful to Suleiman for her permission to continue thinking and writing about Kellner's work, building on our work together.
28. Tatana Kellner, unpaginated.
29. Paul Celan, "Ash-Aureole" ("Aschenglorie"), in *Selected Poems and Prose of Paul Celan*, trans. John Felstiner (New York: Norton, 2001), 261.
30. Tatana Kellner, unpaginated.
31. Ibid.
32. Hirsch and Suleiman, "Material Memory," 101, 102.
33. Jeffrey A. Wolin, *Written in Memory*, 23.
34. Ibid.
35. Ibid., cover.
36. Geoffrey H. Hartman, *The Longest Shadow*, 8.
37. Shoshana Felman, "Camus' The Plague, or a Monument to Witnessing," in Shoshana Felman and Dori Laub, eds., *Testimony*, 108.

38. James Young, *The Art of Memory*, 19.
39. Art Spiegelman, *Maus I*, 158.

4. SURVIVING IMAGES

1. Susan Sontag, *On Photography*, 19–20.
2. Alice Kaplan, *French Lessons*, 29–30.
3. Sontag, *On Photography*, 19.
4. Ibid., 20.
5. Ibid., 21.
6. Geoffrey H. Hartman, *The Longest Shadow*, 152.
7. Ibid.
8. Barbie Zelizer, *Remembering to Forget*.
9. Susan A. Crane, "Choosing Not to Look," 309.
10. Susan Sontag, *Regarding the Pain of Others*, 105.
11. Ibid., 111. For a series of critical engagements with these questions, see Geoffrey Batchen et al., *Picturing Atrocity*.
12. See, e.g., the photographs collected in the controversial exhibition and catalog prepared by the Hamburg Institute for Social Research, *The German Army and Genocide*, which documents not only the atrocities committed but the passion for documenting atrocities photographically.
13. Georges Didi-Huberman, *Images in Spite of All*.
14. See Mendel Grossman, *With a Camera in the Ghetto [Lódz]*; Peter Hellman, ed., *The Auschwitz Album*; Joe Julius Heydecker, *Where Is Thy Brother Abel?*; Ulrich Keller, ed., *The Warsaw Ghetto in Photographs*; Jürgen Stroop, *The Stroop Report*; Gerhard Schoenberner, *Der gelbe Stern*; Teresa Swiebicka, ed., *Auschwitz: A History in Photographs*; Georges Didi-Huberman, *Images in Spite of All*.
15. Sybil Milton, "Photographs of the Warsaw Ghetto." Milton's judgment has more recently been repeated by two scholars who have attempted to historicize and thus to demystify the "atrocity photos" taken by the liberators in 1945. In her rich *Remembering to Forget*, Barbie Zelizer says: "Certain atrocity photos resurfaced time and again, reducing what was known about the camps to familiar visual cues that would become overused with time" (158). See also Cornelia Brink, *Ikonen der Vernichtung*: "The number of images that spontaneously come to mind when one speaks of concentration and death camps, is limited, and the impression imposes itself that since 1945 the very same images have repeatedly been reproduced" (9; my translation).
16. In *Remembering to Forget*, Zelizer traces in detail how certain liberator images, some of which were originally associated with specific dates and individual camps, eventually were mislabeled and associated with other camps,

or came to signal more and more general and abstract images of "death camps" or "the Holocaust," or became unspecific "signifiers of horror." Even at the time of their production, most of these images were not carefully attributed, but now the credits identify neither the photographers nor the original photo agencies for which they worked, but merely the contemporary ownership of the images. Attribution and content are even more difficult to determine when it comes to perpetrator images. The controversy that temporarily closed the Wehrmacht exhibition concerned eight or nine photographs that depicted German soldiers standing next to civilian victims: what is not readable from the images themselves is whether the corpses were the victims of documented Wehrmacht and SS killings or of the Soviet NKVD massacres that preceded those killings. (See Hamburg Institute for Social Research, *The German Army and Genocide*, 82–83.)

17. See Eric Santner's useful notion of "narrative fetishism" in "History Beyond the Pleasure Principle," 144ff.

18. Alison Landsberg, *Prosthetic Memory*.

19. See Dominick LaCapra's useful notions of "muted trauma" and "empathic unsettlement," as well as his distinction between "acting out" and "working through," in *Representing the Holocaust* and *History and Memory After Auschwitz*.

20. It is important to note that, as my initial quotations from Sontag and Kaplan indicate, my inquiry in this chapter is restricted to the memory and postmemory of victims and bystanders, not of perpetrators. For an appreciation for the different issues raised by German encounters with Holocaust photographs, see Cornelia Brink, *Ikonen der Vernichtung*, and Dagmar Barnouw, *Germany 1945*. Both focus specifically on liberator images and their use in Germany in 1945 and after. The Alice Kaplan passage illustrates what happens when images migrate from one context to another, in this case, from their juridical use at Nuremberg to the childhood drama of a third-grader in Ohio. See also Bernd Hüppauf, "Emptying the Gaze": "There is no simultaneity and hardly any exchange of ideas between the U.S. discourse on representations of the Holocaust and the German discourse on the subject (19)." For a discussion of the redeployment of Holocaust photographs in the representations of contemporary artists, see Andrea Liss, *Trespassing Through Shadows*, and some of the chapters in James Young's *At Memory's Edge*. And on iconic images more generally, see the enormously useful *No Caption Needed*, by Robert Hariman and John Louis Lucaites, a volume that explicitly excludes Holocaust images.

21. Robert Jay Lifton, *The Broken Connection*, 176 (cited in Santner, "History Beyond the Pleasure Principle," 152).

22. Bernd Hüppauf stresses the necessity of just such a reading: "Theories of perception and visuality have hardly made an inroad into discourse on the

Holocaust, and, in more general terms, the violent practices of the Third Reich." ("Emptying the Gaze," 14.)

23. Ida Fink, "Traces," in her *A Scrap of Time*, 135–37.

24. Ibid., 135.

25. Ibid. For an elaboration on photographs' indexical *ça-a-été* quality, see Roland Barthes, *Camera Lucida*, 76, 77, 80, and 81, and my discussion of Barthes in chap. 1.

26. Fink, "Traces," 135.

27. Ariella Azoulay, *The Civil Contract of Photography*, 16.

28. W. G. Sebald, *Austerlitz*, 182. On the aural quality of the photograph, see Fred Moten, *In the Break*.

29. Zelizer, *Remembering to Forget*, 9.

30. Ibid., 10.

31. Patricia Yaeger's "Consuming Trauma" serves as a powerful cautionary note against textualizing and theorizing on the basis of the dead bodies of others. I am painfully aware of the risks I take in discussing as figures images that are as uncompromisingly literal, present, and pervasive as these. And yet I am also convinced that their power need not be undermined by a discussion of the metaphoric roles they have come to play. As arresting as they are, these emblematic images have undoubtedly reduced our ability to understand or envision the multifaceted reality of concentration camps. As Dan Stone has said in his "Chaos and Continuity," "ever since the first photos of Auschwitz, the meaning imputed to it has been encompassed in the symbolic framework of the barbed wire, the ramp, or the famous entrance gate. These things are of course important parts of the camp, yet they are not the camp *but only how we wish to keep seeing it*" (emphasis added), 27.

32. Debórah Dwork and Robert Jan van Pelt "Reclaiming Auschwitz," 236–37.

33. Debórah Dwork and Robert Jan van Pelt even suggest that the part of Auschwitz I that was preserved as a museum was determined by the location of the gate. See "Reclaiming Auschwitz," 236–37.

34. The centrality of this image in *Maus* is underscored by the introduction to the DVD edition in *MetaMaus* in which Spiegelman uses it to illustrate his construction of a page: "The size of the panel gives weight, gives importance," he says. "This is the largest panel in the book, too big to be contained by the book—the entrance into Auschwitz."

35. Jacques Lacan's discussion of the simultaneously literal and figural functioning of doors and gates might be useful in explaining the importance these two images have assumed in Holocaust representation. See "Psychoanalysis and Cybernetics, or on the Nature of Language," in *The Seminar of Jacques Lacan, Book II*, ed. Jacques-Alain Miller, trans. Sylvana Tomaselli (New York: Norton, 1988), 294–308. Just as doors can be opened only because they can also be closed, things can be remembered only because they can also be

forgotten. In the cultural remembrance of the Holocaust, the gate is both memory and a defense against memory.

36. See my discussion of the co-implication of these two kinds of Holocaust photographs in my *Family Frames*, 20, 21. See also Cornelia Brink's response to and elaboration of my argument, "'How to Bridge the Gap.'" Gerhard Schoenberner implicitly makes a similar point in *The Yellow Star* when he juxtaposes, on facing pages (280 and 281), the bulldozer image from Bergen-Belsen with a poster that Louis Lazar from Nyons, France, made of images of his lost relatives.

37. Fink, "Traces," 136.

38. See the next chapter for a lengthy discussion of the Nazi gaze.

39. Nadine Fresco, "Remembering the Unknown," 419.

40. Santner, "History Beyond the Pleasure Principle," 151.

41. Ibid., 146.

42. Hal Foster, *The Return of the Real*, 132.

43. Michael Rothberg, *Traumatic Realism*. See also Saul Friedlander's notion of "allusive or distanced realism" in his "Introduction" to *Probing the Limits of Representation*, 17.

44. On Lorie Novak, see the artist's website: http://www.lorienovak.com.

5. NAZI PHOTOGRAPHS IN POST-HOLOCAUST ART

1. Jaroslaw M. Rymkiewicz, *The Final Station*, 324–26. Ellipses are not in the text.

2. Rymkiewicz, *Final Station*, 23–24.

3. Lawrence Langer, *Preempting the Holocaust*, 111.

4. Stewart Justman, ed., *The Jewish Holocaust for Beginners*; Götz Aly, *"Final Solution": Nazi Population Policy and the Murder of the European Jews* (London: Arnold, 1999); *Lest We Forget: A History of the Holocaust*.

5. Jürgen Stroop, *The Stroop Report*.

6. Primo Levi, "The Chemical Examination," 105, 106.

7. In the latter two cases, I have chosen to reproduce not the actual images themselves but the contemporary works that incorporate them. I will argue that these works to some degree retain and perpetuate the power of the Nazi gaze, and I would feel that I am myself contributing to the problem were I to expose these archival images to further viewing.

8. On our relationship to these images, see the moving chapter on perpetrator photographs by Nadine Fresco in her *La mort des juifs*.

9. Susan Sontag, *On Photography*, 70.

10. See my discussion of this retrospective scene of looking and its devastating ironies in the analysis of Ida Fink's "Traces" in chap. 4.

11. Sontag, *On Photography*, 70. For a much more complicated look at Roman Vishniac's *A Vanished World*, see Alana Newhouse, "A Closer Reading of Roman Vishniac," *New York Times Magazine*, April 1, 2010.

12. Christian Metz, "Photography and Fetish," 158.

13. See esp. Jacques Lacan, *Four Fundamental Concepts of Psychoanalysis*; Jonathan Crary, *Techniques of the Observer*; and Kaja Silverman, *The Threshold of the Visible World*.

14. Lacan, *Four Fundamental Concepts*, 106.

15. Ibid., 109.

16. It is interesting to note that some contemporary German theories of visuality, esp. feminist theories, continue to stress the violence of photographic technology and thus of the photographic act. See, e.g., the work of Christina von Braun and Silke Wenk.

17. The controversy in Israel's Yad Vashem illustrates the particular issues facing Jewish viewers of these images. Citing the taboo against female nudity, Orthodox Jews argued against the display of images of nude or scantily dressed women in the photographic exhibitions of the destruction of European Jews. For them the issue is the potential arousal of male viewers by the exposed female bodies. Although, in contrast to the Orthodox line, one might well argue that pedagogy demands that the worst be shown, one might also worry about the violation inherent in such displays: these women are doomed in perpetuity to be displayed in the most humiliating, demeaning, dehumanizing position. Given the invisibility many European Jews worked so hard to enjoy, perpetrator images are also fundamentally troubling in their hyperbolic identification of Jews as Jews and as victims. The act of looking, in these cases, is marked in complicated ways by power, religion, and gender.

18. I am grateful to James Young for bringing these images to my attention, and to Alexander Rossino for discussing them with me at length. These are clearly images of professional quality, indicating that they were taken by an official propaganda corps. Bernd Hüppauf explains this work: "Photos and descriptions inform us about groups of soldiers positioned at the edge of the killing sites, often in elevated positions that provided an unrestrained field of vision. . . . There they watched for an hour or more and sometimes took photographs." ("Emptying the Gaze," 27.) The angle of vision in this group of images does indeed indicate the photographers' elevated position.

19. For a suggestive discussion of perpetrator representations, see Gertrud Koch's analysis of some perpetrator images from the Łódz ghetto in the context of Nazi aesthetic in *Die Einstellung ist die Einstellung*, 170–184. Koch looks specifically at devices like lighting and framing that clearly identify the subjects of the images as "Jews" and as "other," distinguishing them from similar images of German subjects.

20. Bernd Hüppauf traces his own analysis of the alienated, decorporealized technological gaze characterizing the Nazi regime back to Ernst Jünger's extensive writings on the photography of the First World War in "Über den Schmerz," in *Essays I, Werke 5* (Stuttgart: Klett-Cotta, 1963): "A photograph then is 'outside of the zone of sensibility.' . . . It captures the flying bullet as well as the human being at the moment when he is torn to pieces by an explosion. And this has become our characteristic way of seeing; photography is nothing else but an instrument of this, our own character." (Jünger quoted in Hüppauf, "Emptying the Gaze," 25.) Hüppauf describes the images of perpetators as embodying an "empty gaze from no-where." For a dissenting interpretation of soldiers' photographs, see Alexander B. Rossino, "Eastern Europe through German Eyes." See also the exhibition catalog by Petra Bopp, *Fremde im Visier*.

21. See, e.g., Kaja Silverman's discussion of the picture of a woman arriving in Auschwitz that is included in Harun Farocki's film *Bilder der Welt und Inschrift des Krieges*. Silverman and Farocki perceive in the woman's look at the camera a resistant posture: it is a look one might use on the boulevard rather than in the concentration camp, Silverman writes. "The critical problem faced by the Auschwitz inmate is how to be 'photographed' differently—how to motivate the mobilization of another screen" (Silverman, *Threshold of the Visible World*, 153). There are moments when this seems like an impossible task. See Ariella Azoulay, *The Civil Contract of Photography*, for a different model of looking at perpetrator images, resting not on identification or empathy but on a "civil contract" encompassing, equally, photographer, subject, and viewer.

22. For other useful analyses of Nazi photographic practices, see Sybil Milton, Judith Levin, and Daniel Uziel, "Ordinary Men, Extraordinary Photos"; Bernd Hüppauf, "Emptying the Gaze"; Alexander B. Rossino, "Eastern Europe Through German Eyes"; and Daniel Jonah Goldhagen, *Hitler's Willing Executioners*, 245–47, 405–406. While there is considerable disagreement among these writers about how Nazi photographic acts are to be interpreted, they all attest to the importance of a careful contextual analysis of these images.

23. The 1944 SS photo album depicting the leisure-time activities of the Nazi leadership in Auschwitz, donated to the U.S. Holocaust Memorial Museum in 2007, is another revelatory document whose very existence and survival are in themselves astounding. See http://www.ushmm.org/museum/exhibit/online/ssalbum/.

24. See Lawrence Langer's discussion of Samuel Bak in *Preempting the Holocaust* (chap. 5).

25. Aleksandar Tišma, "Mein Photo des Jahrhunderts," *Die Zeit* (October 14, 1999), my translation.

26. Ibid.

27. Geoffrey H. Hartman, *The Longest Shadow*, 131.

28. See my discussion of this more triangulated exchange in the next chapter.

29. Judy Chicago, *Holocaust Project*.

30. I am grateful to Sidra deKoven Ezrahi for calling this play to my attention. The passage is cited from her discussion of this moment in "Revisioning the Past."

31. David Levinthal, *Mein Kampf*.

32. See chap. 8, "Objects of Return," for a discussion of the very different use of one of these images in the work of Bracha Lichtenberg-Ettinger.

33. James Young, *At Memory's Edge*, 44.

34. David Levinthal, quoted in Young, *At Memory's Edge*, 51.

35. Ibid., 55.

36. See Yitzhak Arad, Shmuel Krakowski, and Shmuel Spector, eds., *The Einsatzgruppen Reports: Selections from the Dispatches of the Nazi Death Squads' Campaign Against the Jews, July 1941–January 1943* (New York: Holocaust Library, 1989); Christopher Browning, *Ordinary Men*; and Goldhagen, *Hitler's Willing Executioners*.

37. Silke Wenk, "Pornografisierungen—Einrahmungen des Blicks auf die NS Vergangenheit."

38. Ruth Klüger, *Von hoher und niedriger Literatur*.

39. Wenk, "Pornografisierungen."

40. For a discussion of these photographs, see Nechama Tec and Daniel Weiss, "The Heroine of Minsk."

41. This installation was first shown at the 1993 Whitney Biennial. See John Bird, Jo Anna Isaak, and Sylvère Lotringer, *Nancy Spero*.

6. PROJECTED MEMORY

1. Marjorie Agosín, *Dear Anne Frank*, v–viii. Ellipses are not in text.

2. Ibid.

3. Artist talk, Hood Museum of Art, Dartmouth College, Hanover, N.H., May 1996.

4. For the definition of memory as an "act," see Pierre Janet, *Les Médications psychologiques*, and the gloss on Janet's argument by Bessel A. van der Kolk and Onno van der Hart, "The Intrusive Past."

5. Kaja Silverman, *The Threshold of the Visible World*, 185. See my discussion of Silverman's distinctions in chap. 3.

6. Bruno Bettelheim, "The Ignored Lesson of Anne Frank." See also Cynthia Ozick, "Anne Frank's Afterlife," and Francine Prose, *Anne Frank*.

7. Agosín, *Dear Anne Frank*, 6–7.

8. Lucy S. Dawidowicz, *The War Against the Jews: 1933–1945* (New York: Bantam, 1975), 166.

9. See Debórah Dwork, *Children with a Star*, xxxiii. The most moving illustration of the special vulnerability of children is *French Children of the Holocaust: A Memorial*, ed. Susan Cohen, Howard Epstein, and Serge Klarsfeld, a monumental volume that lists the deportation of 11,400 French Jewish children and reproduces 2,500 of their photographs. The book, as the author writes in the introduction, is a "collective gravestone."

10. Froma Zeitlin, "The Vicarious Witness."

11. *Hatred*, dir. Mitzi Goldman, Australia (1996).

12. Discussion following a public showing of *Hatred* in Cape Town, South Africa, August 1996.

13. Yala Korwin, *To Tell the Story*, 75.

14. Ibid.

15. On this split subject position, see Jean Laplanche and Jean-Bertrand Pontalis, "Fantasy and the Origins of Sexuality."

16. Silverman, *Threshold of the Visible World*, 183.

17. Dominick LaCapra, *Representing the Holocaust*, 198.

18. Ibid., 198–200. See Jacques Derrida's *Memoires for Paul de Man* for his reflections on the cannibalistic and appropriative modes of self/other relation that make mourning and identification after the Second World War impossible. See also Diana Fuss, *Identification Papers*, 40: "Trauma is another name for identification, the name we might give to the irrecoverable loss of a sense of human relatedness."

19. LaCapra, *Representing the Holocaust*, 199.

20. Shoshana Felman and Dori Laub, eds. *Testimony*; in the edited collection, see esp. Shoshana Felman, "Education and Crisis, or the Vicissitudes of Teaching," 1–56; Dori Laub, "Bearing Witness or the Vicissitudes of Listening," 57–74; and Dori Laub, "An Event Without a Witness: Truth, Testimony, and Survival," 75–92.

21. Laub, "An Event Without a Witness," 86.

22. Ibid., 88.

23. Felman, "Education and Crisis," 46.

24. Ibid., 47.

25. Ibid., 48.

26. Ibid., 50.

27. Ibid., 52.

28. Ibid., 50.

29. Laub, "An Event Without a Witness," 75.

30. Ibid., 76.

31. Ibid.

32. Ibid., 77.

33. Saul Friedlander, "Trauma, Transference, and 'Working Through' in Writing the History of the *Shoah*," 51.

34. I stress these moments of resistance and indirection in order precisely to circumvent what Susannah Radstone, in response to an earlier publication of this chapter, saw as a trend in contemporary academic writing about trauma—the critic's assumption of the victim position through identification. Images of children, as I argue, are so easily available for projection that it may well be extraordinarily difficult to maintain any distance from them. However, I would not agree with Radstone that an acknowledgment of identification with perpetrators is necessary in order to establish triangulation and mediation. See Susannah Radstone, "Social Bonds and Psychical Order."
35. Silverman, *Threshold of the Visible World*, 189.
36. Ibid.
37. Laub, "Bearing Witness," 72.
38. Ibid., 73.

7. TESTIMONIAL OBJECTS

1. Cara De Silva, introduction to *In Memory's Kitchen*.
2. Terezín (known as Theresienstadt in German) was built by the Habsburg emperor Joseph II as a walled military garrison town and named after his mother, the empress Maria Theresa. Connected to this fortified town was a smaller fortification that was used as a military and political prison. In 1940, after Czechoslovakia fell under Nazi control, this "Small Fort" became a Gestapo prison, and in 1941 the larger fortified town, called by the Nazis "Ghetto Theresienstadt," began to be used as a Jewish concentration and transit camp. Although tens of thousands of persons died there, and multiple thousands more were deported to extermination camps in Poland until Terezín was liberated in 1945, Nazi propagandists presented the camp as a "model Jewish settlement," sanctioning—but for the most part compelling—artistic and cultural production by inmates for propaganda newsreels, and staging social and cultural events to convince International Red Cross visitors in 1944 of the positive nature and high quality of their Jewish ghetto resettlement schemes. See Ludmila Chádková, *The Terezín Ghetto* (Prague: Nase vojsko, 1995); H. G. Adler, *Theresienstadt, 1941–1945: Das Antlitz einer Zwangsgemeinschaft* (Tübingen: Mohr, 1958); Ruth Schwertfeger, *Women of Theresienstadt: Voices from a Concentration Camp* (New York: Berg Publishers, 1989); and Norbert Troller, *Theresienstadt: Hitler's Gift to the Jews* (Chapel Hill: University of North Carolina Press, 1991).
3. Israeli archives (Beit Theresienstadt at Givat Chaim-Ichud) even contain one recipe collection written by a man, Jaroslav Budlovsky; there is also another recipe book written by male prisoners-of-war in the Philippines during the

Second World War entitled *Recipes Out of Bilibid*. See De Silva, introduction to *In Memory's Kitchen*, xxx.

4. See chap. 2 for a definition and discussion of points of memory.

5. On Transnistria and Vapniarka, see Jean Ancel, ed., *Documents Concerning the Fate of Romanian Jewry During the Holocaust*. 12 vols. (New York: Beate Klarsfeld Foundation, 1986 and 1993); Ihiel Benditer, *Vapniarca* (Tel Aviv: Anais, 1995); Felicia Steigman Carmelly, ed., *Shattered! 50 Years of Silence: History and Voices of the Tragedy in Romania and Transnistria* (Scarborough, Ontario: Abbeyfield, 1997); Julius Fischer, *Transnistria: The Forgotten Cemetery* (New York: Yoseloff, 1969); Radu Ioanid, *The Holocaust in Romania: The Destruction of Jews and Gypsies Under the Antonescu Regime, 1940–1944* (Chicago: Ivan R. Dee; in assoc. with the United States Holocaust Memorial Museum, Washington, D.C., 2000); Marianne Hirsch and Leo Spitzer, " 'There was never a camp here': Searching for Vapniarka"; Marianne Hirsch and Leo Spitzer, *Ghosts of Home*; Marianne Hirsch and Leo Spitzer, " 'Solidarité et souffrance': Le camp de Vapniarka parmi les camps de Transnistrie," *Revue de l'histoire de la Shoah* 194 (janvier/juin 2011), 343–68.

6. Marianne Hirsch and Leo Spitzer, videotaped interview with David Kessler (Suceava, Romania, July 2000).

7. At the end of December 1942, almost five months after Ukrainian prisoners in Pavilion III of the camp and some three and a half months after other prisoners had been introduced to a chickling pea (*lathyrus sativus*) soup diet, the first among them showed the symptoms of a strange illness: severe cramps, paralysis of the lower limbs, and loss of kidney functions. Within a week, hundreds of others throughout the camp were also paralyzed. By late January 1943, some 1,000 in the camp were suffering from this disease in its early and intermediate stages; 120 were totally paralyzed; a number had died. *Lathyrus sativus*, occasionally mixed lightly into animal fodder in times of food shortage or famine, was widely known to be toxic to humans by the local peasantry and, presumably, since it was fed only to camp inmates, by Romanian authorities and officials as well. See Arthur Kessler, "Lathyrismus."

8. Matei Gall, *Finsternis: Durch Gefängnisse, KZ Wapniarka, Massaker und Kommunismus, Ein Lebenslauf in Rumänien 1920–1990* (Konstanz: Hartung-Gorre Verlag, 1999), 150. Our translation.

9. Gall, *Finsternis*, 152. For images of additional objects and artworks produced in Vapniarka, see the Yad Vashem photo archives: http://collections. yadvashem.org/photosarchive/en-us/photos.html

10. Roland Barthes, *Camera Lucida*, 49–51.

11. All Arthur Kessler quotes in this essay are from his "Ein Arzt im Lager." This memoir, in typescript, is based on notes taken in the camp and written not

long after the war. An English translation by Margaret Robinson, Marianne Hirsch, and Leo Spitzer, edited and with an introduction and annotations by Leo Spitzer and Marianne Hirsch, is in preparation.

12. Marianne Hirsch and Leo Spitzer, videotaped interview with Polya Dubs (Rehovoth, Israel, September 6, 2000).

13. Some of the artists' names are not clearly readable in the pages of the little book, and our transcriptions of their names are, in these cases, no more than approximations.

14. Herman Hesse's short story from *Fontaine*, a French literary journal published during the Second World War in Algiers and France, is quoted in Gaston Bachelard, *The Poetics of Space*, 150.

15. Susan Stewart, *On Longing*, xii.

16. Gall, *Finsternis*, 151.

17. Stewart, *On Longing*, 54.

8. OBJECTS OF RETURN

1. Lily Brett, *Too Many Men*, 514.

2. Ibid., 518.

3. On the contemporary phenomenon of return and its recent prevalence, see Marianne Hirsch and Nancy K. Miller, eds., *Rites of Return*.

4. For a classic feminist reading of narrative implausibility, see Nancy K. Miller, "Emphasis Added: Plots and Plausibilities in Women's Writing," *PMLA* 96, 1 (January 1981), 36–48.

5. Ghassan Kanafani, *Palestine's Children*, 99.

6. Ibid., 102.

7. For related analyses of the embodied qualities of return journeys, see Marianne Hirsch and Leo Spitzer, "The Tile Stove" and *Ghosts of Home*.

8. Paul Connerton, *How Societies Remember*, 95.

9. Miriam is one of the first Jewish Israeli characters in Palestinian literature, and a remarkably sympathetic one.

10. Kanafani, *Palestine's Children*, 129. I am grateful to Amira Hass for pointing this incongruity out to me.

11. Brett, *Too Many Men*, 526.

12. Ibid., 527.

13. Ibid., 113.

14. Aleida Assmann, *Der lange Schatten der Vergangenheit*.

15. Assmann's distinction is comparable to Diana Taylor's theorization of a distinction between the "archive" and what she terms "the repertoire"— those stored behaviors and embodied practices that exceed the conventional

structures of the cultural archive. (Diana Taylor, *The Archive and the Repertoire*.) While Taylor specifically writes about cultural memory, Assmann's distinction here is centered on individual embodied recall.

16. Assmann, *Der lange Schatten der Vergangenheit*, 122.

17. Saidiya Hartman, *Lose Your Mother*.

18. Brett, *Too Many Men*, 526.

19. Ibid., 5.

20. Joseph Roach, *Cities of the Dead*.

21. The phantom sibling, or "memorial candle," is a ubiquitous and determining figure in narratives of massive trauma and loss. See esp. Richieu in Art Spiegelman's 1986 *Maus*, but also, more recently, the figure of Simon in Phillippe Grimbert's novel and Claude Miller's 2008 film *A Secret*. On the notion of "memorial candle," see Dina Wardi, *Memorial Candles*. On "replacement children," see Gabriele Schwab, *Haunting Legacies*, chap. 5.

22. On perpetrator photographs of executions, see chap. 5.

23. Griselda Pollock, *Encounters in the Virtual Feminist Museum*.

24. See esp. Bracha Lichtenberg-Ettinger, *Artworking, 1985–1999*; *The Eurydice Series*; *Matrix: Carnets 1985–1989*; *The Matrixial Gaze*; and *Que dirait Eurydice? What Would Eurydice Say?*

25. Pollock, *Encounters*, 175.

26. On unconscious optics, see Walter Benjamin, "The Work of Art in the Age of Mechanical Reproduction," and Marianne Hirsch, *Family Frames*.

27. For a full account, see Dalia Karpel, "With Thanks to Ghassan Kanafani," *Ha'aretz* (April 15, 2005). Sami Michael's novel has not been translated into English.

28. Rebecca Harrison, review of "The Return to Haifa," by Ghassan Kanafani, *Ha'aretz*, April 15, 2008.

29. Ibid.

9. POSTMEMORY'S ARCHIVAL TURN

1. Hal Foster, "An Archival Impulse."

2. Ibid., 21.

3. Ibid.

4. Ibid.

5. On the album, see Martha Langford, *Suspended Conversations*. I am grateful to Annegret Pelz and Anke Kramer for their invitation to speak and think about the album in Vienna in 2009.

6. The terms are Jacques Derrida's; see *Archive Fever*, 2–3.

7. Margaret Olin, *Touching Photographs*, 149.

8. See Andrew Hoskins, "Digital Network Memory."

9. Golda Tencer and Anna Bikont, eds., *And I Still See Their Faces*, 5.
10. Ibid., 6.
11. Kristen Lubben, ed., *Susan Meiselas: In History*, 242.
12. E-mail correspondence with the artist (November 25, 2010).
13. Lubben, *Susan Meiselas*, 244.
14. Personal communication from the artist.
15. Susan Meiselas, *Kurdistan: In the Shadow of History*, xv.
16. Personal communication from the artist.
17. Tencer and Bikont, *And I Still See Their Faces*, 174.
18. Ibid., 5
19. Barthes, *Camera Lucida*, 96. See the discussion of photography and death in chap. 5.
20. Meiselas, *Kurdistan*, xvii.
21. Olin, *Touching Photographs*, 151.
22. E-mail correspondence with the artist (November 25, 2010).
23. Meiselas, *Kurdistan*, xvii.
24. *And I Still See Their Faces*, The Simon Wiesenthal Center.
25. *Aka Kurdistan: A Place for Collective Memory and Cultural Exchange.*
26. E-mail correspondence with the artist (November 25, 2010).
27. Boym, *The Future of Nostalgia*, 347.
28. E-mail comment from the artist (November 25, 2010).
29. Elizabeth Edwards, "Entangled Documents: Visualized Histories," 330.
30. Jeff Wall, "Photography and Liquid Intelligence," 109–110.
31. Ibid.
32. Tencer and Bikont, *And I Still See Their Faces*, 5.
33. See Jan Gross, *Neighbors: The Destruction of the Jewish Community of Jedwabne, Poland* (Princeton: Princeton University Press, 2001).
34. Art Spiegelman, *Maus I*, 114–16.
35. Régine Robin, *L'Immense fatigue des pierres*.
36. Patricia J. Williams, *The Rooster's Egg*, 208–9.

SELECTED BIBLIOGRAPHY

Abraham, Nicolas, and Maria Torok. *The Shell and the Kernel: Renewals of Psychoanalysis*. Translated by Nicholas Rand. Chicago: University of Chicago Press, 1994.

Adorno, Theodor W. *Prisms*. Translated by Samuel Weber and Shierry Nicholson. Cambridge, Mass.: MIT Press, 1967.

Agosín, Marjorie. *Dear Anne Frank*. Translated by Richard Schaaf. Washington, D.C.: Azul Editions, 1994.

Aka Kurdistan: A Place for Collective Memory and Cultural Exchange, http://www.akakurdistan.com (accessed January 16, 2012). .

And I Still See Their Faces, The Simon Wiesenthal Center, http://motlc.wiesenthal.com/site/pp.asp?c=jmKYJeNVJrF&b=478527 (accessed January 16, 2012).

Appignanesi, Lisa. *Losing the Dead*. London: Chatto & Windus, 1999.

Assmann, Aleida. *Der lange Schatten der Vergangenheit: Erinnerungskultur und Geschichtspolitik*. München: Beck, 2006.

——. *Erinnerungsräume: Formen und Wandlungen des kulturellen Gedächtnisses*. München: Beck, 1999.

——. "Re-framing Memory: Between Individual and Collective Forms of Constructing the Past." In *Performing the Past: Memory, History, and Identity in Modern Europe*, edited by Karin Tilmans, Frank van Vree, and Jay Winter, 35–50. Amsterdam: Amsterdam University Press, 2010.

Assmann, Jan. *Das kulturelle Gedächtnis: Schrift, Erinnerung und politische Identität in früheren Hochkulturen.* München: Beck, 1997.

Azoulay, Ariella. *The Civil Contract of Photography.* Translated by Rela Mazali and Ruvik Danieli. New York: Zone Books, 2008.

Bachelard, Gaston. *The Poetics of Space.* Translated by Maria Jolas. New York: Orion Press, 1964.

Baer, Elizabeth R., and Hester Baer. "Postmemory Envy?" *Women in German Yearbook: Feminist Studies in German Literature and Culture* 19 (2003): 75–98.

Baer, Elizabeth R., and Myrna Goldenberg, eds. *Experience and Expression: Women, the Nazis, and the Holocaust.* Detroit: Wayne State University Press, 2003.

Baer, Ulrich. *Spectral Evidence: The Photography of Trauma.* Cambridge, Mass.: MIT Press, 2002.

——. "To Give Memory a Place: Holocaust Photography and the Landscape Tradition." *Representations* 69 (2000): 38–62.

Bal, Mieke, Jonathan Crewe, and Leo Spitzer, eds. *Acts of Memory: Cultural Recall in the Present.* Hanover: University Press of New England, 1998.

Ball, Karyn. "Unspeakable Differences, Unseen Pleasures: The Holocaust as an Object of Desire." *Women in German Yearbook: Feminist Studies in German Literature and Culture* 19 (2003): 20–49.

Barnouw, Dagmar. *Germany 1945: Views of War and Violence.* Bloomington: Indiana University Press, 1996.

Barthes, Roland. *Camera Lucida: Reflections on Photography.* Translated by Richard Howard. New York: Hill and Wang, 1981.

——. *Roland Barthes by Roland Barthes.* Translated by Richard Howard. Berkeley: University of California Press, 1977.

Batchen, Geoffrey, Mick Gidley, Nancy K. Miller, and Jay Prosser, eds. *Picturing Atrocity: Reading Photographs in Crisis.* London: Reaktion Books, 2012.

Baumel, Judith Tydor. *Double Jeopardy: Gender and the Holocaust.* London: Vallentine Mitchell, 1998.

Benjamin, Walter. "A Short History of Photography." Translated by P. Patton. In *Classic Essays on Photography,* edited by Alan Trachtenberg. New Haven: Yale University Press, 1980.

——. "The Work of Art in the Age of Mechanical Reproduction." In *Illuminations,* translated by Harry Zohn and edited by Hannah Arendt, 217–51. New York: Harcourt, Brace & World, 1968.

Bennett, Jill. "The Aesthetics of Sense-Memory: Theorising Trauma Through the Visual Arts." In *Trauma und Erinnerung/Trauma and Memory: Crosscultural Perspectives,* edited by Franz Kaltenbeck and Peter Weibel, 81–96. Vienna: Passagen, 2000.

——. *Empathic Vision: Affect, Trauma, and Contemporary Art.* Palo Alto: Stanford University Press, 2005.

Berger, Alan L. *Children of Job: American Second-Generation Witnesses to the Holocaust*. Albany: State University of New York Press, 1997.

Bernstein, Michael André. *Foregone Conclusions: Against Apocalyptic History*. Berkeley: University of California Press, 1994.

Bettelheim, Bruno. "The Ignored Lesson of Anne Frank." In *Surviving and Other Essays*. New York: Knopf, 1979.

Bilder der Welt und Inschrift des Krieges (Images of the World and the Inscription of War). Dir. Harun Farocki, 1988.

Bird, John, Jo Anna Isaak, and Sylvère Lotringer. *Nancy Spero*. London: Phaidon, 1996.

Boltanski, Christian, Lynn Gumpert, and Mary Jane Jacob. *Christian Boltanski: Lessons of Darkness*. Chicago: Museum of Contemporary Art, 1988.

Bopp, Petra. *Fremde im Visier: Foto-Erinnerungen an den Zweiten Weltkrieg*. Bielefeld: Kerber, 2010.

Bos, Pascale. "Positionality and Postmemory in Scholarship on the Holocaust." *Women in German Yearbook: Feminist Studies in German Literature and Culture* 19 (2003): 50–74.

Boym, Svetlana. *The Future of Nostalgia*. New York: Basic Books, 2001.

Breaking the Silence: The Generation After the Holocaust. Directed by Edward Mason. Public Broadcasting System, 1984.

Brett, Lily. *Too Many Men*. New York: HarperCollins Perennial, 2002.

Brink, Cornelia. " 'How to Bridge the Gap': Überlegungen zu einer fotographischen Sprache des Gedenkens." In *Die Sprache des Gedenkens: Zur Geschichte der Gedenkstätte Ravensbrück*, edited by Insa Eschebach, Sigrid Jacobeit, and Susanne Lanwerd. Berlin: Edition Hentrich, 1999.

——. *Ikonen der Vernichtung: Öffentlicher Gebrauch von Fotografien aus nationalsozialistischen Konzentrationslagern nach 1945*. Berlin: Akademie, 1998.

Browning, Christopher. *Ordinary Men: Reserve Police Batallion 101 and the Final Solution in Poland*. New York: HarperCollins, 1992.

Bukiet, Melvin Jules. *After*. New York: St. Martin's, 1996.

——, ed. *Nothing Makes You Free: Writings by Descendants of Jewish Holocaust Survivors*. New York: Norton, 2002.

Caplan, Jane. " 'Indelible Memories': The Tattooed Body as Theatre of Memory." In *Performing the Past: Memory, History, and Identity in Modern Europe*, edited by Karin Tilmans, Frank van Vree, and Jay Winter, 119–46. Amsterdam: Amsterdam University Press, 2010.

——. *Written on the Body: The Tattoo in European and American History*. Princeton: Princeton University Press, 2000.

Caruth, Cathy. *Unclaimed Experience: Trauma, Narrative and History*. Baltimore: Johns Hopkins University Press, 1996.

———, ed. *Trauma: Explorations in Memory.* Baltimore: Johns Hopkins University Press, 1995.

Chambers, Ross. *Untimely Interventions: Aids Writing, Testimonial, and the Rhetoric of Haunting.* Ann Arbor: University of Michigan Press, 2004.

Chicago, Judy. *Holocaust Project: From Darkness into Light.* New York: Penguin, 1993.

Connerton, Paul. *How Societies Remember.* Cambridge: Cambridge University Press, 1989.

Crane, Susan A. "Choosing Not to Look: Representation, Repatriation, and Holocaust Atrocity Photography." *History and Theory* 47 (2008): 309–30.

Crary, Jonathan. *Techniques of the Observer: On Vision and Modernity in the Nineteenth Century.* Cambridge, Mass.: MIT Press, 1990.

Culbertson, Roberta. "Embodied Memory, Transcendence, and Telling: Recounting Trauma, Re-establishing the Self." *New Literary History* 26, no.1 (1995): 169–95.

Cvetkovich, Ann. *An Archive of Feelings: Trauma, Sexuality, and Lesbian Public Culture.* Durham: Duke University Press, 2003.

Dark Lullabies. Directed by Irene Lilienheim Angelico. National Film Board of Canada, 1985.

Delbo, Charlotte. *Days and Memory.* Translated by Rosette Lamont. Marlboro, Vt.: Marlboro Press, 1990.

Derrida, Jacques. *Archive Fever: A Freudian Impression.* Translated by Eric Prenowitz. Chicago: University of Chicago Press, 1995.

———. *Memoires for Paul de Man.* Translated by Cecile Lindsay, Jonathan Culler, Eduardo Cadava, and Peggy Kamuf. New York: Columbia University Press, 1988.

———. *The Work of Mourning.* Edited by Pascale-Anne Brault and Michael Nas. Chicago: University of Chicago Press, 2001.

De Silva, Cara, ed. *In Memory's Kitchen: A Legacy from the Women of Terezín.* Northvale, N.J.: J. Aronson, 1993.

Didi-Huberman, Georges. "Artistic Survival: Panofsky vs. Warburg and the Exorcism of Impure Time." *Common Knowledge* 9, no. 2 (2003): 273–85.

———. *Images in Spite of All: Four Photographs from Auschwitz.* Translated by Shane B. Lillis. Chicago: University of Chicago Press, 2008.

Doane, Marianne. "Indexicality: Trace and Sign: Introduction." *Differences* 18, no. 1 (2007): 1–6.

Dobroszycki, Lucjan, and Barbara Kirshenblatt-Gimblett. *Image Before My Eyes: A Photographic History of Jewish Life in Poland, 1864–1939.* New York: Schocken Books, 1977.

Dwork, Debórah. *Children with a Star: Jewish Youth in Nazi Europe.* New Haven: Yale University Press, 1991.

Dwork, Debórah, and Robert Jan van Pelt. "Reclaiming Auschwitz." In *Holocaust Remembrance: The Shapes of Memory,* edited by Geoffrey Hartman, 232–51. Cambridge: Basil Blackwell, 1994.

——. *Auschwitz*. New York: W.W. Norton, 1996.

Edelman, Gwen. *War Story*. New York: Riverhead, 2001.

Edwards, Elizabeth. "Entangled Documents: Visualized Histories." In *Susan Meiselas: In History*, edited by Kristen Lubben, 330–41. New York: International Center of Photography and Steidl, 2008.

Eigler, Friederike. "Engendering Cultural Memory in Selected Post-Wende Literary Texts of the 1990s." *German Quarterly* 74 (2001): 392–406.

Eng, David L. *The Feeling of Kinship: Queer Liberalism and the Racialization of Intimacy*. Durham: Duke University Press, 2010.

Epstein, Helen. *Children of the Holocaust: Conversations with Sons and Daughters of Survivors*. New York: Putnam, 1979.

Epstein, Julia, and Lori Hope Lefkovitz, eds. *Shaping Losses: Cultural Memory and the Holocaust*. Urbana: University of Illinois Press, 2001.

Ezrahi, Sidra deKoven. "Representing Auschwitz." *History and Memory* 7, no. 2 (Fall–Winter, 1995): 121–54.

——. "Revisioning the Past: The Changing Legacy of the Holocaust in Hebrew Literature." *Salmagundi* (Fall 1985–Winter 1986): 245–70.

Felman, Shoshana, and Dori Laub, eds. *Testimony: Crises of Witnessing in Psychoanalysis, Literature and History*. New York: Routledge, 1992.

Fine, Ellen. "The Absent Memory: The Act of Writing in Post-Holocaust French Literature." In *Writing and the Holocaust*, edited by Berel Lang, 41–57. New York: Holmes & Meier, 1988.

Fink, Ida. *A Scrap of Time*. Translated by Madeline Levine and Francine Prose, 135–37. New York: Schocken, 1987.

Fleckner, Uwe, and Sarkis. *The Treasure Chest of Mnemosyne: Selected Texts on Memory Theory from Plato to Derrida*. Dresden: Verlag der Kunst, 1998.

Foster, Hal. "An Archival Impulse." *October* 110 (Fall 2004): 3–22.

——. *The Return of the Real: The Avant-Garde at the End of the Century*. Cambridge, Mass.: MIT Press, 1996.

Franklin, Ruth. *A Thousand Darknesses: Lies and Truth in Holocaust Fiction*. Oxford: Oxford University Press, 2011.

Fresco, Nadine. *La Mort des Juifs*. Paris: Seuil, 2009.

——. "Remembering the Unknown." *International Review of Psychoanalysis* 11 (1984): 417–27.

Fried, Michael. "Barthes's Punctum." *Critical Inquiry* 31 (2005): 539–74.

Friedlander, Saul, ed. *Probing the Limits of Representation: Nazism and the "Final Solution."* Cambridge, Mass.: Harvard University Press, 1992.

——. "Trauma, Transference, and 'Working Through' in Writing the History of the Shoah." *History and Memory* 4, no. 1 (1992): 39–59.

Fuss, Diana. *Identification Papers*. New York: Routledge, 1995.

Gallop, Jane (photographs by Dick Blau). *Living with His Camera*. Durham: Duke University Press, 2003.

Goldhagen, Daniel J. *Hitler's Willing Executioners: Ordinary Germans and the Holocaust*. New York: Knopf, 1996.

Grossman, David. *See Under: Love*. Translated by Betsy Rosenberg. New York: Farrar, Straus & Giroux, 1997.

Grossman, Mendel. *With a Camera in the Ghetto [Lódz]*. Translated by Mendel Kohansky. Hakibutz Hameuchad: Ghetto Fighters' House, Lohame HaGetaot, 1970.

Grunebaum, Heidi Peta. *Memorializing the Past: Everyday Life in South Africa After the Truth and Reconciliation Commission*. New York: Transaction, 2011.

Halbwachs, Maurice. *On Collective Memory*. Edited and translated by Lewis Coser. Chicago: University of Chicago Press, 1992.

Hamburg Institute for Social Research, ed. *The German Army and Genocide: Crimes Against War Prisoners, Jews, and Other Civilians, 1939–1945*. Translated by Scott Abbott. New York: New Press, 1999.

Hariman, Robert, and John Louis Lucaites. *No Caption Needed: Iconic Photographs, Public Culture, and Liberal Democracy*. Chicago: University of Chicago Press, 2007.

Harris, Stefanie. "The Return of the Dead: Memory and Photography in W. G. Sebald's *Die Ausgewanderten*." *The German Quarterly* 74, no. 4 (2001): 379–91.

Hartman, Geoffrey H. *The Longest Shadow: In the Aftermath of the Holocaust*. Bloomington: Indiana University Press, 1996.

Hartman, Saidiya. *Lose Your Mother: A Journey Along the Atlantic Slave Route*. New York: Farrar, Straus & Giroux, 2007.

Hass, Aaron. *In the Shadow of the Holocaust: The Second Generation*. Ithaca: Cornell University Press, 1990.

Hellman, Peter, ed. *The Auschwitz Album: A Book Based on an Album Discovered by a Concentration Camp Survivor, Lili Meier*. New York: Random House, 1981.

Heydecker, Joe Julius. *Where Is Thy Brother Abel?: Documentary Photographs of the Warsaw Ghetto*. Sao Paolo: Atlantis Livros, 1981.

Heymann, Florence. *Le Crépuscule des Lieux: Identités Juives de Czernowitz*. Paris: Stock, 2003.

Hilberg, Raul. *The Destruction of the European Jews*. 3 vols. New York: Holmes & Meier, 1985.

Hirsch, Marianne. *Family Frames: Photography, Narrative, and Postmemory*. Cambridge, Mass.: Harvard University Press, 1997.

——. "Maternity and Rememory." In *Motherhood and Representation*, edited by Donna Bassin, Margaret Honey, and Meryle Kaplan, 92–110. New Haven: Yale University Press, 1994.

——. *The Mother/Daughter Plot: Narrative, Psychoanalysis, Feminism*. Bloomington: Indiana University Press, 1989.

Hirsch, Marianne, and Nancy K. Miller, eds. *Rites of Return: Diaspora Poetics and the Politics of Memory*. New York: Columbia University Press, 2011.

Hirsch, Marianne, and Valerie Smith. "Feminism and Cultural Memory: An Introduction." *Gender and Cultural Memory*, special issue of *Signs: Journal of Women in Culture and Society* 28, no. 1 (2002): 1–19.

Hirsch, Marianne, and Leo Spitzer. "Gendered Translations: Claude Lanzmann's Shoah." In *Gendering War Talk*, edited by Miriam Cooke and Angela Woollacott, 3–19. Princeton: Princeton University Press, 1993.

——. *Ghosts of Home: The Afterlife of Czernowitz in Jewish Memory*. Berkeley: University of California Press, 2010.

——. "Holocaust Studies/Memory Studies: The Witness in the Archive." In Susannah Radstone and Bill Schwarz, eds., *Memory: Histories, Theories, Debates*. New York: Fordham University Press, 2010.

——. "Incongruous Images: 'Before, During, and After' the Holocaust." *History and Theory* 48, no. 4 (2009): 9–25.

——. " 'There was never a camp here': Searching for Vapniarka." In *Locating Memory*, edited by Annette Kuhn and Kirsten McAllister, 135–54. New York: Berghahn, 2007.

——. "The Tile Stove." *WSQ* 36, nos. 1 & 2 (Spring/Summer 2008): 141–50.

Hirsch, Marianne, and Susan Suleiman. "Material Memory: Holocaust Testimony in Post-Holocaust Art." In *Shaping Losses: Cultural Memory and the Holocaust*, edited by Julia Epstein and Lori Hope Lefkowitz, 87–104. Urbana: University of Illinois Press, 2001.

Hoffman, Eva. *After Such Knowledge: Memory, History, and the Legacy of the Holocaust*. New York: Public Affairs, 2004.

Holocaust. Written by Gerald Green, directed by Marvin J. Chomsky. Four episodes first broadcast in the United States on April 16–19, 1978, by the National Broadcasting Company.

Hornstein, Shelley, and Florence Jacobowitz, eds. *Image and Remembrance: Representation and the Holocaust*. Bloomington: Indiana University Press, 2002.

Horstkotte, Silke. "Literarische Subjektivität und die Figur des Transgenerationellen in Marcel Beyers *Spione* und Rachel Seifferts *The Dark Room*." In *Historisierte Subjekte–Subjektivierte Historie: Zur Verfügbarkeit und Unverfügbarkeit von Geschichte*, edited by Stefan Deines, Stephan Jaeger, and Ansgar Nünning, 275–93. Berlin: Walter de Gruyter, 2003.

Hoskins, Andrew. "7/7 and Connective Memory: Interactional Trajectories of Remembering in Post-Scarcity Culture." *Memory Studies* 4, no. 3 (July 2011), 269–80.

——. "Digital Network Memory." In *Mediation, Remediation, and the Dynamics of Cultural Memory*, edited by Astrid Erll and Ann Rigney, 91–106. Berlin: Mouton de Gruyter.

Hughes, Alex, and Andrea Noble. *Phototextualities: Intersections of Photography and Narrative*. Albuquerque: University of New Mexico Press, 2003.

Hungerford, Amy. *The Holocaust of Texts: Genocide, Literature, and Personification*. Chicago: University of Chicago Press, 2003.

Hüppauf, Bernd. "Emptying the Gaze: Framing Violence Through the Viewfinder." *New German Critique* 72 (1997): 3–44.

Huyssen, Andreas. *Present Pasts: Urban Palimpsests and the Politics of Memory*. Stanford: Stanford University Press, 2003.

———. "Transnationale Verwertungen von Holokaust und Kolonialismus." In *Verwertungen von Vergangenheit*, edited by Elisabeth Wagner and Burkhardt Wolf, 30–51. Berlin: Vorwerk 8, 2009.

Janet, Pierre. *Les Médications psychologiques (1919–25)*. Vol. 2. Paris: Société Pierre Janet, 1984.

Jones, Amelia. "The 'Eternal Return': Self-Portrait Photography as a Technology of Embodiment." *Signs* 27 (2002): 947–78.

Justman, Stewart, ed. *The Jewish Holocaust for Beginners*. London: Writers and Readers, 1995.

Kacandes, Irene. *Daddy's War: Greek American Stories*. Lincoln: University of Nebraska Press, 2009.

Kahane, Claire. "Dark Mirrors: A Feminist Reflection on Holocaust Narrative and the Maternal Metaphor." In *Feminist Consequences: Theory for the New Century*, edited by Elisabeth Bronfen and Misha Kavka, 161–88. New York: Columbia University Press, 2000.

Kanafani, Ghassan. *Palestine's Children: Return to Haifa and Other Stories*. Translated by Barbara Harlow. London: Heinemann, 1984.

Kaplan, Alice. *French Lessons*. Chicago: University of Chicago Press, 1993.

Kaplan, Brett Ashley. *Landscapes of Holocaust Postmemory*. New York: Routledge, 2010.

———. *Unwanted Beauty: Aesthetic Pleasure and Holocaust Representation*. Urbana: University of Illinois Press, 2007.

Karpf, Anne. *The War After: Living with the Holocaust*. London: Heinemann, 1996.

Keller, Ulrich, ed. *The Warsaw Ghetto in Photographs: 206 Views Made in 1941*. New York: Dover, 1984.

Kellner, Tatana. *B-11226: Fifty Years of Silence*. Rosendale, N.Y.: Women's Studio Workshop, 1992.

———. *71125: Fifty Years of Silence*. Rosendale, N.Y.: Women's Studio Workshop, 1992.

Kessler, Arthur. "Ein Arzt im Lager: Die Fahrt ins Ungewisse. Tagebuch u. Aufzeichnungen eines Verschickten" ("A Doctor in the Lager: the Journey in the Unknown. Diary and Notes of a Deportee"). Unpublished manuscript.

———. "Lathyrismus." *Psychiatrie und Neurologie* 112, no. 6 (1947): 345–76.

Kestenberg, Judith. "A Metapsychological Assessment Based on an Analysis of a Survivor's Child." In *Generations of the Holocaust*, edited by Martin S. Bergman and Milton E. Jucovy, 137–58. New York: Basic Books, 1982.

Kidron, Carol A. "In Pursuit of Jewish Paradigms of Memory: Constituting Carriers of Jewish Memory in a Support Group of Children of Holocaust Survivors." *Dapim: Studies on the Shoah* 23, no. 9 (2009): 7–43.

Klarsfeld, Serge. *The Children of Izieu: A Human Tragedy.* New York, Abrams: 1984.

Klarsfeld, Serge, Susan Cohen, and Howard Epstein, eds. *French Children of the Holocaust: A Memorial.* Translated by Glorianne Depondt and Howard Epstein. New York: New York University Press, 1996.

Klüger, Ruth. *Von hoher und niedriger Literatur.* Bonn: Wallstein, 1996.

Koch, Gertrud. *Die Einstellung ist die Einstellung: Visuelle Konstruktionen des Judentums.* Frankfurt: Suhrkamp, 1992.

Korwin, Yala, ed. *To Tell the Story: Poems of the Holocaust.* New York: Holocaust Library, 1987.

Kremer, Lillian. *Women's Holocaust Writing.* Lincoln: University of Nebraska Press, 1999.

Kritzman, Lawrence D. "Roland Barthes: The Discourse of Desire and the Question of Gender." *Modern Language Notes* 103 (1988): 848–64.

Lacan, Jacques. *Four Fundamental Concepts of Psychoanalysis.* Translated by Alan Sheridan. New York: Norton, 1978.

——. "Psychoanalysis and Cybernetics, or on the Nature of Language." In *The Seminar of Jacques Lacan, Book II,* edited by Jacques-Alain Miller and translated by Sylvana Tomaselli, 294–308. New York: Norton, 1988.

LaCapra, Dominick. *History and Memory After Auschwitz.* Ithaca: Cornell University Press, 1998.

——. *Representing the Holocaust: History, Theory, Trauma.* Ithaca: Cornell University Press, 1994.

——. *Writing History, Writing Trauma.* Baltimore: Johns Hopkins University Press, 2001.

Landsberg, Alison. *Prosthetic Memory: The Transformation of American Remembrance in the Age of Mass Culture.* New York: Columbia University Press, 2004.

Lang, Berel. *Writing and the Holocaust.* New York: Holmes & Meier, 1988.

Langer, Lawrence. *Preempting the Holocaust.* New Haven: Yale University Press, 1998.

Langford, Martha. *Suspended Conversations: The Afterlife of Memory in Photographic Albums.* Montreal: McGill University Press, 2008.

Laplanche, Jean, and Jean-Bertrand Pontalis. "Fantasy and the Origins of Sexuality." In *Formation of Fantasy,* edited by Victor Burgin, James Donald, and Cora Kaplan. London: Routledge, 1989.

Lentin, Ronit. *Israel and the Daughters of the Shoah: Reoccupying the Territories of Silence.* New York: Berghahn, 2000.

Lest We Forget: A History of the Holocaust. Belgium: Endless S.A., Sitac, and Media Investment Club, 1998.

Levi, Primo. "The Chemical Examination." In his *Survival in Auschwitz: The Nazi Assault on Humanity*, translated by Stuart Woolf. New York: Collier Books, 1960.

Levin, Mikael. *War Story*. New York: Gina Kehayoff, 1997.

Levinthal, David. *Mein Kampf*. Santa Fe: Twin Palms, 1996.

Levy, Daniel, and Natan Sznaider. *The Holocaust and Memory in the Global Age: Politics, History, and Social Change*. Philadelphia: Temple University Press, 2006.

Leys, Ruth. *Trauma: A Genealogy*. Chicago: University of Chicago Press, 2000.

Lichtenberg-Ettinger, Bracha. *Artworking, 1985–1999*. Brussels: Palais des Beaux Arts, 1999.

——. *The Eurydice Series*. Edited by Catherine de Zegher and Brian Massumi. *Drawing Papers* 24. New York: The Drawing Center, 2001.

——. *Matrix: Carnets 1985–1989*. Artist book, 1992.

——. *The Matrixial Gaze*. Leeds: Feminist Arts and Histories Network, 1995.

——. *Que dirait Eurydice? What Would Eurydice Say? Emmanuel Levinas en/in Conversation avec/with Bracha Lichtenberg-Ettinger*. Amsterdam: Kabinet in the Stedeijk Musem, 1997.

Lifton, Robert Jay. *The Broken Connection: On Death and the Continuity of Life*. New York: Simon & Schuster, 1979.

Liss, Andrea. *Trespassing Through Shadows: Memory, Photography, and the Holocaust*. Minneapolis: University of Minnesota Press. 1998.

Lubben, Kristen, ed. *Susan Meiselas: In History*. New York: International Center of Photography and Steidl, 2008.

Lury, Celia. *Prosthetic Culture: Photography, Memory, Identity*. London and New York: Routledge, 1998.

Mandel, Naomi. *Against the Unspeakable: Complicity, the Holocaust, and Slavery in America*. Charlottesville: University of Virginia Press, 2006.

McClintock, Anne. *Imperial Leather: Race, Gender and Sexuality in the Colonial Contest*. New York: Routledge, 1995.

McGlothlin, Erin. *Second-Generation Holocaust Literature: Legacies of Survival and Perpetration*. Rochester: Camden House, 2006.

Meiselas, Susan. *Kurdistan: In the Shadow of History*. Second ed. Chicago: University of Chicago Press, 2007.

Metz, Christian. "Photography and Fetish." In *The Critical Image: Essays on Contemporary Photography*, edited by Carol Squiers. Seattle: Bay Press, 1990.

Michaels, Anne. *Fugitive Pieces*. New York: Knopf, 1997.

Michaels, Walter Benn. "'You who never was there': Slavery and the New Historicism, Deconstruction and the Holocaust." *Narrative* 4, no. 1 (January 1996): 1–16.

Miller, Nancy K., and Jason Tougaw. *Extremities: Trauma, Testimony and Community*. Urbana: University of Illinois Press, 2002.

Milton, Sybil. "Photographs of the Warsaw Ghetto." *Simon Wiesenthal Center Annual* 3 (1986): 307.

Milton, Sybil, Judith Levin, and Daniel Uziel. "Ordinary Men, Extraordinary Photos." *Yad Vashem Studies*, 26 (1998): 265–79.

Mitchell, Juliet. *Mad Men and Medusas: Reclaiming Hysteria.* New York: Basic Books, 2000.

Morris, Leslie. "Postmemory, Postmemoir." In *Unlikely History: The Changing German-Jewish Symbiosis, 1945–2000*, edited by Leslie Morris and Jack Zipes, 291–306. New York: Palgrave, 2002.

——. "The Sound of Memory." *German Quarterly* 74 (2001): 368–78.

Morrison, Toni. *Beloved.* New York: Knopf, 1987.

Moten, Fred. *In the Break: The Aesthetics of the Black Radical Tradition.* Minneapolis: University of Minnesota Press, 2003.

Night and Fog. Directed by Alain Resnais. France. Distributed by Contemporary Films/McGraw-Hill, 1955.

Nora, Pierre. *Les Lieux de Mémoire.* Paris: Gallimard, 1984.

Olin, Margaret. *Touching Photographs.* Chicago: University of Chicago Press, 2012.

Ozick, Cynthia. "Anne Frank's Afterlife." *The New York Review of Books*, April 9, 1998.

——. *The Shawl.* New York: Knopf, 1989.

Phelan, Peggy. "Francesca Woodman's Photography: Death and the Image One More Time." *Signs* 27 (2002): 979–1004.

Pollock, Griselda. *Encounters in the Virtual Feminist Museum: Time, Space, and the Archive.* London: Routledge, 2007.

——. "Inscriptions in the Feminine." In *Inside the Visible: An Elliptical Traverse of 20th Century Art.* Cambridge, Mass.: MIT Press, 1996.

——. "Rethinking the Artist in the Woman, the Woman in the Artists, and That Old Chestnut, the Gaze." In *Women Artists at the Millenium*, edited by Carol Armstrong and Catherine de Zegher. Cambridge, Mass.: MIT Press, 2006.

Prose, Francine. *Anne Frank: The Book, The Life, The Afterlife.* New York: Harper, 2009.

Prosser, Jay. *Light in the Dark Room: Photography and Loss.* Minneapolis: University of Minnesota Press, 2005.

Rabaté, Jean-Michel. *Writing the Image after Roland Barthes.* Philadelphia: University of Pennsylvania Press, 1997.

Raczymow, Henri. "Memory Shot Through with Holes." Translated by Alan Astro. *Yale French Studies* 85 (1994): 98–106.

Radstone, Susannah. "Social Bonds and Psychical Order: Testimonies." *Cultural Values* 5, no. 1 (2001): 59–78.

Radstone, Susannah, and Bill Schwarz, eds. *Memory: Histories, Theories, Debates.* New York: Fordham University Press, 2010.

Ringelheim, Joan. "Thoughts About Women and the Holocaust." In *Thinking the Unthinkable: Meanings of the Holocaust*, edited by Roger S. Gottlieb, 141–49. New York: Paulist Press, 1990.

———. "The Unethical and the Unspeakable: Women and the Holocaust." In *Simon Wiesenthal Center Annual*, edited by Alex Grobman, 64–87. Chappaqua, N.Y.: Rosssel, 1983.

Rittner, Carol, and John Roth. *Different Voices: Women and the Holocaust*. New York: Paragon House, 1993.

Roach, Joseph. *Cities of the Dead: Circum-Atlantic Performance*. New York: Columbia University Press, 1996.

Robin, Régine. *L'Immense fatigue des pierres*. Paris: Xyz, 2005.

———. *La Mémoire saturée*. Paris: Stock, 2003.

Rosenbaum, Thane. *Second Hand Smoke*. New York: St. Martin's, 1999.

Rossino, Alexander B. "Eastern Europe Through German Eyes: Soldiers' Photographs 1939–42." *History of Photography* 23, no. 4 (Winter 1999): 313–21.

Rothberg, Michael. *Multidirectional Memory: Remembering the Holocaust in the Age of Decolonization*. Stanford: Stanford University Press, 2009.

———. *Traumatic Realism: The Demands of Holocaust Representation*. Minneapolis: University of Minnesota Press, 2000.

Rymkiewicz, Jaroslaw M. *The Final Station: Umschlagplatz*. Translated by Nina Taylor. New York: Farrar, Straus & Giroux, 1994.

Sa'di, Ahmad H., and Lila Abu-Lughod. *Nakba: Palestine, 1948 and the Claims of Memory*. New York: Columbia University Press, 2007.

Said, Edward W. *The World, the Text, and the Critic*. Cambridge: Harvard University Press, 1983.

Santner, Eric. "History Beyond the Pleasure Principle: Some Thoughts on the Representation of Trauma." In *Probing the Limits of Representation: Nazism and the "Final Solution,"* edited by Saul Friedlander, 143–54. Cambridge, Mass.: Harvard University Press, 1992.

Scheler, Max. *The Nature of Sympathy*. Translated by Peter Heath. 1923. Reprint, Hamden, Conn.: Archon Books, 1970.

Schindler's List. Directed by Steven Spielberg. USA. Universal, 1993.

Schoenberner, Gerhard. *The Yellow Star: The Persecution of Jews in Europe 1933–1945*. New York: Fordham University Press, 2004.

Schor, Naomi. *Reading in Detail: Aesthetics and the Feminine*. New York: Methuen, 1987.

Schwab, Gabriele. *Haunting Legacies: Violent Histories and Transgenerational Trauma*. New York: Columbia University Press, 2010.

Schwertfeger, Ruth. *Women of Theresienstadt: Voices from a Concentration Camp*. New York: Berg Publishers, 1989.

Sebald, W. G. *Austerlitz*. Munich: Hanser, 2001.

———. *Austerlitz*. Translated by Anthea Bell. New York: Modern Library, 2001.

Sedgwick, Eve Kosofsky. *Epistemology of the Closet*. Berkeley: University of California Press, 1990.

———. *Touching Feeling: Affect, Pedagogy, Performativity*. Durham: Duke University Press, 2003.

Seiffert, Rachel. *The Dark Room*. New York: Vintage, 2002.

Shachan, Avigdor. *Burning Ice: The Ghettos of Transnistria*. Translated by Shmuel Himelstein. East European Monographs, no. CDXLVII. Boulder and New York: Columbia University Press, 1996.

Shoah. Directed by Claude Lanzmann; distributed by New Yorker Films. France, 1985.

Silverman, Kaja. *The Threshold of the Visible World*. New York: Routledge, 1996.

Snyder, Timothy. *Bloodlands: Europe Between Hitler and Stalin*. New York: Basic, 2010.

Sontag, Susan. *On Photography*. New York: Anchor Doubleday, 1989.

———. *Regarding the Pain of Others*. New York: Farrar, Straus & Giroux, 2003.

Spiegelman, Art. *Maus I: A Survivor's Tale: My Father Bleeds History*. New York: Pantheon, 1986.

———. *Maus II: A Survivor's Tale: And Here My Troubles Began*. New York: Pantheon, 1991.

———. *MetaMaus*. New York: Pantheon Books, 2011.

Spivak, Gayatri C. "Acting Bits/Identity Talk." In *Identities*, edited by Kwame Anthony Appiah and Henry Louis Gates, 147–80. Chicago: University of Chicago Press, 1995.

Stein, Arlene. "Feminism, Therapeutic Culture, and the Holocaust in the United States: The Second-Generation Phenomenon." *Jewish Social Studies: History, Culture, Society* 16, no. 1 (2009): 27–53.

Steinitz, Lucy Y., and David M. Szonyi, ed. *Living After the Holocaust: Reflections by Children of Survivors in America*. Second ed. New York: Bloch, 1979.

Stewart, Susan. *On Longing: Narratives of the Miniature, the Gigantic, the Souvenir, the Collection*. Durham: Duke University Press, 1993.

Stone, Dan. "Chaos and Continuity: Representations of Auschwitz." In *Representations of Auschwitz: Fifty Years of Photographs, Paintings and Graphics*, ed. Yasmin Doosry. Oswiecim: Auschwitz-Birkenau State Museum, 1995.

Stroop, Jürgen. *The Stroop Report: The Jewish Quarter of Warsaw Is No More!* Translated by Sybil Milton. New York: Pantheon, 1979.

Suleiman, Susan Rubin. *Crises of Memory and the Second World War*. Cambridge, Mass.: Harvard University Press, 2006.

———. "The 1.5 Generation: Thinking about Child Survivors and the Holocaust." *American Imago* 59, no. 3 (2002): 277–95.

———. "War Memories: On Autobiographical Reading." In *Auschwitz and After: Race, Culture, and "the Jewish Question" in France*, edited by Lawrence D. Kritzman, 47–62. New York: Routledge, 1995.

Swiebicka, Teresa, ed. *Auschwitz: A History in Photographs*. Oswiecim, Bloomington, Warsaw: Auschwitz-Birkenau State Museum and Indiana University Press, 1990.

Taylor, Diana. *The Archive and the Repertoire: Performing Cultural Memory in the Americas*. Durham: Duke University Press, 2003.

Tec, Nechama, and Daniel Weiss. "The Heroine of Minsk: Eight Photographs of an Execution." *History of Photography* 23, no. 4 (Winter 1999): 322–30.

Tencer-Szurmiej, Golda, and Anna Bikont, eds., *And I Still See Their Faces: Images of Polish Jews*. Warsaw: Shalom Foundation, 1998.

Tsvi Nussbaum: A Boy from Warsaw. Directed by Ilkka Ahjopalo. Ergo Media, 1990.

Van Alphen, Ernst. *Art in Mind: How Contemporary Images Shape Thought*. Chicago: University of Chicago Press, 2005.

——. *Caught by History: Holocaust Effects in Contemporary Art, Literature, and Theory*. Palo Alto: Stanford University Press, 1997.

——. "Second-Generation Testimony, the Transmission of Trauma, and Postmemory." *Poetics Today* 27, no. 2 (2006): 473–88.

Van der Kolk, Bessel A., and Onno van der Hart. "The Intrusive Past: The Flexibility of Memory and the Engraving of Trauma." In *Trauma: Explorations in Memory*, edited by Cathy Caruth, 158–82. Baltimore: Johns Hopkins University Press, 1995.

Van Dijck, J. "Flickr and the Culture of Connectivity: Sharing Views, Experiences, Memories." *Memory Studies*, 4, no. 4 (September 2011).

Von Braun, Christina. *Die Schamlose Schönheit der Vergangenheit: Zum Verhältnis Von Geschlecht und Geschichte*. Frankfurt: Neue Kritik, 1989.

Wall, Jeff. "Photography and Liquid Intelligence" (1989). In *Selected Essays and Interviews*, 109–10. New York: Museum of Modern Art, 2007.

Warburg, Aby. "The Absorption of the Expressive Values of the Past" (1929). Translated by Matthew Rampley. In *Art in Translation* 1, no. 2 (July 2009): 273–83.

Wardi, Dina. *Memorial Candles: Children of the Holocaust*. New York: Routledge, 1992.

Weigel, Sigrid. " 'Generation' as a Symbolic Form: On the Genealogical Discourse of Memory since 1945." *Germanic Review* 77, no. 4 (2002): 264–77.

Weissman, Gary. *Fantasies of Witnessing: Postwar Efforts to Experience the Holocaust*. Ithaca: Cornell University Press, 2004.

Wenk, Silke. "Pornografisierungen—Einrahmungen des Blicks auf die NS Vergangenheit." Unpublished manuscript, 1999.

Williams, Patricia J. *The Rooster's Egg: On the Persistence of Prejudice*. Cambridge: Harvard University Press, 1995.

Wolin, Jeffrey A. *Written in Memory: Portraits of the Holocaust*. San Francisco: Chronicle Books, 1997.

Yaeger, Patricia. "Consuming Trauma; Or, the Pleasures of Merely Circulating." In *Extremities: Trauma, Testimony, and Community*, edited by Nancy K. Miller and Jason Tougaw, 25–51. Urbana: University of Illinois Press, 2002.

Young, James. *The Art of Memory: Holocaust Memorials in History*. Munich and New York: Prestel, 1994.

——. *At Memory's Edge: After-images of the Holocaust in Contemporary Art and Architecture*. New Haven: Yale University Press, 2000.

——. "Toward a Received History of the Holocaust," *History and Theory* 36, no. 4 (1997): 21–43.

Zeitlin, Froma. "The Vicarious Witness: Belated Memory and Authorial Presence in Recent Holocaust Literature." *History & Memory* 10, no. 2 (Fall 1998): 5–42.

Zelizer, Barbie. *Remembering to Forget: Holocaust Memory Through the Camera's Eye*. Chicago: University of Chicago Press, 1998.

——, ed. *Visual Culture and the Holocaust*. New Brunswick: Rutgers University Press, 2001.

ACKNOWLEDGMENTS

Two of this book's chapters were written collaboratively with Leo Spitzer, and thus the book's voice shifts between the singular and the plural first person. All the chapters reflect their production in the context of our concurrent collaboration on our co-authored book *Ghosts of Home* and thus my thinking is often inextricable from his. They reflect as well the many interdisciplinary conversations we were both lucky to share with colleagues encountered at conferences, workshops, and meetings of reading groups, and in the pages of collected volumes and special journal issues. The dialogues that undergird this argument are palpable throughout these pages, and I am grateful to have had the opportunity to engage these difficult subjects during the remarkable growth of several interdisciplinary fields: Holocaust and memory studies and visual culture, in connection with women, gender, and sexuality studies.

A book written over a number of years incurs endless personal debt. I owe immeasurably to several close colleagues and friends with whom I have taught, written, coedited, collaborated, and co-conspired during the writing of this book, and whom I deeply admire: in addition to Leo Spitzer, Diana Taylor, Nancy K. Miller, Irene Kacandes, Susan Rubin

Suleiman, Valerie Smith, Andreas Huyssen, Jean Howard, Annelise Orleck, Hannah Naveh, Orly Lubin, Ivy Schweitzer, Marta Peixoto, and Jane Coppock. At times, I have talked with some of you on a daily basis, and you will find your ideas and approaches refracted throughout this work.

Fellow members of the postgenerations, whether the third, second, or 1.5, have contributed enormously to my thinking about postmemory, through their skepticism and their hard questions, and through their engaged and creative responses to the heavy legacies we share. I thank Amira Hass, Gail Reimer, Bella Brodski, Pascale Bos, Judith Greenberg, Atina Grossman, Régine Robin, Florence Heymann, Gabriele Schwab, Alice Kessler-Harris, Lori Lefkowitz, Julia Epstein, Heidi Grunebaum, Susannah Heschel, and Susan Gubar. Among the large group of trauma and memory scholars throughout the world, I am most grateful for the lively and provocative discussions I have shared with Lila Abu-Lughod, Jan and Aleida Assman, Mieke Bal, Carol Bardenstein, Susan Brison, Ross Chambers, Mary Marshall Clark, Sarah Cole, Jonathan Crewe, Ann Cvetkovich, Sidra deKoven Ezrahi, Yifat Gutman, Geoffrey Hartman, Brett Kaplan, Temma Kaplan, Barbara Kirshenblatt-Gimblett, Dominick LaCapra, Dori Laub, Michael Levine, Rosanne Kennedy, Erin McGlothlin, Griselda Pollock, Susannah Radstone, Ann Rigney, Michael Rothberg, Ronnie Scharfman, Marita Sturken, Thomas Trezise, Liliane Weissberg, Gary Weissman, Susan Winnett, Ernst van Alphen, Patricia Yaeger, James Young, and Froma Zeitlin.

I am grateful to colleagues working on photography and visual culture who have enabled me to think further about the powers of visual media, especially Elizabeth Abel, Geoffrey Batchen, Jill Bennett, Tina Campt, Saidiya Hartman, Andrea Liss, Agnes Lugo-Ortiz, Diane Miliotes, Peggy Phelan, Jay Prosser, Silvia Spitta, Andy Szegedy-Mazsak, Laura Wexler, and Barbie Zelizer.

Participants in seminars, working groups, and reading groups have provided tough readings and suggestive comments on some of these chapters—at Dartmouth, the Feminist Inquiry Seminar and the Humanities Institute on Cultural Memory and the Present; and at Columbia, the University Seminar on Cultural Memory, the Engendering Archives Group of the Center for the Critical Analysis of Social Difference, and my wonderful feminist reading group.

For their helpful and at times tough editorial work, I thank the editors and readers of the chapters that have appeared, mostly in earlier versions, in essay form: Silke Horstkotte, Nancy Pedri, Meir Sternberg, Annelies Schulte Nordholt, Cornelia Brink, Omer Bartov, Molly Nolan, Jason Tougaw, Andrea Noble, Alex Hughes, Anne-Marie Baronian, Jakob Lothe, James Phelan, Victoria Rosner, Geraldine Pratt, Silke Wenk, and Insa Eschebach, as well as a few multitaskers already named above.

I am grateful to the artists and writers who have inspired this work with theirs and who have generously granted permission for the reproduction of their images. It is fortunate that some of them are also regular interlocutors from whom I have learned immeasurably. For this precious friendship, I thank Muriel Hasbun, Eva Hoffman, Bracha Lichtenberg-Ettinger, Susan Meiselas, Lorie Novak, and Art Spiegelman,

My thinking has been shaped in conversation with students working on memory at Dartmouth, Columbia, and the School of Criticism and Theory. The graduate students I've been fortunate to work with, in particular, have spurred me to look toward the future with greater hope in the possibilities of justice and repair through activist and feminist scholarship that they believe in and themselves practice. Warm thanks for this to Jenny James, Kate Stanley, Joanna Scutts, Sonali Thakkar, and Kate Trebuss, co-organizers of Columbia's Cultural Memory Seminar, and to Lauren Walsh, Susanne Knittel, Chad Diehl, Rachel Frankel, Ofrah Amihai, Sherally Munshi, and many others for their stimulating investigations into the workings of memory.

Enormous thanks to Jenny James, Sonali Thakkar, Emily Cersonsky, and Marta Bladek for their research help and for reading and helping me edit the entire manuscript, and to Vina Tran for putting it all together with such grace and expertise. I thank Jennifer Crewe and everyone at Columbia University Press for the personal warmth they add to their professional skills.

The Columbia University Seminar on Cultural Memory has provided an enriching discussion forum for many of the questions motivating this book. I especially want to acknowledge the Schoff fund for its generous assistance.

As always, I thank our sons and their partners, Alex and Martina, Oliver and Alanna, Gabriel and Meghan, for cheering and encouraging me as I delve into the catastrophes of the past. Through their creative and committed engagements in the world, they continue to remind me to have hope. In the spirit of that hope for a future that is yet to be imagined—a better future that knows the past but is not shadowed by its darknesses—this book is dedicated, with love, to our grandchildren, Quinn, Freya, Chloë, and Lucas.

Earlier versions of a number of chapters were previously published. All have been significantly revised, updated, and integrated into the book's larger argument, though, of course, each still betrays the conventions of its moment of composition and circulation:

"The Generation of Postmemory." *Poetics Today* 28, no. 1 (Spring 2008).

"What's Wrong with This Picture? Archival Photographs in Contemporary Narratives" (with Leo Spitzer), in *Journal of Modern Jewish Studies* 5, no. 2 (2006). trans. "Erinnerungspunkte: Schoahfotografien in zeitgenössischen Erzählungen," *Fotogeschichte: Beiträge zur Geschichte und Ästhetik der Fotografie* (2005).

"Marked by Memory: Feminist Reflections on Trauma and Transmission," in *Extremities*, ed. Nancy K. Miller and Jason Tougaw (Urbana and Chicago: University of Illinois Press, 2002).

"Surviving Images: Holocaust Photographs and the Work of Postmemory," in *Yale Journal of Criticism* 14, no. 1 (Spring 2001). Reprinted in *Visual Culture and the Holocaust*, ed. Barbie Zelizer (New Brunswick: Rutgers University Press "Depth of Field" series, 2001).

"Nazi Photographs in Post-Holocaust Art: Gender as an Idiom of Memorialization," in *Crimes of War: Guilt and Denial*, ed. Omer Bartov, Atina Grossman, and Molly Noble (New York: New Press, 2002). Reprinted in *Phototextualities: Intersections of Photography and Narrative*, ed. Andrea Noble and Alex Hughes (Albuquerque: University of New Mexico Press, 2003).

"Projected Memory: Holocaust Photographs in Personal and Public Fantasy" in *Acts of Memory*, ed. Mieke Bal, Jonathan Crewe, and Leo Spitzer (Hanover: University Press of New England, 1998).

"Testimonial Objects: Memory, Gender, Transmission" (with Leo Spitzer), in *Poetics Today* (2006). Reprinted in *Diaspora and Memory*, ed. M. Baronian, S. Besser, and Y. Janssen (Amsterdam: Amsterdam University Press, 2006).

INDEX

Abraham, Nicolas, 82, 255*n*13

absent memory, 3

acts of return, 24, 203–25; body and sense memory triggered by, 211–13; sequels to, 224–25; surrogations in, 213–16; visual returns as, 216–21

acts of transfer, 31. *See also* intergenerational acts of transfer; transgenerational acts of transfer

affiliative postmemory, defined, 36, 40, 41, 42, 48, 97, 109, 122, 161, 180

affiliative structures of transmission: in child victim images, 155–74; and cultural acts of affiliation, 159; in familial postmemory, 22, 23, 98–99; figures as, 113–20; in Fink's "Traces," 109–12; in iconic images, 103–24; and identification, 166; in Levinthal's *Mein Kampf*, 145–49; in mother/daughter transmissions, 93;

in Novak's *Night and Fog*, 122–24; in perpetrator images, 127–52; screens as, 120–22; in Spero's *The Torture of Women*, 149–52; in testimonial objects, 177–200

After Such Knowledge (Hoffman), 1, 3. *See also* Hoffman, Eva

"After Such Knowledge: Culture and Ideology in Twentieth-Century Europe" (course), 10

Agosín, Marjorie, 156, 161–62, 165

Aka Kurdistan (Meiselas), 240–41, 242, 246

albums: as archives of postmemory, 228, 230–33; evidentiary power of, 65; limits of, 237–43; as transitional period creations, 232–33

allo-identification, 85, 87, 90, 97, 98

alterity, 166, 172–73

alternative histories, 15–16, 243–47

Améry, Jean, 44
And I Still See Their Faces: Images of Polish Jews (Tencer & Bikont), *102*, 226, 229, 230–35, 237–43
Anfal campaign (1988), 231
archives of postmemory, 24, 227–49; albums as, 230–33; alternative histories and counter-memories in, 243–47; digital archives, 228, 230, 242; gaps and silences in, 247–49; limits of, 237–43; photographs as, 68–73, 233–36
Arendt, Hannah, 16
Arkadyev, Lev, 149
Assmann, Aleida, 31–32, 33, 34, 211, 212, 271*n*15
Assmann, Jan, 31–32, 33, 255*n*7
Attie, Shimon, 13
Auschwitz Album, 228
Auschwitz I, 113, *114*, 116
Auschwitz II–Birkenau, 113, *114*, 117–18
Austerlitz (Sebald), 22, 40–48
authentication: in familial postmemory, 41; photographs as, 38; and testimonial objects, 186
auto-identification, 85
"Avadani" (artist), 189–91, *191*
Azoulay, Ariella, 111, 266*n*21

B-11226: Fifty Years of Silence (Kellner), 87–93, *88–89*
Bachelard, Gaston, 195
backshadowing, 63, 74
Baer, Ulrich, 61
Bak, Samuel, 129, 140, *141*, 142
Barbie, Klaus, 156
Barthes, Roland: and maternal images, 47; and notion of punctum, 22, 61–62, 63, 86; on photography, 37, 38, 50, 74, 110–11, 258*n*5

belated memory, 3
Beloved (Morrison), 11, 81, 83, 259*n*7
Benjamin, Walter, 13, 47
Bennett, Jill, 39, 80
Bercovici, Dora, 187
Bergen-Belsen, 103, *116*
Berger, Alan L., 20
Bergman, Ingmar, 129
Bernstein, Michael André, 63
Bettelheim, Bruno, 161
Beyond the Pleasure Principle (Freud), 121
Bikont, Anna, *102*, 226, 234, 244
Birkenau, 113, *114*, 117–18
body memory, 79–99; and acts of return, 211; in Kellner's *Fifty Years of Silence*, 87–93; and photographs, 111–12; rememory vs. postmemory, 82–87; in Wolin's *Written in Memory*, 93–98
Boltanski, Christian, 13, 98
Bourke-White, Margaret, 30, 36, 122
Boym, Svetlana, 242
Brecht, Bertolt, 151
Brett, Lily, 203–205
Bromberg, Zahava, 234–35
Bruskina, Masha, 130, 149–52
Buchenwald prisoners (photo), 30, 122
Budlovsky, Jaroslav, 269*n*3
Bukiet, Melvin, 20
bulldozer image, 113, *116*, 118–19, 136, 264*n*36
Burgin, Victor, 13
Buxbaum, Arthur, 177

Camera Lucida (Barthes), 47, 63, 138, 258*n*8
Caruth, Cathy, 16
catastrophic memory, 86
Celan, Paul, 44, 89, 170

Cernăuți: history of, 56; photographs from, 55–56; postmemories of, 4; yellow stars worn in, 59, 60. See also Czernowitz

Chambers, Ross, 35

Chicago, Judy, 129, 142–44, *143*

children: affiliation and identification with images of, 23, 155–74, 269*n*34; and lost child trope, 210, 212–13, 215–16, 224, 272*n*21; survivors as the 1.5 generation, 15, 41; vulnerability of, 156, 162–63, 173; as witnesses, 163–67. *See also* familial postmemory

The Children of Izieu album, 229

Children of Job (Berger), 20

Children of the Holocaust (Epstein), 251*n*9, 254*n*3

"Choosing Not to Look: Representation, Repatriation, and Holocaust Atrocity in Photography" (Crane), 106

Cities of the Dead (Roach), 214

Cohen, Gavriel, 193–94, *194*

collective memory, 32, 62, 115

collective resistance, 180, 184–85

communicative memory, 32, 33

connective histories, 201–49; in acts of return, 203–25; in archives of postmemory, 227–49; defining, 21

Connerton, Paul, 31, 38, 207

"Consuming Trauma" (Yaeger), 263*n*31

counter-memories, 15–16, 243–47

Crane, Susan A., 106, 108

cropping of images, 68, 140

Culbertson, Roberta, 80

cultural memory: and acts of return, 214; and archives of postmemory, 227; and child images, 159, 173; defined, 32, 33, 255*n*7; and perpetrator images, 135; and

projection, 159; and punctum, 62–63; and testimonial objects, 178

Cypora and Rachela (photo), 243–45, 244

Czernowitz, 4, 55, 59, 60. *See also* Cernăuți

Dachau, 103

The Dark Room (Seiffert), 63–67

Dartmouth College, 7, 12

Das kulturelle Gedächtnis (Assmann), 32

daughters as agents of transmission, 99. *See also* mother/daughter transmission

Dawidowicz, Lucy, 162

DB, 193–94, *194*

De Silva, Cara, 178

Dean, Tacita, 227

Dear Anne Frank (Agosín), 156

decontextualization, 142

deep memory, 82

dehumanization, 23, 118, 148, 179, 184, 196

Delbo, Charlotte, 80, 82

depersonalization of perpetrators, 133

Der lange Schatten der Vergangenheit (Assmann), 211

Derrida, Jacques, 268*n*18

The Destruction of the European Jews (Hilberg), 2

Didi-Huberman, Georges, 38, 107

digital archives, 228, 230, 242

displacement, 161, 163, 208

dissociated memories, 212

Doves in Trafalgar (Michael), 224

Dubs, Polya, 187

Durant, Sam, 227

Duras, Marguerite, 13

Dwork, Debórah, 113–14, 263*n*33

Edwards, Elizabeth, 242
Einsatzgruppen, 130, 138–39, 218
Eliach, Yaffa, 229
empathic identification, 140–41
empathic unsettlement, 262n19
Entrance to Vapniarka (Leibl & Ilie),
182
Epstein, Helen, 251n9, 254n3
Ermarth, Michael, 10
eroticization of murder, 148, 151
escape fantasies, 195
The Eurydice Series
(Lichtenberg-Ettinger), 205–206,
216–21, 219, 222–23, 225

familial gaze, 13, 135
familial look, 13, 135
familial postmemory, 22–23, 27–99;
and affiliative postmemory, 36, 41,
98–99; generation of, 29–52; in
Kellner's *Fifty Years of Silence*,
87–93; markings of, 79–99;
and photographs, 36–40, 55–76;
and points of memory, 61–63; and
projection, 68–73; reasons for,
34–36; rememory vs., 82–87;
and reparative looking, 73–76;
romanticization and mythmaking
in, 49–52; in Sebald's *Austerlitz*,
40–48; in Seiffert's *The Dark Room*,
63–67; in Wolin's *Written in
Memory: Portraits of the
Holocaust*, 93–98
Family Frames (Hirsch), 13, 135
Farocki, Haroum, 266n21
Felman, Shoshana, 16, 80, 97, 168,
170–73
feminist approaches: and acts of
return, 206; and affiliative
postmemory, 98; and memory
studies, 15, 17, 253n21; and
nonappropriative identification

and empathy, 86; and photography,
258n8; and postmemory as activist
platform, 6, 16, 252n20; and
subjectivity and intersubjectivity,
87; and testimonial objects, 179
feminization of victims, 23, 133,
140–45, 147–48
Fifty Years of Silence (Kellner), 87–93,
88–89, 92
The Final Station: Umschlagplatz
(Rymkiewicz), 128
Fine, Ellen, 3
Fink, Ida, 109–12, 113, 119
Finkielkraut, Alain, 98
Finsternis (Gall), 183
The First Maus (Spiegelman), 28,
29–30, 43
Fogelman, Eva, 251n9
Foster, Hal, 121, 227
foster writing, 35
Foucault, Michel, 16, 227
Frank, Anne, 154, 155–56, 161–62, 165
Franklin, Ruth, 20, 253n21
French Children of the Holocaust
(Klarsfeld), 229
French Lessons (Kaplan), 104
Fresco, Nadine, 3, 120
Freud, Sigmund, 16, 51, 82, 121
Friedlander, Saul, 10, 173
Fugitive Pieces (Michaels), 98
The Führer Gives a City to the Jews
(film), 44–46, 45
Fuss, Diana, 260n22

Gall, Matei, 183, 184
Gaon, Boaz, 224–25
gaps in archives of postmemory,
247–49
Geisinger, Berthold, 59, 60
gender: and acts of return, 24; in
affiliative postmemory, 98–99; and
Bruskina's heroization, 151; and

cultural memory, 63; and dehumanization, 179; and familial postmemory, 39–40, 48; and iconic images, 23; and memory, 10, 17–18; and miniaturization, 195–96; in perpetrator images, 144–45, 147–48; and testimonial objects, 179; and witnessing acts, 23
"Gender and Cultural Memory" (Hirsch & Smith), 17
"Gender and War: Roles and Representations" (humanities institute), 12
"Gendered Translations: Claude Lanzmann's *Shoah*" (Hirsch & Spitzer), 12
The German Army and Genocide exhibition, 261n12
Ghosts of Home: The Afterlife of Czernowitz in Jewish Memory (Hirsch & Spitzer), 14
Ginsburg, Carlo, 10
Glazerowa, Zofia Olzakowska, 243–45
Godard, Jean-Luc, 107
Goldman, Mitzi, 163–67, *164*, 173
Goldstein-Rosen, Deborah, 234
Greenberg, Judith, 244, 245
Grossman, David, 98
Grossman, Mendel, 107
Gulf War, 231

Halbwachs, Maurice, 16, 31–32
Hamburg Institute for Social Research, 261n12
HaPatriot (Levin), 144
Hartman, Geoffrey, 7, 8, 35, 80, 105–106, 142
Hartman, Saidiya, 213
Hasbun, Muriel, 68–73, *69–70*, *72–73*, *75–76*
Hatred (Goldman), 163–67, *164*, 173
Haunting Legacies (Schwab), 255n13

Heartfield, John, 227
Hélène's Eye (Hasbun), 71, *73*
Hesse, Hermann, 195
heteropathic identification, 85–86, 161, 163, 166, 168, 173
Heydecker, Joe, 107
Hilberg, Raul, 2, 10
Hirsch, Carl & Lotte, *54*, 55, 57–61, *58*, 74
Hirschhorn, Thomas, 227
historical withholding, 93, 99
Hoess, Rudolf, 214, 224
Hoffman, Eva, 1, 3, 13, 31, 34, 35–36
The Holocaust (Yad Vashem), 129
The Holocaust and Memory in a Global Age (Levy & Sznaider), 21
Holocaust Project (Chicago), 142
Hoskins, Andrew, 21–22
How Societies Remember (Connerton), 207
Human Rights Watch, 232
Hüppauf, Bernd, 262–63n22, 265n18, 266n20
Huyssen, Andreas, 3, 21, 41, 211
hypermasculinization of perpetrators, 133, 144, 147–48

iconic images: as figures, 113–20; in Fink's "Traces," 109–12; in Novak's *Night and Fog*, 122–24; repetition of, 23, 106–107, 108, 120–21, 122; as screens, 120–22
identification: and body memory, 82, 83, 84; in child images, 160, 163–67, 269n34; cultural act of, 159; in familial postmemory, 97; and perpetrator images, 140–41, 142; processes of, 260n22; transgenerational acts of, 158
Identification Papers (Fuss), 260n22
idiopathic process of identification, 85, 161, 163

Im/Balance of Power (Chicago), 142,
  143, 144
Image Before My Eyes, 229
Images in Spite of All (Didi-
  Huberman), 38
*In Memory's Kitchen: A Legacy
  from the Women of Terezín* (De
  Silva, ed.), 178, 178–79
incorporation, 82
index of identification, 48
indexicality of images, 46, 47–48, 61,
  71, 90, 134, 159
infantilization of victims, 23, 133,
  140–45, 147–48, 173
intergenerational acts of transfer:
  in acts of return, 205; and body
  memory, 83; postmemory as, 2, 6;
  role of, 18–19
intersubjectivity, 87
introjection, 82
Isaac Bashevis Singer festival, 238, 239
Izieu children (photo), 156, 158, 159,
  165

Jeşive (artist), 191–92, *192*
Jünger, Ernst, 266*n*20

Kahane, Claire, 17
Kanafani, Ghassan, 205, 206–10,
  214–15, 224
Kaplan, Alice, 104, 108–109, 120,
  262*n*20
Karpf, Anne, 84–85
Kellner, Eva and Eugene, 89–90
Kellner, Tatana, 87–93, *88–89*, *92*
Kessler, Arthur, 180–200
Kessler, David, 180, *182*
Kessler, Judith, 197
Kestenberg, Judith, 83
Kidron, Carol A., 254*n*30
Kincaid, Jamaica, 13
Klarsfeld, Serge, 229

Klein, Melanie, 16
Klepfisz, Irena, 151
Klüger, Ruth, 148
Koch, Gertrud, 265*n*19
Korwin, Yala, 129, 165
Kramer, Anke, 272*n*5
Kraus, Dora, *102*
Kraus, Jozef, *102*
Kurdistan: In the Shadow of History
  (Meiselas), 24, 229, 230–33, 235–36,
  237, 239

Lacan, Jacques, 135, 263*n*35
LaCapra, Dominick, 82, 167, 262*n*19
Landsberg, Alison, 3, 108
Landscapes of Jewish Experience
  (Bak), 140
Lang, Berel, 10
Langer, Lawrence, 129
Lanzmann, Claude, 7–10, 12, 107
latent memories, 212
lathyrism, 180, 182, 185, 187, 270*n*7
Latvia: mass executions in, 136;
  perpetrator images from, 145
Laub, Dori, 168, 170, 171–73, 174
Lazar, Louis, 264*n*36
Le Colonel Chabert (Balzac), 51
Leibl, Moshe, 182, *182*
Levi, Primo, 130
Levin, Hanokh, 144
Levinthal, David, 130, *131*, 145–49, *146*
Levy, Daniel, 21
liberator images, 113, *116*, 118–19,
  136–37, 261–62*n*16, 262*n*20, 264*n*36
Lichtenberg-Ettinger, Bracha, 202,
  216–21, *219*, 222–23
Lifton, Robert Jay, 109
L'Immense fatigue des pierres (Robin),
  247–48
Liss, Andrea, 74, 252*n*13
Lithuania: mass executions in, 136;
  perpetrator images from, 145

Lódz, 107, *217*
The Longest Shadow (G. Hartman),
 105
Lose Your Mother (S. Hartman), 213
lost child trope, 210, 212–13, 215–16,
 224, 272*n*21
Lury, Celia, 3

Mahmoud, Saring, 237
Mann, Sally, 13
Mărculescu, Aurel (artist), 192–94, *193*
Marker, Chris, 174
masculinization of perpetrators, 133,
 144, 147–48
materiality, 221, 239–40
maternal images, 30, 42–46, 47, 220
Maus (Spiegelman), 9, 22, 28, 29–30,
 34, 37, 40–48, *43*, 98
Maus II (Spiegelman), 13
McClintock, Anne, 256*n*18
mediation: in acts of return, 205, 208;
 and body memory, 83; of cultural
 conventions, 135; in familial
 postmemory, 33, 39; in *Maus*, 9; of
 memory, 25; in testimonial objects,
 189
Mein Kampf (Levinthal), *131*, 145–49,
 146
Meiselas, Susan, 229, 230–36, *231*, *239*,
 239–41, 246
mémoire des cendres, 3
mémoire ordinaire, 82
mémoire profonde, 82
mémoire trouée, 3
Memoires for Paul de Man (Derrida),
 268*n*18
memorial candle narrative, 272*n*21
memory: formats, 32; reasons for,
 31–34; tasks of, 18–25. *See also*
 familial postmemory; postmemory
Memory: Histories, Theories, Debates
 (Radstone & Schwarz), 252*n*19

Menachem S., 168–71, *169*, 171–73
Mes enfants/Photographe Sanitas
 (Hasbun), 68, 71, 72, 75–76
Metz, Christian, 134–35
Michael, Sami, 224
Michaels, Anne, 98
Miller, Nancy K., 257*n*41
Milton, Sybil, 107, 261*n*15
miniaturization, 195–96, *196–97*
Mitchell, Juliet, 82
Modiano, Patrick, 55, 98
Morgensztern, Irma, *78*, 93, *94*, 97
Morris, Leslie, 3
Morris, Rosalind, 5
Morrison, Toni, 11, 16, 23, 79–80, 83,
 259*n*7
The Mother/Daughter Plot (Hirsch),
 11, 13
mother/daughter transmission, 83,
 86–87, 93–98
multidirectional memory, 21
*Multidirectional Memory:
 Remembering the Holocaust in the
 Age of Decolonization* (Rothberg),
 21
Museum of Jewish Heritage (New
 York), 35
muted trauma, 262*n*19
mythmaking: in familial postmemory,
 49–52; in perpetrator images, 146;
 and resistance heroes, 151

narratives: incongruity in, 213; as
 media of memory and loss, 13;
 narrative memory, 82; of return, 205
The Nature of Sympathy (Scheler),
 260*n*22
Nazi gaze, 133–39
Night and Fog (Novak), 122–24, *123*
Night and Fog (Resnais), 7, 107, 122, 129
nonappropriative identification and
 empathy, 86

Nora, Pierre, 16
Nothing Makes You Free (Bukiet), 20
Novak, Lorie, *x*, 13, 25, 122–24, *123*,
   156–60, *157*
Nussbaum, Tsvi, 129

Olin, Margaret, 47, 48, 229, 236
On Photography (Sontag), 134
"1.5 generation," 15, 41
Only a Shadow? (Ester I) (Hasbun),
   68, *70*
Only a Shadow? (Lódz Family)
   (Hasbun), 68, *69*
ordinary memory, 82
Ozick, Cynthia, 10–11

Pächter, Mina, *177*
paranoid reading, 74
Past Lives (Novak), 156, *157*, 160
Payne, Lewis, 138
Peirce, C. S., 37
Pelz, Annegret, 272*n*5
performative index, 47, 48, 49, 61
perpetrator images, 23, 127–52; and
   acts of return, 218; archives of,
   228–29; attribution for, 262*n*16;
   and infantilization/feminization
   of victims, 140–45; in Levinthal's
   Mein Kampf, 145–49; and Nazi
   gaze, 133–39; in Spero's *The
   Torture of Women*, 149–52;
   survival of, 106–107
Persona (Bergman), 129
phantom sibling narrative, 272*n*21
photographs: in archives of
   postmemory, 233–36; and body
   memory, 97; and death, 258*n*5;
   and desensitization, 105–106; as
   evidence, 63–67, 110–11; in familial
   postmemory, 36–40, 55–76;
   history-telling role of, 233–36;
   materiality of, 239–40; as media of

memory and loss, 13, 14; as
   perpetrator images, 127–52; as
   projection spaces, 38, 46, 67, 68–73;
   as revenants, 51; as screens, 38;
   symbolic power of, 112, 115
Pinkasova synagogue (Prague), 89
poetry, 2, 151, 156
points of memory, 22, 61–63
Polish Jews, 24, *102*, 145, 226, 229,
   230–35, 237–43
political memory, 32, 33
Pollock, Griselda, 220, 221
"Pornographizations of Fascism"
   (Wenk), 148
postfeminism, 5
postgeneration, 3, 4
postmemory: defining, 4–6, 252*n*13;
   and parental past, 3; rememory vs.,
   82–87. *See also* affiliative structures
   of transmission; familial
   postmemory
Postmemory (Novak), *x*, 25
postmodernism, 5
poststructuralism, 5
Prince, Richard, 227
"Probing the Limits of Representation"
   (conference), 10
projection: in child images, 155–74;
   in familial postmemory, 68–73,
   97; in Novak's *Night and Fog*,
   123; and perpetrator images,
   140; photographs as, 38, 46, 67,
   68–73; postmemory mediated
   through, 5
prosthetic memory, 3
Protegida/Watched Over (Hasbun), 68,
   72, *73*
Proust, Marcel, 16
punctum, 22–23, 47, 61–63, 86, 185,
   194–95, 235

The Queen's Page (Sebald), 49

Raczymow, Henri, 3
Radstone, Susannah, 252*n*19, 269*n*34
Rauschenberg, Robert, 227
received history, 3
recipe books, 177–80, 196, 269*n*3
reframing of images, 68, 71
Regarding the Pain of Others (Sontag), 106
Remembering to Forget (Zelizer), 261*n*15
rememory, 23, 82–87
reparative looking, 73–76
reparative reading, 24, 75
representation: in familial postmemory, 39; gender as vehicle for, 189; in *Maus*, 9–10; in testimonial objects, 194–95
Representing the Holocaust (LaCapra), 167
repressed memories, 212
resistance, 180, 184–85
Resnais, Alain, 7, 107, 122, 129
retrospective witnessing, 130
return. *See* acts of return
Return to Haifa (Kanafani), 205, 224
Richter, Gerhard, 227
Roach, Joseph, 214
Robin, Régine, 247–48
Rodchenko, Alexander, 227
Roland Barthes by Roland Barthes (Barthes), 47
Romania, map of, *181*
romanticization of familial postmemory, 49–52. *See also* mythmaking
Romăscanu (artist), *188*, 188–89
The Rooster's Egg (Williams), 248
Rosenberg, Ethel, 156–57, 158
Rosenberg, Julius, 157
Rossino, Alexander, 265*n*18
Rothberg, Michael, 21, 122

Russia: mass executions in, 136; perpetrator images from, 145
Rymkiewicz, Jaroslaw, 128, 141

Sachs, Nelly, 151
Saddam Hussein, 231
Said, Edward, 255–56*n*18
Sanders, Marie, 151
Sans Soleil (Marker), 174
Santner, Eric, 121
saturation point, 105
Savran, Bella, 251*n*9
Scheler, Max, 85, 260*n*22
Schindler's List (Spielberg), 136, 147
Schmueli, Ilana, 59, 60
Schoenberger, Gerhard, 107, 264*n*36
School of Criticism and Theory (SCT), 7
Schwab, Gabriele, 3, 21, 255*n*13
Schwarz, Bill, 252*n*19
Schwitters, Kurt, 227
A Scrap of Time (Fink), 109
screens: as affiliative structures of transmission, 120–22; child images as, 174; mediation of cultural conventions through, 135; photographs as, 38
Sebald, W. G., 22, 40–48, 49, 112
"second generation": appropriation of suffering by, 20; and evidentiary force of photographs, 110–11; and familial postmemory, 3, 15, 34, 251*n*9
Sedgwick, Eve Kosofsky, 24, 74, 85, 86
See Under Love (Grossman), 98
Seiffert, Rachel, 63–67, 73
sense memory: acts of return as trigger for, 211–13; in familial postmemory, 23, 79–99; and photographs, 111–12. *See also* body memory
Serbia, perpetrator images in, 136–37, *137*

71125: Fifty Years of Silence (Kellner), 3, 87–93, 92
sexual humiliation, 148
sexualization of murder, 148, 151
"The Shawl" (Ozick), 10–11
Sherman, Cindy, 13
Shoah (Lanzmann), 7–10, 12
Shope, Rebecca, 140
Showalter, Elaine, 7, 8
silences in archives of postmemory, 247–49
Silver, Brenda, 10
Silverman, Kaja, 85–86, 161, 166, 174, 260n22, 266n21
Simon, Nathan, 187
Smith, Valerie, 17
social memory, 32
¿Sólo una Sombra? (Only a Shadow?) (Hasbun), 68, 69, 70
Sontag, Susan, 2, 103, 104–105, 106, 134
South African Truth and Reconciliation Commission, 19
souvenirs, 186
spatiality of images, 61
spectral evidence, 61
Spero, Nancy, 130, 132, 149–52, 150
Spiegelman, Anja, 13, 43, 44, 98
Spiegelman, Art: and cultural memory, 22; and familial postmemory, 28, 29–30, 35–36, 40; iconic images used by, 115, 117, 117–18; on Levinthal's *Mein Kampf*, 147; and lost objects, 247; as male narrator, 98; photographs used by, 13, 43, 44
Spiegelman, Vladek, 13, 98
Spielberg, Steven, 136
Spitzer, Leo, 8–9, 12–14, 22–23, 55, 176, 177
Spivak, Gayatri C., 79, 81
Steichen, Edward, 13
Stein, Arlene, 251n9, 252n20
Stern, Anny, 177, 180, 197

Stewart, Susan, 195–96
Stone, Dan, 263n31
storytelling: and familial postmemory, 30; historians' use of, 2
Stroop, Jürgen, 126, 129–30, 139
Stroop Report, 139, 228
Study F (Bak), 141
Stupp, Heini, 59, 60
subjectivity, 87, 248
Suleiman, Susan Rubin, 252n13, 260n27
surrogations in acts of return, 213–16
survivor fantasies, 51–52, 160
symbolic status of images, 37, 112, 115
Sznaider, Nathan, 21

tattoos, 81–82, 90, 91, 96
Taylor, Diana, 271n15
temporality of images, 61, 64, 75, 96, 138
Tencer, Golda, 102, 226, 229, 230–36, 234, 239, 244, 245–46
Terezín camp, 269n2
Terezín camp recipe book, 177–80, 196
testimonial objects, 23–24, 177–200; and acts of return, 206; Terezín camp recipe book, 177–80; Vapniarka miniature book, 180–200, 188, 190–94, 199
Testimony (Felman & Laub), 168, 174
Theweleit, Klaus, 12
A Thousand Darknesses (Franklin), 20, 253n21
The Threshold of the Visible World (Silverman), 85
Tišma, Aleksandar, 141–42
Too Many Men (Brett), 203–205, 213, 224
Torok, Maria, 82, 255n13
The Torture of Women (Spero), 132, 149–52, 150
Tower of Faces (Eliach), 35, 229
"Traces" (Fink), 109–12, 119

transgenerational acts of transfer: and identification, 136; postmemory as, 4, 6

Transnistria, 56, 180, *181*

transposition, 83, 84–85

trauma: and body memory, 81–82; defined, 80; and memory, 82; traumatic realism, 122; traumatic seeing, 66

Trespassing Through Shadows (Liss), 252*n*13

Tsvi Nussbaum: A Boy from Warsaw (documentary), 129

Uncomfortably Close (Brett), 224

United States Holocaust Memorial Museum, 13, 35, 135

universalization, 149, 151

van Alphen, Ernst, 254*n*3

van der Hart, Ono, 82

van der Kolk, Bessel, 82

van der Zee, James, 47, 62

van Dijck, José, 22

van Pelt, Robert Jan, 113–14, 263*n*33

Vapniarka, 180, *181*, 182, 183

Vapniarka miniature book, 180–200, *188, 190–94, 199*

vicarious witnessing, 3

victims: child victim images, 23, 155–74; infantilization/feminization of, 140–45; perpetrator images of, 127–52

Vietnam War, 163, *164*

Vishniac, Roman, 134

visual acts of return, 216–21

Vogel, Mišo, 95, *96*

vulnerability of children, 156, 162–63, 173

Waal, Edmund de, 227

Wall, Jeff, 243

The War After (Karpf), 84

Warburg, Aby, 22, 39, 42

Warhol, Andy, 121

The Warsaw Ghetto Is No More (Stroop), *126*, 127–30, 134, 139, 144

Weissman, Gary, 20, 254*n*3

Wenk, Silke, 148

White, Hayden, 10

Williams, Patricia, 248, 249

Winnett, Susan, 258*n*12

witnessing: by adoption, 35, 97; gendered nature of, 23; retrospective, 130; testimonial transfers of, 256*n*21; vicarious witnessing, 3

Wolff, Ghiță, 189, *190*

Wolin, Jeffrey, 78, 93–98, *94, 96*

women: maternal images, 30, 42–46; *Shoah* lacking stories from, 8; in Vapniarka, 186–87. *See also* gender

Woolf, Virginia, 16

World Wide Web, 240–41

"Writing and the Holocaust" (conference), 10

Written in Memory: Portraits of the Holocaust (Wolin), 78, 93–98, *94, 96*

Yad Vashem, 129, 143, 265*n*17

Yaeger, Patricia, 263*n*31

Yale Fortunoff Video Archive for Holocaust Survivor Testimony, 168

yellow star, 56, 57, 59, *60*

The Yellow Star (Schoenberger), 107, 264*n*36

Young, James, 3, 97, 147, 211, 265*n*18

You've Gotta Have Balls (Brett), 224

Zawadzka, Sabina, 243

Zeitlin, Froma, 3, 163

Zelizer, Barbie, 105–106, 111, 112, 261*nn*15–16

Zonshtajn, Cyporah, 243–45, *244*

GENDER AND CULTURE
A SERIES OF COLUMBIA UNIVERSITY PRESS

Nancy K. Miller and Victoria Rosner, Series Editors
Carolyn G. Heilbrun (1926–2003) and Nancy K. Miller, Founding Editors

In Dora's Case: Freud, Hysteria, Feminism
EDITED BY CHARLES BERNHEIMER AND CLAIRE KAHANE

Breaking the Chain: Women, Theory, and French Realist Fiction
NAOMI SCHOR

Between Men: English Literature and Male Homosocial Desire
EVE KOSOFSKY SEDGWICK

Romantic Imprisonment: Women and Other Glorified Outcasts
NINA AUERBACH

The Poetics of Gender
EDITED BY NANCY K. MILLER

Reading Woman: Essays in Feminist Criticism
MARY JACOBUS

Honey-Mad Women: Emancipatory Strategies in Women's Writing
PATRICIA YAEGER

Subject to Change: Reading Feminist Writing
NANCY K. MILLER

Thinking Through the Body
JANE GALLOP

Gender and the Politics of History
JOAN WALLACH SCOTT

The Dialogic and Difference: "An/Other Woman" in Virginia Woolf and Christa Wolf
ANNE HERRMANN

Plotting Women: Gender and Representation in Mexico
JEAN FRANCO

Inspiriting Influences: Tradition, Revision, and Afro-American Women's Novels
MICHAEL AWKWARD

Hamlet's Mother and Other Women
CAROLYN G. HEILBRUN

Rape and Representation
EDITED BY LYNN A. HIGGINS AND BRENDA R. SILVER

Shifting Scenes: Interviews on Women, Writing, and Politics in Post-68 France
EDITED BY ALICE A. JARDINE AND ANNE M. MENKE

Tender Geographies: Women and the Origins of the Novel in France
JOAN DEJEAN

Unbecoming Women: British Women Writers and the Novel of Development
SUSAN FRAIMAN

The Apparitional Lesbian: Female Homosexuality and Modern Culture
TERRY CASTLE

George Sand and Idealism
NAOMI SCHOR

Becoming a Heroine: Reading About Women in Novels
RACHEL M. BROWNSTEIN

Nomadic Subjects: Embodiment and Sexual Difference in Contemporary Feminist Theory
ROSI BRAIDOTTI

Engaging with Irigaray: Feminist Philosophy and Modern European Thought
EDITED BY CAROLYN BURKE, NAOMI SCHOR, AND MARGARET WHITFORD

Second Skins: The Body Narratives of Transsexuality
JAY PROSSER

A Certain Age: Reflecting on Menopause
EDITED BY JOANNA GOLDSWORTHY

Mothers in Law: Feminist Theory and the Legal Regulation of Motherhood
EDITED BY MARTHA ALBERTSON FINEMAN AND ISABELLE KARPIN

Critical Condition: Feminism at the Turn of the Century
SUSAN GUBAR

Feminist Consequences: Theory for the New Century
EDITED BY ELISABETH BRONFEN AND MISHA KAVKA

Simone de Beauvoir, Philosophy, and Feminism
NANCY BAUER

Pursuing Privacy in Cold War America
DEBORAH NELSON

But Enough About Me: Why We Read Other People's Lives
NANCY K. MILLER

Palatable Poison: Critical Perspectives on The Well of Loneliness
EDITED BY LAURA DOAN AND JAY PROSSER

Cool Men and the Second Sex
SUSAN FRAIMAN

Modernism and the Architecture of Private Life
VICTORIA ROSNER

Virginia Woolf and the Bloomsbury Avant-Garde: War, Civilization, Modernity
CHRISTINE FROULA

The Scandal of Susan Sontag
EDITED BY BARBARA CHING AND JENNIFER A. WAGNER-LAWLOR

Mad for Foucault: Rethinking the Foundations of Queer Theory
LYNNE HUFFER

Graphic Women: Life Narrative and Contemporary Comics
HILLARY L. CHUTE

Gilbert and Sullivan: Gender, Genre, Parody
CAROLYN WILLIAMS

Nomadic Subjects: Embodiment and Sexual Difference in Contemporary Feminist Theory, 2d ed.
ROSI BRAIDOTTI

Rites of Return: Diaspora Poetics and the Politics of Memory
EDITED BY MARIANNE HIRSCH AND NANCY K. MILLER

Unlikely Collaboration: Gertrude Stein, Bernard Faÿ, and the Vichy Dilemma
BARBARA WILL

The Global and the Infinite: Feminism in Our Time
EDITED BY GERALDINE PRATT AND VICTORIA ROSNER

GENDER AND CULTURE READERS

Modern Feminisms: Political, Literary, Cultural
EDITED BY MAGGIE HUMM

Feminism and Sexuality: A Reader
EDITED BY STEVI JACKSON AND SUE SCOTT

Writing on the Body: Female Embodiment and Feminist Theory
EDITED BY KATIE CONBOY, NADIA MEDINA, AND SARAH STANBURY